D0170551

WITHDRAWN

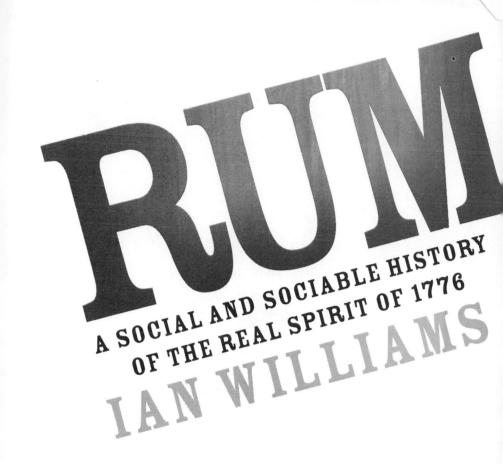

RUM

A SOCIAL AND SOCIABLE HISTORY
OF THE REAL SPIRIT OF 1776

IAN WILLIAMS

NATION BOOKS
NEW YORK

Rum
A Social and Sociable History of the Real Spirit of 1776

Published by
Nation Books
An Imprint of Avalon Publishing Group Inc.
245 West 17th St., 11th Floor
New York, NY 10011

AVALON
publishing group incorporated

Copyright © 2005 by Ian Williams

Nation Books is a co-publishing venture of the Nation Institute and Avalon
Publishing Group Incorporated.

Library of Congress Cataloging-in-Publication Data is available.

ISBN 1-56025-651-6

9 8 7 6 5 4 3 2 1

Book design by Maria Elias
Printed in the United States of America
Distributed by Publishers Group West

There are too many people who have helped in the intensive, hands-on on-site research that was necessary for this book to name and thank adequately. And it is in the nature of such research that memories for names become a little hazy.

However, the book would not have been started without the help and encouragement of Jamaican friends like Joy Elliot and Winston Coles, and it would not have been completed so soon without the enthusiastic encouragement of agent Colin Campbell and the Simon Legree–like encouragement of editor Carl Bromley.

In the meantime, the burden was relieved by research assistant Jacob Parakilas, who sorted out the materials even more quickly than baby Ian could shuffle them, and by Anora Mahmudova, who shared with the baby the burden of my being at editorial beck and call for so long.

Thanks to them, and on a more somber note, thanks and a moment's silence to all who suffered and died over the centuries for the darker side of this subject.

CONTENTS

PART III:
ROLLING AROUND THE WORLD

I t is the distinctive and evocative aroma of rum from the Christmases of my childhood that gave birth to this book. Growing up on a council estate—the equivalent of a New York housing project—in Liverpool after the Second World War was a much more prosperous experience than it would have been prewar, but it was hardly affluence. Food, candy, and newspapers were still rationed, but that was almost irrelevant. We couldn't have afforded them anyway.

Christmas was the occasion for splashing out with what little we could afford. The first time I tasted chicken was from a tin that was part of a Christmas hamper. For my father's Christmas gift, we children would save our pocket money and buy him cigars. In our Christmas stockings, which were our regular socks pressed into action for the occasion, was always a tangerine at the darned toe along with cheap toys from Hong Kong. My father, normally a beer drinker, and a prodigious one at that, indulged in a bottle of rum for Christmas, usually Demerara, in nostalgia for his days in the merchant navy in the Second World War. I would crouch at the foot of the Christmas tree and study the bottle's label with its hint of tropical exoticism—three barrels on a beach with a background of palm trees.

The resulting combination of smells that permeated the house—cigar smoke, peeled tangerines, and rum—has always evoked Christmas for me, and a Christmas of particular childhood innocence, before the pressures of nine of us living in a three-bedroom house built up to fissiparous levels and before that prodigious beer drinking transformed the head of the family. But it was bitter beer, not the demon rum, that effected the changes.

As a precocious teenager in the sixties—obviously still influenced subliminally—while others would bring bottles of beer to parties, I would show off with a small bottle of dark rum, costing ten shillings and six pence. Girls in those days were supposed to drink Babycham (a fizzy alcoholic drink made of pear juice) or cherry brandy. I discovered that rum would do nicely in a pinch.

For many years afterward, rum was just one more gargle in my extensive drinking repertoire but not a subject of particular interest, although a cold or flu would have me going with the folkloric crowd and downing a tot, or two, or more.

But then, in Martinique, while researching another subject entirely, I discovered vintage rums. I studied their taste, the methods of distilling, and, increasingly, the history. I discovered that the French Antillean rums were not as uniquely excellent as the French thought, and that many other islands aged and matured their rums to equal and even greater excellence.

I began to collect rum on my travels, and my collection includes Kazakh, Czech, Croat, Thai, Hawaiian, Indian, Nepalese, Argentinean, Australian, and German rums. I began to collect labels—the iconography of rum, which showed how consumers and producers viewed the spirit— and various advertisments and rum-drinking paraphernalia.

My collection of "rumabilia" has been growing and it may yet breed another volume.

This book has been an intermittent project, and I have to confess that much of the hands-on, intensive, on-site research I have carried out in the Caribbean was not strictly necessary for the way this volume has turned out. Other people have chronicled the varieties and tastes of modern brands of rum, and there is no particular reason for me to try to follow in their wobbly footsteps.

Dipping into the history of rum, I found that it was more than just an interesting drink. "Nelson's blood" was the lubricant and fuel for the whole engine of commerce that made the modern world. It put a whole new light on the motives for the founding fathers of the American Republic. I do not want to be censorious of the founders, for, as a onetime shop steward and union official, I have always appreciated the winning motivational force of linking high principles to naked self-interest when trying to call a strike.

This book is an attempt to share the excitement I felt as I looked under the rug beneath which a lot of that history has been discreetly swept. But throughout the project, it has always helped that the warehouses and distilleries I visited had the pervasive, alluring smell of maturing rum, continually evoking the happiness of a child's Christmas in Liverpool.

RUM: THE GLOBAL SPIRIT WITH ITS HEART IN THE CARIBBEAN

Even while Prohibition blighted the United States and rumrunners defied it, Charles William Taussig, the young, precocious president of the American Molasses Company and a future member of Franklin D. Roosevelt's inner circle, romanced the spirit in his 1928 book, *Rum, Romance and Rebellion:* "Where we find rum, we find action, sometimes cruel, sometimes heroic, sometimes humorous, but always vigorous and interesting," he wrote, adding that "Rum both as a beverage and as a medium of exchange, appears to have released the energies of brave men, and much of that strength and resource was used in creating our Western civilization."[i] As an American, he was well aware that it was not tea but rum and the molasses for making it that really incited the American colonists to rebellion. Rum, he argued, has a strong claim to be "The Spirit of '76."

In conclusion he remarked, "It is not strange that we should find so much history corked up in a bottle of rum ...rum was a symbol, as well as a fact."[ii] He was right. Rum has a history every bit as rich as its distinctive flavor and aroma. Even though it is often relegated to a synonym for sin or, perhaps worse, merely a useful mixer for a cocktail, it has always been a commodity with a worldwide reach and depth: a global spirit with its beating heart in the Caribbean. Its very imagery and iconography bespeak a history with more universal effect and appeal than other, more bland, and less cosmopolitan spirits.

Rum began as a heady Mediterranean cocktail that mixed Islamic science and technology with European enterprise. It added the effect of that Iberian enterprise to northwest Europe's developing Protestant capitalism and mercantilism. Together they set in motion the great cycle of circum-Atlantic trade, fueling the slave trade and the massive population shifts that make the present-day Caribbean and North American populations look the way they do, and in the process started up the modern capitalist economy of the north Atlantic.

Much of what we see in the modern America has the sugary savor of old rum about it—even up to the present trade wars between Cuba and Washington. And in the worship of Mammon, rum has been a medium of exchange and a globalized commercial commodity almost from the first time English settlers in Barbados discovered that you could get interesting results from fermenting and distilling the syrupy residue of sugar refining. Since its invention, rum has flowed across the world with the trade routes, but while it is made—and drunk—from Australia to Austria, Brazil to Bohemia, no matter how damp and chilly the customer's home, rum brings with it warm connotations of the Caribbean in particular, of the tropics in general, and of the sea.

Even though rum's role as a major commodity in the slave trade has tarnished its reputation, it was then and is now a favorite drink of the slavers, the slaves, and their descendants alike. In fact, rum is the one common factor of a recognizable common Caribbean culture. The Dutch-, English-, French-, and Spanish-speaking islands have separate strands of culture, and even within the different language blocks, the islands are similar but distinct. On each island, the scars of slavery manifest themselves in different ways. But on all of them, islanders make, drink, and relish the rum that was at once the means of and the purpose for their ancestral servitude.

In the English-speaking world, those images were enhanced by nautical, indeed piratical, overtones, and so the drink certainly lacked the prestige of, for example, fine Cognac. It was a drink to be gulped, not one to sip. The French historian of rum, Alain Huetz de Lemp, declared that it remained "the drink of the Blacks, the buccaneers, and all the vagabonds who scoured the new world."[iii]

For centuries, the ritual of serving the grog ration on the decks of the Royal Navy marked the passage of a voyage for most of the crews far more memorably than any bells or logbooks, or even the sight of land. Rum has had an intimate relationship with warfare: it provided the causes for wars, the finance for them, and the pharmacological support for those fighting them. However, more important than its role in lubricating the war god's chariot, rum has been one of the major motivators of warfare, and in particular the War of American Independence.

Unlike whiskey, tequila, Cognac, gin, or vodka, rum is more than just a beverage, having spiritual as well as spirituous connotations. The "demon rum" of American evangelists is also the preferred drink of the gods at Haitian Voodoo ceremonies, where it provides a potent and palatable alternative to holy water.

There are reasons why rum's role in history, particularly American history, has been overlooked. Looking at the past through the prism of present prejudices is common to all nations, and a century of fiery temperance campaigning culminating in Prohibition certainly led to an erosion of references in the hagiographies of the founding fathers to their bibulous habits. In addition, a combination of factors after the Revolution—the opening up of the West, the breach in trade ties with the Caribbean, and patriotic sentiment, which largely led to whiskey replacing rum as *the* American drink—obscured for later historians the importance of rum.

There is another important reason for writing about rum. It is a wonderful and greatly underappreciated drink. For the connoisseurs, an aged rum can match and even surpass a single malt scotch or a fine old Cognac. And for the do-gooders who want an enhanced conscience as well as the enhanced consciousness a good rum can give, almost every tot downed helps the Third World develop.

Admittedly, for lots of people in the Caribbean, aged

rum is almost an oxymoron. They'd drink the stuff warm
from the still and be horrified at the thought of leaving it
undrunk to mature. Only the brave would sip at the undi-
luted overproof spirit sold by the gallon in Caribbean rum
shops or imbibe the Haitian moonshine *clairin*.

However, I share Taussig's ambivalence: "There is in the
sweet aromatic redolence of old rum, a mystic charm, a soft
soothing fragrance that beguiles one into forgetting its
more sinister and vicious history."[iv] Rum has been undervalued as a fine spirit. It is one of life's pleasures that more
people should share. I hope that this book will help raise its
profile and its prestige to make that possible.

PART I
ORIGINS—"A HOT HELLISH LIQUOR"

1. WHAT IS IT, WHERE IS IT?

Like the other British export, the English language, rum is so ubiquitous and globally pervasive that people tend to forget where it came from and automatically naturalize it. Whiskey always carries its Celtic roots, vodka will always be Slavic, and the French have a lien on Cognac and even brandy. But half the world treats rum as its very own.

At the beginning of the nineteenth century, it was still tied to its imperial strings. For example, although we automatically associate Russia with vodka, rum had its proponents as a road to ruin and was drunk as intemperately as vodka. But when Tolstoy in *War And Peace* had Dolokhov in a rum-drinking wager that entailed downing a full bottle while sitting unsupported in a third-story window sill, it was with an English sailor, which showed that for Tolstoy, rum was a British thing.

In the best traditions of scholasticism, over the years there have been determined efforts to overlook the most obvious etymology for rum, which is from *rumbullion,* the word that first accompanied descriptions of the spirit almost four centuries ago, and at least one reason for that is attempts by other nations to claim rum as their very own. Taussig, the patriotic American rum-lover, claimed "The name 'Rum' is without doubt American: in fact it is an early manifestation of the American fancy for abbreviation, having been derived from a West Indian word, 'Rumbullion.'"[1] This is far-fetched. The British lower orders who provided the folk-ways and language of colonial America were no slouches at contraction and abbreviation themselves. And *rumbullion* to rumbo or rum is well within the linguistic tropes of British settlers. Richard Ligon's fascinating descriptions of life in Barbados testify to the verbal ingenuity of the first thirsty settlers there. *Rumbullion* was used again in wonderful context in 1660, when the Assizes in Bermuda recorded a rollicking tale of Celtic rumbunctiousness:

> John, an Irishman, having presumptuouslie under-taken to deliver a cask of rumbullion to the Governor's Negroe woman Sarah Simon to keep, if not to retaile the same for his advantage, and thereby having occasioned great disorder and drunkenesse amongst the Governor's Negroes and others, the same Rumbullion having been discovered by Mr. John Briscoe Marhdall, it is unanimously Ordered that the same shall be sould and the produce thereof be bestowed upon the Scotchman latelie wounded by Matthew Makennie for his maintenance.[2]

Others have suggested that *rumbullion* is derived from Rom or Romany, for Gypsy, and bouillon, but this is etymology of the falsest kind. The Oxford English Dictionary has *Romany* as an obsolete term for Romania, the Roman Empire, until it became a description for the Gypsies in the nineteenth century. It has been suggested that *rumbo*, the name for a punch, used by Tobias Smollet in *The Adventures of Peregrine Pickle* is the origin—but this is a good half-century later than the first recorded use of *rum* and seems more likely to be an expansion of *rum* than a contraction of *rumbullion*, certainly within the inventive phonetic framework of, for example. English West Country dialect words for drink and, indeed, up to present-day usages such as *scrumpy* for (very) hard cider.

John Josselyn claimed that Captain Wannerton in New England drank a pint of "Kill Devil or Rhum" with him in 1639, but Josselyn did not write about it until 1674, and his memory may have been at fault—indeed if he made a habit of drinking pints of rum, it almost certainly was. Even if it was rum he drank then, it is possible that he did not use the actual word. The word *rum* first appears in its monosyllabic glory in 1661 in an order of the Governor and Council of Jamaica, which had been accidentally conquered by Cromwell's men six years before. The settlers from Barbados who accompanied the Roundhead troops obviously wasted no time in setting up their stills on the new island.

· In French Martinique, the open-minded distillers accept that the word *rum* entered the language during the English occupations of the island and that originally it was spelled without the *h* that the French Encyclopediasts later put in—probably out of sheer pedantry to make it seem apothecary-like. Some of the French have suggested that *saccharum,* medieval Latin for *sugar,* is the root of *rum,* but that seems, to say the least, highly unlikely. We may be unsure about who first fired up a still and refined rum, but we can be fairly sure that it was no scientist or apothecary. They certainly did not use sugar itself to make rum—and it was not until the eighteenth century that Linnaeus gave sugarcane the scientific name of *Saccharum officinarum.*

In fact, the English Barbadian origins for rum are strongly persuasive for both the spirit and its name. By 1647, as the people back in the motherland were embroiling themselves in the English Civil War, there were already references, which lasted for a century, to "Barbadoes Waters," and the only real lexicographical rival to *rum* is *kill-devil,* as attested to on the island. Rum was known as *kill-devil* for centuries, even up to modern times in Newfoundland, which may be why the most popular rum of that region is called Screech.[3] The Danes, of similar disposition to the Celts, took the name *kiel-dyvel* from the colonists and were recorded using both the name and its referent in 1674.[4] The Dutch in Surinam called it *keldiuvel* in the late eighteenth century. And in that engaging Gallic way that turned a beefsteak into *bifteck,* the French originally transformed *kill-devil* into *guildive,* and in Haiti that is still the name for the still. In the nineteenth century, the Spanish took to calling it *ron,* while Russians, Swedes, and the like called it *rom.*

And then there is the irrefutable argument that the British made more rum and drank more of it for longer than any of the other pretenders. While Spain, Portugal, and France forbade imports of rum and molasses from their colonies, the British domestic market developed rapidly, if not as quickly as in the New England colonies, where, without grain or grapes to spare, there were few alternatives— whether beer, wine, or gin—to compete with rum.

Beyond the question of what the stuff is called is the existential question of what rum is. With one Teutonic exception, there is, at least, general agreement on the answer. The European Union has taken the issue in hand. In its dry, unromantic Directive 1576, issued in 1989, rum is described as an alcoholic drink obtained from the distillation of either molasses or other syrups from sugarcane or of the whole sugarcane juice. The distillations should be at least 96 percent to conserve the various nonethanol substances that give rum its the distinctive flavor and aroma. But rum is, of course, much more fun than a mere chemical formula.

2. Sugar: The Seed of Rum

The European bureaucrats are right, of course. You can't have rum without sugar, and once you have sugar, it is only a matter of time before trial leads to alcoholic error in one form or another.

In 325 B.C., Nearchus, one of Alexander's generals, remarked on how the Indians made "a sort of honey from reeds, without the help of bees."[5] India, however, was only a way station on sugar's journey around the globe. Botanists suggest that it began its journey westward from Papua New Guinea,[6] where archaeologists have found evidence of some of the earliest cultivation in the world of many tropical-zone crops. Sugarcane has been grown there for seven thousand years, and it is remarkable that the actual name of sugar is almost as old, surprisingly preserved across the globe. It had been in use in India for hundreds of years when the Greeks turned up and history, in

Western eyes at least, began. In Sanskrit, it was *karkara,* which meant sand or gravel, suggesting that it was already being refined and crystallized. The Pakrit language, which superseded that of the Gitas, transmuted it to *sakkara,* which the Arabs turned to *sukkur,* the word they still use and which the Europeans adopted and used.[7]

Udoy Chand Dutt, the compiler of a Sanskrit pharmacopoeia, refers to a drink made from pure sugarcane juice called *sidhu* and another made from the molasses called *gaud.*[8] Neither seems to have been a big seller. As precociously advanced as the ancient Indians were, they had not developed distillation—and most people agree that fermented sugar on its own will never win any gold medals at any international exposition.

While sugar has since been found in beets, sorghum, and other plants, in no form is it as plentiful and accessible as in sugarcane. Technically the cane is a grass, *Saccharum officinarum,* and can be propagated easily by planting cuttings. In fact, it grows as rapidly as grass, and over centuries of selective cultivation, the sugar content of the cane has risen steadily. Either the Indians or the Persians and Arabs to whom sugarcane cultivation passed discovered how to crystallize it. The crop also spread north and east to China, the Philippines, and the Pacific Islands, where the Spanish conquistadors found that the locals had already been growing it for over a thousand years.

• The Filipinos fermented the cane juice to make their local tipple, *bawsis,* without distilling it. Because of the mercantilist principles of the age, in 1786 the Spanish banned the locals from drinking it to help promote imports of wine from the Spanish vineyards on the other side of the world.

The ban, similar to those that were imposed in Spanish America against rum production, provoked a revolt that lasted twelve days. One can't help but suspect it may have lasted longer if the filipinos had learned how to make rum before the ban was imposed.

In the view of the modern world, it was the Arabs who perfected the cultivation and production of sugarcane. According to Marco Polo, even though the Chinese had originally studied its cultivation in India during the T'ang dynasty, Genghis Khan sent to Egypt for expertise in refining. There, the ingredients of sugar cultivation came together—technical expertise, plentiful water, sun, and a biddable labor force. Sugarcane needs very specific environmental conditions: lots of sunshine and water. This restricts it to the tropics, hence its spread along the tropical band of the Eurasian and African landmasses. As with peppers and spices, which the increasingly prosperous medieval West also came to crave, it could not usually be grown in the temperate lands that has such insatiable appetites for it. It also needed some quite specific social conditions as well; the intensive labor needed to cut, cart, and process the cane under a broiling tropical sun has never appealed to people who had other career options.

To get the best results, the cane should be cut close to the ground, which of course adds to the strain for the cutters. It must then be milled very quickly after harvesting, while the sugar content is high. And then it must be boiled, rendered down quickly once the juice, the *vesous,* is squeezed out, because otherwise it will rapidly ferment—which is, of course, another story.

· As the juice is progressively concentrated in a series of

open boilers, in the final stages the actual sugar, the sucrose, crystallizes out, leaving molasses to drain off as a by-product. Although laden with complex sugars and other nutritious compounds, molasses will not crystallize. It has been used as a cheap sweetener, as a medical compound—*treacle,* as the British call it—and later for fermenting as the feed-stock for rum distilleries. We shall return to that aspect. But the molasses by-product was originally a problem for the early producers. No one was quite sure what to do with it. It was used as fertilizer, sometimes it was tipped into the sea, and it is still used for animal feeds, being one of the causes of the "rich" smell of manure from intensively reared livestock.

Because sugar tends to burn easily, or caramelize, the application of heat during the refining process is a careful and exact science. The combination of fires, boiling pans, and tropical heat with the heavy physical labor involved in a sugar mill and refinery must have made Dante's Inferno seem like a vacation spot. In general, people had to be coerced to do it. All too often, as it spread around the tropical zone, sugarcane brought with it a demand for an industrial-scale slave force: out of sweetness came forth slavery, a connection often brought up by British abolitionists who made the ultimate sacrifice—refusing sugar in their tea.

Even in the ninth century there were slave revolts in what is now Iraq, where East African slaves had been set to work growing sugar. During the Crusades, when the Northern barbarians were exposed to a superior culture and lifestyle, sugar became a prized luxury. The Arab's enemies stole the technology; the Normans in Sicily and

Cyprus were soon growing sugar, and Venice became a major sugar-refining center. It may not be coincidental that Venice was a major slave-trading center; although the slaves were Slavs, brought by the Tartars from Russia and the Ukraine for sale in the Mediterranean.

In Cyprus, the Venetians and the crusading Order of Hospitallers have left elaborate remains of the sugar pans, mills, and other equipment they used to maintain commercial dominance. Their technology was scarcely different from those to be found rusting even now in the preindustrial refineries of the Caribbean plantations, except that they used copper rather than iron and steel for the pans and wood for the mills. Appropriately enough, one of the medieval refineries is near the reputed birthplace of Aphrodite. The two would stay linked. As Ogden Nash put it, "Candy is dandy / But liquor's quicker."

In Sicily, the unique and flourishing mix of Byzantine, Arab, and Norman culture left behind a hybrid pan-Mediterranean civilization that, among other commodities, used the best Arab techniques for sugar production to sell to the North. In 1449, the Sicilians made a significant breakthrough—the three-rollered mill, which allowed two passes of the sugarcane for more efficient extraction of the juice. The Crown of Spain later inherited the island, which added to Iberian expertise, since on the Spanish mainland the Arabs had had 75,000 acres under cane.

The Spaniards picked up what the Arabs left behind when they were driven out of their last Iberian stronghold in 1492. Indeed, southern Spain is the only part of the mainland European Union that still grows cane rather than sugar beet and where there is still an indigenous rum made from local cane, grown on the Costa Tropica along the coastal area spiked with the old Moorish hill forts that are still the centers of Spanish towns. There is, of course, significance in that date. Christopher Columbus went to petition Ferdinand and Isabella for help in his voyage to the Indies even as they were besieging Arab Granada.

The Portuguese did not want to be excluded from such a lucrative business. Their explorations were not just to find oriental sources of spice; they were also prospecting for suitable sugar-growing terrain. Almost as soon as they had discovered Madeira in 1418, Portugal's ruler, Henry the Navigator, ordered the cultivation of sugarcane there, since Portugal, on the chillier Atlantic side of the Iberian Peninsula, was unsuitable. The fields were, of course, worked by slaves, Africans from the nearby coast. A few decades later, the Portuguese had reproduced the process in the Cape Verde Islands and in the Azores.

As a result, Portugal has the dubious honor of being the first to use African slaves, transplanting the cane and slaves from Madeira and its African outposts and eventually to Brazil. Although it seems likely that slave labor had been used in the Mediterranean, those slaves were not necessarily African. They could have been Arab prisoners or white Slavs imported from the Ukraine and Russia. We are not sure whether the slaves used in Madeira and the Azores were Berbers or Moors or from the sub-Sahara. We do know, however, that African slavery in its modern form made its first fatal association with sugar in 1490, when the Portuguese imported slaves from Benin to work the sugar plantations on the island of São Tomé, off the West African coast.[9]

The Spanish, also searching for suitably warm and wet terrain to grow this major money earner, had discovered the Canary Islands and transplanted sugarcane there. To do so, they first enslaved the native people, the Guanche. Then, when they had exterminated them in a dry run for their later practice with the Amercan Indians in the Caribbean, they brought in African slaves. It may be a small mitigating factor in any charges of racism that the Guanches were blond and blue-eyed. But in their isolation they had over-looked becoming Catholic, so they were fair game for slavery.

Having traversed the Eurasian landmass from east to west, it now seemed that sugar had reached a dead end with the Azores in its human-assisted search for suitable growing environments. But then came Christopher Columbus. On his second voyage, he took with him to Hispaniola sugarcane cuttings from the Canaries and began the whole story of sugar, rum, and African chattel slavery in the New World.

Cortez and Pizarro took the cane to the American mainland along with smallpox, gunpowder, and slavery. For their part, the Portuguese transferred the plant, the skills, and the technicians for sugar-making from Madeira to Brazil.[10] And with them went the slaves from Africa, since the American Indians perversely followed the Guanches into overworked oblivion so quickly when they were put to work in the fields or mines.

3. THE CARIBBEAN CONNECTION: PREPARING THE GROUND

I t was in the Caribbean that the crucial connections between peoples, European, African, and American, with their respective technologies, came together to be distilled into rum. This fervid, humid region is steeped in history—and in holocausts. The ovoid formed by the Caribbean islands and the Spanish Main is the dinosaurs' grave marker. The islands are a ring of volcanoes, some extinct but many still active, that formed when a massive meteor hit the Earth some sixty-five million years ago, smashing the crust. All across the world, the geological record shows the fallout from this spectacular event, which marks a complete change in the amount and variety of the fossil records. The resulting conflagration, tidal waves, and proto-nuclear winter cleared the planet for the mammals to come out from their hiding places under the feet of the reigning lizards.

Even now, in a weaker imitation of its baleful past, the region is often the birthplace of the weather systems that sweep up the east coast of North America and the west coast of Europe, and it is the warm wellspring of the Gulf Stream that takes them there. But with Columbus, the tides of history joined up with those of meteorology and geology to reconnect the islands with the rest of the world. The prevailing winds brought ships across from European waters to hit land in the Caribbean. There, the locals were already behaving as humans do. The Caribs were moving north through the island chains, reputedly annihilating and eating the previous Arawak inhabitants. Whether this was true or simply propaganda put out by the Spanish to justify their enslavement, the Caribs in turn were effectively expunged, though not ingested, first by the incoming conquistadors and then by the English and French settlers in the Leeward and Windward islands.

On the Caribbean islands, a system evolved that was as ruthless as the predatory dinosaurs whose doom had been delivered there eons before. It was to move millions of souls from Africa and swallow up whole armies and fleets from Europe. Arabic alchemy and agriculture, transmitted respectively via northern Europe and the Iberian peninsula, combined with the northwest European spirit of commerce and enterprise, not to mention the Spanish and Portuguese industrial-scale adoption of the Arab idea of chattel slavery and their exclusive application of it to Africans. Together they helped begin modern history as we know it. The collective suffering it brought, with millions of casualties, was enormous, but, for good or evil, it gave birth to the modern world, from the growth of capitalism to the birth of the United States. And the whole bloody enterprise was launched upon a sea of rum.

Within two centuries of Columbus setting forth, the Atlantic seaboards of Europe, Africa, and the Americas were tied in complex currents and eddies of commerce. While the silver and gold bullion from the Spanish Main had its effects on the European economy and history, it did not so much transform Spain as allow its rulers to postpone the reforms that would have allowed them to flourish longer. Instead of the plundered bullion providing capital for trade and industry, the Hapsburgs squandered their treasure on imperial ambitions while their domestic economy puttered along as before. Indeed the one part of their realms that could have benefited from the trading link was the Netherlands, where the American bullion paid instead for the century-long religious wars of repression that ensured that neither the Dutch, the Spanish, nor the Hapsburgs could benefit fully from the transatlantic connection.

But more important in their long-term economic and historical effects were those fifteen hundred sugarcane shoots from the Canary Islands that Columbus carried on his second voyage in 1493, along with Arab prisoners to work them. Making their base in Hispaniola, his settlers took time off from rooting for gold to plant the cane—or rather to make the Moors plant it. They noticed that many of the prison laborers died, and the implications were noted for the future. Columbus's son, Ferdinand, also noted that the cane cuttings germinated in only seven days. As that indicated, the Caribbean islands proved to be exceptionally productive for cultivating cane—but not very productive of the gold and silver that the Spanish had crossed the ocean to find. That might explain why Spain did not defend the islands as vigorously as it might have done, allowing interlopers like the Dutch, English, and French to take possession of Barbados and Jamaica, Martinique and Guadeloupe. Like a nefarious vacuum, these interlopers and their sugar cultivation eventually sucked in black slaves from across the Atlantic.

This is the background for rum's "more sinister and vicious history."[11] While there may have been a few Africans in the motley crew of Moorish prisoners and slaves that the Spanish took to Cuba in 1502, the Portuguese can be said to have truly pioneered the Middle Passage eight years later, in 1510. They took the first consignment of African slaves across the Atlantic as commodities rather than captured prisoners of war. Indeed, not only did the Portuguese pioneer the trade, they and their Brazilian successors were the last to relinquish it. Emancipation in Brazil waited until 1888, competing for the dishonor with the Spanish in Cuba, where it had been abolished a mere two years earlier.

São Tomé, a colonial backwater where the slave trade had started, was the last place where slavery lingered on into the twentieth century. Angolans were kidnapped and sent by steamer to São Tomé for a one-way trip. Officially they went voluntarily as contract laborers, but in reality they went as slaves. They cultivated cocoa rather than sugar, but the principle was the same. In the end as at the beginning, Africans died in bondage to assuage the sweet tooth of Europe and the Americas.[12]

It was not until 1516 that the first Caribbean sugar, in the form of sugar loaves, was presented to King Charles V, ironically by the inspector of gold mines in Hispaniola. In the absence of serious gold mines, he did not have over-much work to match his official job description, but the sugar did become a gold mine in the metaphorical sense. The conquistadors of Hispaniola also planted much more than sugar; they planted the seeds for the dark history of Haiti and its slave rebellions and brutal repressions in which sugar and rum were to play a major part. Gradually over the decades of the sixteenth century, the Spanish and Portuguese, as they abandoned hope of striking gold, began planting sugar in the various islands that are now the homes of renowned rum distilleries—Hispaniola (now Haiti and the Dominican Republic), Puerto Rico, Cuba, Jamaica—and also along the coast, the Spanish Main, as the English termed it later when many of the islands had been wrested from His Hispanic Majesty's control.

Father Jean Labat, the seventeenth-century French Dominican friar who spent as much time dealing with dis-tilled spirits as holy spirits and who perfected the pot still that bears his name, claimed that the French found sugarcane growing wild on Martinique, Saint Kitts, and Guadeloupe, but one cannot help but suspect that this may have been the vegetable remains of the earlier Spanish attempts at colo-nization and cultivation or that escaped slaves or Arawaks brought it over.

Islam's Contribution to the Modern World—Alcohol

So much for the sugar. But the Spanish did not make the final connection. It was the Arabs, of all people, who, despite claimed Koranic injunctions against alcohol, provided the science for both sugar and distillation, without going into rum production themselves.

One Arab scholar suggested to me that the prophet's prohibition was not of wine as such but of a local wine made from dates, and on aesthetic grounds he applauded the prophet's taste and decision. "The stuff is really bad," he told me, "But the Prophet was silent about Black Label, which is just as well, since I like it—a lot." Recent experience suggests that his attractively pragmatic exegesis is a distinctly minority view in Islamic jurisprudence, although several of the Sufi schools would doubtless go along with it.

It is perhaps fitting that the alchemy that produces such a flavorsome and satisfying drink should ultimately be based on the work of the alchemists themselves. As the repositories of ancient knowledge during the western European Dark Ages, the Arabs passed on the Greek *ambix,* which, with the addition of the Arabic definite article *al* became the *alembic.* In its essence, it prefigured every still that has been made since: a vessel in which the original mixture is heated, sending vapors along a tube into a condenser, which cools the vapors into a solid or liquid form. As a piece of apparatus it had many uses, such as isolating mercury. The purpose of the alchemical researchers was, of course, to transmute dull, workaday material into gold, which was perfectly feasible if you thought there were just four elements that made up the universe. Like the Star Wars antimissile research of modern times, it just needed a little jiggling, a bit more research funding.

But just as the Spanish went looking for gold and discovered sugar, the Arabs found something else in their search. The alembic allowed all sorts of magical tricks, in

the course of which someone discovered that by heating
fermented liquids, notably wine, to a temperature we now
know is 78.4 degrees Celsius, the product that evaporates,
leaving behind most of the water, is *al kohl,* alcohol, a clear
liquid that burnt the taste buds and itself burned when lit.
When the vapors were run through a cooler, they would
precipitate, or *sublimate,* in alchemical terms, on the sides
of the vessel.

Originally *al kohl* was *kohl,* the sublimate of antimony, used
to enhance the appearance of the eyes, but it soon came to
mean any sublimate or distillate. In its early use, *alcohol,* even in
English, meant the distillate, so, for example, *alcohol of wine*
referred to brandy, in much the same sense as we would use
"spirits." In the Arabic and Muslim world, the word *alcohol* was
not used for the spirits of wine; the term used was *arrack,*
which means "sweat," referring to the droplets of condensing
alcohol on the side of the vessel. In various forms, such as *raki,*
the name has spread from the Adriatic to the Indian Ocean
and even to the steppes of Mongolia, which suggests some
assiduous trading by the less-devout kind of Muslims.

For fairly obvious religious reasons, modern Arab historians, generally otherwise eager to demonstrate how much
Islam contributed to modern science, have not promoted
their national primacy in this field of endeavor. In earlier
days, they were less reticent. Muslim scientists such as Ibn
Sina (Avicenna), whose complete works were translated into
Latin by the great university of Salerno, publicized their dis-
coveries on distillation. Avicenna, who lived in what is now
Uzbekistan in the late tenth century, seems to have used the
process to make perfume. Ironically, in the last days of the
Soviet Union, his thirsty compatriots were reduced to

drinking eau de cologne when Mikhail Gorbachev added the already failed tactic of prohibition to the tail end of the failed Soviet experiment. Collaterally, he also trashed the Cuban economy by banning imports of rum.

While Avicenna may have had perfume in mind, not all his colleagues were so pure. Marco Polo also mentioned that the Persians made a "very good wine" out of it, but he did not leave enough details for us to know whether Islamic alchemy had introduced distillation to the cane juice.

Arnold of Villanova called the product *aqua vitae,* the water of life, a name publicized by his disciple Raymond Lull, the Catalan philosopher who has good claims to have invented the computer and allegedly made gold from mercury and tin for King Edward III of England in between making the hard stuff in the interests of science. Al-Antaki (d. 1599) mentions the *'araq* of sugarcane and of grapes, which suggests that the Arabs were making rum even as Columbus was shipping his cane cuttings across to the Caribbean.[13]

People who drank beer instead of wine soon realized that the spirits of the ferment could be distilled in the same way. In Holland, cereals were used to make gin, in Russia and Poland, vodka, and in Scotland and Ireland, whiskey. Naturally, there are big issues of national pride involved here, right down to spelling—in Scotland, whisky; in Ireland, whiskey. We can fairly safely give as much credence to the tale of Saint Patrick bringing a still back to Ireland as to the story of him driving the snakes out of it.

Allegedly, when King Henry II of England received the papal franchise of "Lord of Ireland," his soldiery were much taken with the local aqua vitae, and claims have been made that the Bushmills distillery was founded in that period. However, this tale is not copper-bottomed evidence of Hibernian primacy and is likely to be the result of a combination of too much drinking of the product and kissing the Blarney Stone.

The first direct mention of Scottish whisky distillation is in the Scottish Exchequer Rolls of 1494, accounting for "Eight bolls of malt to Friar John Cor wherewith to make aquavitae." The malt is a key reference. In much of Scotland, and Ireland too, wheat does not grow easily, so the main crops were oats and barley, much hardier grains. Barley has a very distinctive trait for the brewer or distiller: if the grain is *malted,* germinated for a few days, it becomes very rich in sugars— not nearly as much as sugarcane but far more so than other grain crops and enough to incite the yeasts to ferment it much more actively than mere starches. Those "bolls of malt" reflect a distinctive Celtic advantage in developing an alcohol-rich mash for the stills.

How could history combine the Celtic skills in distillation with sugarcane? By bringing the various actors together in the Caribbean.

4. Barbados, the Birthplace of Rum

The Mount Gay distillery is perched at the top of a ridge in the northern part of Barbados, positioned to catch the wind so its windmills could grind the sugarcane—and also to keep the heat and mosquitoes of the lower reaches of the island at bay. The distillery claims to be the oldest rum-maker in the world and celebrated its tercentenary in 2003. While such claims of corporate continuity are not always verifiable, it is true that the company is still making rum on a site where its manufacture was recorded as far back as 1703, when a legal deed lists "two stone windmills . . . one boiling house with seven coppers, one curing house and one still house" as part of the estate, implying that it was already a going concern then.

More significantly, Barbados is the (almost) undisputed home of rum, both of the drink and the name. The first direct literary reference to rum was on the island, when a much-quoted anonymous author wrote in 1651 that "the chief fudling they make in the island is Rumbullion, alias Kill-Devil, and this is made of sugar canes distilled, a hot, hellish and terrible liquor."[14] Even the French historian of rum, Alain Huetz de Lemp, while allowing the possibility that the Portuguese and Spanish may have tried distillation in the Canaries and Azores, credits Barbados with literary primogeniture for rum, which he claimed was being made there by 1638, within a few years of settlement.[15] As we shall see, the stills were certainly steaming away there by the middle of the century.

Why Barbados? Our answers lies in the convergence of the long lineages of invention and commerce from the various parts of the Eurasian land mass that recombined in the cultural alembic of Barbados in the fourth and fifth decades of the seventeenth century. The original skills of Neolithic East Asian subsistence farmers, Greek and Arab science, early modern commerce, the Mediterranean abuse of slavery for sugar cultivation, and the Iberian discovery of Africans as readily available slaves were stirred with Protestant enterprise from England and Holland and the Celtic taste for strong liquor and skills in meeting their needs. Together, these streams of history all mixed in one small island to produce the heady cocktail of rum, which was to foment wars, industries, and revolutions around the Atlantic for centuries to come.

Barbados was, in a sense, discovered in what one might call good spirits. The English first discovered it in 1609, when Sir John Summer was driven there in a hurricane that left the ship in peril of foundering. To console themselves, he and his crew dipped into their cargo of "comfortable waters," the name for spirits at that time.[16]

With no locals to do the Thanksgiving thing and help out the incoming settlers, the *William and John,* the ship that later brought the first English settlers to Barbados, had to sail on to the Dutch ports on the mainland to find food that the settlers could recognize. Along with seeds and cuttings for food cultivation, its captain, Henry Powell, brought back sugarcane, which was certainly not on the manifest when the ship left England.

And there we have the equation in a small tot—thirsty settlers who knew how to make spirits, and sugarcane, the most potent source of fermenting alcohol *for the still.* Barbados had the year-round heat, the water, and the flat lands that sugarcane needs for growing. It soon had the labor, the commercial contacts, and the expertise to produce and sell sugar—and its by-products, such as rum—and to export its new social structure.

Barbados is unique among the Antilles. It is almost the only island that is not a product of the volcano belt that surrounds the Caribbean. It is a coral island with, as contemporary rum producers on the island are quick to tell you, clean water filtered through the coral limestone—ideal for rum production. It is also fairly low-lying and hence easily cultivatable, without the upland *mornes* of the French islands or the mountains of Jamaica for the slaves to escape to. The easternmost of the Caribbean islands, astride the trade winds from Africa, Barbados was the first port of call for sailing ships from northern Europe.

In those days, latitude was relatively easy to calculate but longitude involved a lot of guesswork, so ships cast about carefully looking for the island on the appropriate latitude. They were not helped in this by the fact that Barbados, with less than two hundred low-lying square miles, was neither a big nor a very visible target. As Sir Henry Colt, who visited it in 1630, said, "It is like a sixpence thrown upon Newmarkett Heath."[17] However, the availability of the fine harbor at Carlisle Bay, with water, stores, markets, and information at Bridgetown, made it a highly advisable stop for ships that had just crossed the Atlantic, short of water, stores, and possibly even structure if they had met bad weather en route.

The difficulty of returning to Barbados by sail against the prevailing winds from the islands further west and north meant that it was one of the few islands not yo-yoed from one European empire to another, nor even wasted and burned in the usual form of economic warfare in the Caribbean over the ensuing two centuries. Compared with most colonial enterprises, the Barbados colony was born without original sin, even if it soon added some quite original ones of its own. When the first English settlers landed in 1627, they found no trace of the original native inhabitants except the bridge they had left to give the current capital, Bridgetown, its name. Barbados was an insular *Marie Celeste,* and no one has ever found out what happened to the bridge-builders, who left many signs of their existence that archaeologists are still excavating. It is possible that the Spanish had taken them as slaves, but they were not around to be asked, so the English colonists were spared the temptation of replicating the ethnic cleansing of other ventures in the Caribbean and North America.

We have a chatty, sharp, and engaging narrative about the

island that brings together all aspects of its future development just as the future was in the process of happening: sugar planting, slavery, the accompanying deforestation—and rum. Its author, Richard Ligon, *Gent.,* was a Cavalier ruined during the English Civil War by riots at home that culminated in the decapitation of King Charles. Like many of his Royalist kind, he had come to Barbados to repair his fortune. It was not an entirely successful attempt, since he was sick for most of his three years on the island and was in the Upper Bench Prison in London, probably for debt, when he wrote his book in 1657. It is a rare narrative, since while the pious New Englanders had gone to the New World for reasons of theology, most Caribbean settlers were far more concerned with making money than making any intellectual or spiritual mark on the world.

Ligon was a polymath: a gourmet (responsible for the first recipe containing rum—calvesfoot pie, made with minced and spiced pig skin and a "dramme cup *of Kill-Devill*"),[18] an architect, something of an economist, and a lover of nature. His rapturous descriptions of his contented meditations in the forests of Barbados call to mind his political opponent but poetical soul mate, the "Puritan" poet Andrew Marvell:

> *The mind, that ocean where each kind*
> *Does straight its own resemblance find;*
> *Yet it creates, transcending these,*
> *Far other worlds, and other seas;*
> *Annihilating all that's made*
> *To a green thought in a green shade*

However, Ligon could already see paradise being lost: the

island's native flora and fauna were rapidly coming to a sticky end, as indeed was its founding social composition. While he was lyrically content with the natural state of the island, Ligon was positively enraptured with its economic prospects. He may have been a Royalist, but his enthusiasm for "improvement" rivaled that of dissenter Daniel Defoe. Wearing his botanist's hat as he sketched its tropical wonders for his readers, Ligon differentiated between the species "planted there by the great Gardiner of the World," and one other, sugarcane:

> brought thither as a stranger; from beyond the Line, which has a property beyond them all; which though it has but one single taste, yet that full sweetness has such a benign faculty, as to preserve all the rest from corruption, which, without it, would taint and become rotten, and not only the fruits of this Island, but of the world, which is a special preheminence due to this plant, above all others.[19]

He meant that you could make preserves, jam, jellies, or marmalade with it, but one must admit that he said it in a much nicer way.

The first colonists were land-hungry farmers, for whom the island must have seemed even more attractive since their homeland was undergoing the severe winters of the Little Ice Age that blighted the years of the Commonwealth and saw ice fairs held on a frozen Thames. Ligon inadvertently revealed the perils of paradise when he recommended anyone taking trade goods to the island to stock up with "Black Ribbon for mourning," which he says "is much worn there, because their mortality is greater."[20] The death rate was high among the planters, and even higher among the indentured servants they brought along to do the work.

"The slaves and their posterity, being subject to their Masters for ever, are kept and preserv'd with greater care than the servants, who are theirs but for five years,"[21] Ligon comments, in a way that almost anticipates Karl Marx's patron, Frederick Engels, commenting on how much cheaper it was to employ cotton-mill workers in Lancashire than slaves in the fields. Most of the white workers were indentured for five years to repay the cost of their passage, so, Ligon said, they "have the worser lives, for they are put to very hard labour, ill lodging, and their dyet very sleight."[22] As one example, Ligon records how the "negroes" ate roasted corn on the cob but the "Christian servants" were fed "lob lollie," maize porridge, pounded in a large mortar, boiled, and served cold in trays for "seven or eight" of them, "and scarce afford them salt with it."

Within a few years of the island's settlement, Sir Henry Colt, who had managed to navigate his way to "the six-pence on Newmarkett Heath," recorded in his diary that his ship was overrun with servants trying to flee the island and that it took a day's search to remove the stowaways before they could voyage on to Saint Kitts. It is clear that even a "free" servant's lot was not a happy one.

Significantly, many of these white "servants" came from the Celtic fringes of the British islands—Devon, Cornwall, Scotland, and Ireland—where people have had a long and colorful relationship with alcohol in all its forms and where, as we have seen, whiskey-making was well attested.

Many of them were no more voluntary than the African immigrants. The Venetian ambassador reported that in 1656 alone he saw 1,200 people collected from the streets of London and put on ships for Barbados.[23] One indentured servant later wrote that he was the only survivor of 1,300 prisoners sent in 1654. Ominously, the word "barbadosed" carried some of the connotations of "shanghaied."[24] Even before the English Civil War, there are records of ships from Ireland bringing servants—for example, fifty-six Irish men and women from Kinsale who signed up in 1636. They thought they were going to be indentured in Saint Kitts but ended up in Barbados, where they were sold for 500 pounds of tobacco each.[25] Sugar was neither a product nor a commodity at that stage, but it soon became one.

Ligon tells what he considers an amusingly illustrative anecdote of planter who wanted to exchange a sow at "a groat [four pence] a pound for the hogs flesh" with a white woman servant at "sixpence for the woman's flesh." The woman was so heavy that he reneged on the deal. Tastes in both women and jokes have changed—or maybe it was the rum.

One prominent group of workers whose plight did at least attract attention, if not much mercy, were the seventy-three Royalist prisoners taken at the Battle of Colchester in 1648. The Parliamentarians let the pressed men go but sent the volunteers to Barbados and sold them to the planters on the island. Sold on the boat as they arrived for fifteen hundred pounds of sugar each, the Cavalier prison-laborers had a lot of capital to amortize with their labor.[26] While landless workers traditionally signed indentures that, like those of an apprenticeship, bound them to their masters for a period of five years, this was not usually the fate of "gentlemen," which in the context of the plantations pragmatically meant those who paid their own fare out. Of course, these gentlemen had not paid their fare. To add to their humiliation of being bound to manual labor, as prisoners the Royalists seem to have been indentured indefinitely.

· Their fate was the subject of a major parliamentary debate in 1659. "Bought and sold still from one planter to another, attached as horses or beasts for the debts of their masters, whipped at the whipping post at their masters' pleasure and mercy, and in other ways made miserable beyond expression or Christian imagination. . . . They are now generally grinding at the mills and attending at the furnaces or digging in the scorching land," said Sir John Lenthall, M.P., who suggested that all English servants should be withdrawn from fieldwork, which he said should be left for "Blacks and Irishmen." With similar ethnic sensitivity, Major Knight asked why his parliamentary colleagues were wasting their time on Cavaliers and inquired rhetorically: "What will you do with the Scots taken at Dunbar, and Durham and Worcester. Many of them were sent to Barbadoes." He was not expressing care for their fate. Rather the opposite. It is perhaps symptomatic of the hard-nosed attitude of the plantocracy in Barbados that despite the strong Royalist sympathies of so many of the plantation owners—they had even staged a rebellion against Cromwell and Parliament—they did not try to "buy" and redeem their Royalist counterparts from their servile labors.

Certainly no one in Parliament in London or on the island saw anything wrong with African slaves suffering the same fate. And so harsh was the treatment of the white workers that they mounted several major revolts. There was one in 1634, and another in 1647 that the local magnates dealt with as summarily as any slave revolt. In the latter, Ligon says, eighteen ringleaders were put to death.[27] Indeed while a "servant" still technically had legal civil rights, the exercise of those rights was not easy in the face of a legal establishment of masters. Barbadian historian Hilary Beckles reports that in 1640, two servants who had the temerity to complain about their treatment were "Adjudged malicious and publicly flogged."[28] Ligon describes servants who complained being "beaten by the Overseer; if they resist, their time is doubled. I have seen an Overseer beat a Servant with a cane about the head, till the blood has followed."[29]

In the circumstances, it is perhaps not surprising that the masters' houses were "built in the manner of Fortifications, and Lines, Bulwarks and Bastions to defend themselves. In case there should be any uproar or commotion in the island, either by the Christian servants, or Negroe slaves." Already the paranoia of classical plantation life had taken hold. Each household was to "discharge a Musquet, which gives the Alarum to the whole island" in the event of any overt mutiny in other plantations.[30] Barbados was pioneering "the custom of the country," the institutionalization of slavery in defiance of the laws of England. There is some evidence that in the early days black slaves were treated as if they were indentured, but eventually the indentured were treated like slaves.

Although there was heavy stress in the early days, it became worse. Ligon reports that on his arrival in September 1647, "the great work of sugar making was but ncwly practiced by the inhabitants there." By the time he left in 1650, "they were much better'd." He lists the new technologies they had adopted: letting the canes grow fifteen months, instead of the twelve months considered the appropriate period for a crop by farmers accustomed to annual seasons in the temperate zone; plating mill rollers with iron, which improved extraction; and getting the right sequence for the boilers. "And now this commoditie, Sugar, hath gotten so much the start of all the rest of those, that were held the staple commodities of the island, and so much over-top't them as they are for the most part slighted and neglected." It had become truly the "soul of trade in this island."[31]

As another correspondent wrote to Henry Winthrop in New England, "Men are so intent upon producing sugar that they had rather buy foods at very deare rates than produce it by labour"—a phenomenon that the New Englanders soon took advantage of.[32] The Dutch, who did not go much for planting and settling themselves, played a catalytic role. While the French and British warred for control of fertile islands, first jointly against the Spanish and then against each other, the Dutch were much happier arbitraging goods produced by others. The Dutch colonies were generally trading posts with good harbors but poor harvests, such as Saint Eustatius or Curaçao. The exception was the coast of Brazil near Pernambuco, where the Dutch developed the existing sugar plantations with the aid of Sephardic Jews, whom the Portuguese eventually expelled along with the Dutch when they reclaimed the territory.

The Portuguese estates had been run on a semifeudal basis, with sharecropping playing a major role. The *senhor de engheno,* the lord of the mill, exacted his half-share from the sublessees, who of course used slaves to produce the cane. In contrast, the Dutch were happier with the openly capitalist cash-based system that the British had also brought with them to the Caribbean. Following the example of the Dutch plantations in Brazil around 1640, when Colonel James Drax bought a triple-roller sugar mill and a set of copper cauldrons from Pernambuco, Barbados began the switch to sugar monoculture, setting the course for much of the Caribbean for the next three centuries. The technology of the three rollers came from Sicily via the Canaries and Azores to Brazil, where the Dutch and their Sephardic protégés developed it and then transferred to Barbados when the Portuguese threw them out after 1645. At the same time, Captain James Holdip imported sugarcane cuttings, which he spread around the island—in one contract swapping fifty acres–worth of cuttings for twenty-five servants.[33]

The Dutch encouraged the cultivation. Initially they sold slaves, tools, and food to the settlers and then bought the resulting sugar for resale in Europe. With the fighting in Pernambuco, Barbados was a replacement producer for the Dutch, not competition. They took profits on the food, slaves, and tools and also on sales of the resulting products, at each stage taking a high markup.

Ligon was impressed with the intensity of the labor. In English traditional agriculture, as in much of the world, seasons varied, and often there was little to do except wait for the crops to grow. In the seasonless tropics, the planting, weeding, and harvesting of sugar demanded a continuous round of toil all year. The actual sugar mill, *the ingenio* itself set new standards for industrial production-line techniques.

But it took a northern European Protestant work ethic to develop a workweek that began at 1 A.M. on Monday and continued around the clock in four-hour shifts until midnight the following Saturday, when religion, at least, forbade such toil. Any minor interruption anywhere on the line, from the mills to the furnaces to the boiling vats, brought the whole process to a halt and had everyone else standing idle. The cane could not be stockpiled while waiting for the line to restart, because within a day the sugar content was lost "For all these depend upon one another, as wheels in a Clock," Ligon says, adding significantly, "or if the Stills be at fault, the kill-devil cannot be made."[34]

His diagram of the mill shows, with a draftsman's eye, the capstan-like structure turned by animal power, the array of coppers and pots for the sugar, and the gravity-fed pipes leading to a cistern in the stillhouse, where the skimmings of the later stages of refining were drawn off and kept until they were *soure*, or fermented, before being twice distilled in the two stills. Ligon explains that "the first time it [the rum] comes over the helme [the head of the still], it is but small, and is called Low-wines, but second time comes off the strongest spirit or liquor that is potable."[35] When Ligon left Barbados in 1650, the distillery had already become an integral part of the machinery of production that had begun to move the trading fleets in their stately progress around the Atlantic seaboards.

· To show how this production line centering on the *ingenio* spanned the globe, jeopardizing the whole enterprise Ligon also diagrammed the triangle of trade that was, with various apexes, to create the modern world. "A Master of a ship . . . having transported goods of several kinds from—

England to a part of Africa, the River of Gambra, had there exchanged his commodities for Negroes which is what he intended to make his voyage of," was surprised by a slave uprising, and blew up the ship with himself and all the slaves. "These and several other wayes there will happen, that extreamly retard the world of Sugar-making."[36] Indeed!

It is worth noting that Ligon does not seem to have spoken in any social way with the white servants but often refers to his conversations with black and Indian slaves. He clearly took a great interest in their lives and had a deep appreciation of their intelligence and skills, which were so necessary for the settlement to survive. And yet, just as Daniel Defoe's Robinson Crusoe appreciated Man Friday's sterling qualities but still sold him as a slave, Ligon questions the conditions of white servitude but does not challenge black or Indian slavery at all.

Barbados thus assembled a unique social and commercial cocktail of Arab, Mediterranean, and northern European technologies, tastes, and people and a particular early-modern attitude to slavery, all stirred but not shaken, protected as the island was by geography and meteorology from the naval and military vicissitudes of the islands farther to the west. In retrospect, it is not surprising that this small island seems to have been the original home of rum or that for many generations the finer forms of it were also known as Barbadoes Water.

Who Done It?

Although the evidence all points to the time and place for the invention of rum, we have no record of who on the island made the crucial intuitive leap between sugarcane and rum cask. Once sugarcane cultivation began, anyone familiar with brewing beer or making whiskey would soon have noticed that in the fecund tropical air, natural fermentation began in any sugarcane juice that was not concentrated rapidly in the coppers or in the molasses when mixed with water. In the rhummeries of Guadeloupe and Martinique, where they use the full sugarcane juice to make their rums, I saw several that fermented the *vesous,* the sugar juice, in open vats. Within hours, the tanks looked like freshly poured pints of Guinness with froth bubbling on the top.

Concentrated sugar or molasses alone will not ferment. As Ligon notes, it is a preservative. But add water, and it is a distillers' dream. The high sugar, content makes for a high alcohol level, and the complexity of the material ensures that the alcohols are varied and laced with all those congeners that guarantee hangovers when taken in excess.

Initially, neither the "skimmings" taken off the top of the copper vats to concentrate the sugar, nor the molasses that drained from the bottom had much commercial value. They were not nearly as valuable or as transportable as the sugar loaves. Molasses can be used as a flavoring or sweetener in its own right, and the Spanish recognized that, calling it *melaza,* after the word for honey, while it is known as *blackstrap* in the United States and treacle in Britain. It can also be used as an additive to animal feeds or it can be used as God intended—to make spirits.

Present-day distillers unite in declaring the brew from fermented sugarcane juice (*vesous*) or molasses to be obnoxious to the taste and dangerous to intestinal comfort as well. However, the history of human relations with alcohol suggests that people who feel the urge will drink anything that contains it. I adduce in evidence *koumiss,* the drink the Mongols make by fermenting mares' milk, to confirm that taste is a cultural artifact. (In fact it is quite a refreshing aperitif, sour in taste compared with *shubat,* fermented camel's milk, which is much creamier.) I asked one modern stillmaster why no one drank the wash, and he suggested that there "were a lot of reasons. The yeast, some dead and some alive, and the bacteria—and you don't want to risk the fermentation continuing in your stomach."

However, anyone who knew that you could distill the enjoyable and active spirit from the otherwise noxious brew of fermented molasses would soon make the connection—and rum. Without being too stereotypical, we can hypothesize that some thirsty and inventive Scot or Irishman landed, voluntarily or involuntarily, in Barbados in its early days. Any exiled Celt who had dealt with malt to make a mash for a still would not need to be an Einstein to make the connection with molasses, not least on an island like Barbados, where traditional cereal production was insufficient for food, let alone brewing. So the odds are high that it may well have been an aesthete Celt, desperate for a decent drink, who decided that all those spirits needed releasing from their distasteful, wet, and murky brown shroud.

The urge to make alcohol is always strong, and when such eminently suitable materials as molasses were at hand it must have been near-irresistible. In fact, between 1644 and 1673, various colonial councils in the Leeward Islands forbade using the full sugarcane juice to make rum.[37] The task of the islands was to make sugar for hard currency, not hard drink to keep the locals soaked.

Ligon wrote as if torn between writing a prospectus to attract settlers and his concern as a good reporter when he described what the Barbadians in their ingenuity drank:

> good English Beer, French and Spanish wines, with others, some from the Maderas, some from Fiall, one of the islands of Asores; so we cannot justly complain of want, either of bread or drink, and, from England, Spirits, some of Anniseeds, some of Mint, some of Wormwood, &c. And from France, Brandy, which is extream strong, but accounted very wholesome."[38]

However, he also spends much time describing the shifts the colonists went to in adapting cornmeal, cassava, potatoes, and similar local staples to replace the expensive imports. Then he testifies to the ingenuity of the Barbadian colonists in the ways they used to alleviate the pangs of exile: *mobbie,* made from potatoes; *perino,* made from cassava root; *grippo plantine,* a drink brewed from plantains mashed and fermented; *punch,* made from sugar and water left to ferment; and a derivative made with added oranges. Most of these had to be drunk quickly when the fermentation finished, and all of them were a happy product of tropical temperatures and tropical air filled with natural yeasts rather than the cold and yeast-unfriendly atmosphere of England.[39] And he mentions again the main potation, "the drink of the Island, which is made of the skimmings of the Coppers, that boyl the sugar, which they call kill-Devil."[40] This is what Ligon later called:

the seventh sort of drink . . . infinitely strong, but not
very pleasant in taste. It is common and therefore the
less esteemed: the value of it is half a crown a gallon.
The people drink much of it, indeed too much, for
it often lays them asleep on the ground and that is
accounted a very unwholesome thing.

However, Ligon sings its praises for its lubrication of the
productive process:

This drink is of great use to cure and fresh the poor
negroes, whom we ought to have a special care of, by
the labour of whose hands, our profit is brought in. . . .
It is helpful to our Christian servants too; for when
their spirits are exhausted, by their hard labour, and
sweating in the Sun, ten hours every day, they find their
stomacks debilitated and much weakned in their vigour
every way, a dram or two of this Spirit, is a great comfort and refreshing to them.

One could almost drink to that!

As an underemployed architect and draftsman, Ligon complains about the colonists'"preposterous" style of building—
their failure to build high-ceilinged buildings with cellars,
thick walls, and good ventilation. Implying that tobacco and
rum were so ubiquitous as to make the homes potential fire-
bombs, he writes,"truly, in a very hot day, it may raise a doubt,
whether so much heat without, and so much Tobacco and
kill-devil within, might not set the house to fire: for these
three ingredients are strong motives to provoke it, and they
were ever there."[41]

While revealing that the settlers were more likely to be drinking rum than imported brandy, wine, or beer, he also implies that the rum was distilled and left overproof—nearly pure alcohol—without the dilution that would have made it less of a fire risk and more drinkable. He describes an accident that killed one slave who brought a lit candle near the bung of a cask: "If he had in the instant of firing, clapt his hand on the bung, all would have been saved; but he knew not that cue, lost the whole vessel of Spirits, and his life to boot." One worries about the implied sense of priorities here that puts the vessel of spirits before a life, but he mitigates it with his testimonial to rum's medicinal qualities: "though it had the ill hap to kill one Negro, yet has had the virtue to cure many."[42]

On the other hand, he shows mixed feelings even as he recommends the product to counter the enervating heat of the island, complaining that the remedy is "almost as ill as the disease; liquors so strong, as to take away the breath as it goes down, and red pepper for spice, which wants little of the heat of a fire coale."[43] In 1667 rum was commonly twice as strong as brandy. And a few decades later, George Warren called it "Stronger than brandy," and "drawn from Dreggs of sugar for the most part, yet sometimes from fruits and Rows of Fish."[44]—though fish-roe spirit is not a drink that would pass modern standards for rum.

By 1684, Thomas Tenison, who was later to attend to high spiritual rather than spirituous affairs by becoming the Archbishop of Canterbury, visited Barbados and wrote that rum had risen up the social scale. Referring to "Coow woow," a drink made from "molosses and ginger," he claims that its "being the cheapest and most common, is sufficient reason with most that have the wherewithal to make more chargeable liquors, to reject it." Those who could afford it drank "Rumm," he explains, though in terms no modern advertising copywriter would use. The islanders took the sugarcane juice, he writes, and then:

> the Scum, Dregs and excrementious Parts, which are separated from the finer and more essential parts, in the making of Sugar are of some value, for from the same being fermented and distilled, is extracted a strong Spirit, which they call Rumm; so that you see Sir, that the Juice of the Cane is made into three considerable Commodities, viz, Sugar, Treacle, and Rumm.[45]

The unholy spirit of this trinity was not just rum, but slavery, with depopulation and deforestation thrown in.

· But just as the rum crossed the ethnic divide in the plantations, it also bridged the class divide. It was a major revenue source for the planters, who sold up to thirty shillings–worth of it a week in addition to what they consumed in-house. Some of the revenue came from selling to local planters who lived without the spiritual benefit of an on-site still, but the rest was sent down to Bridgetown to be sold to ships, where it was "transported to foraign parts, and drunk by the way,"[46] showing that there was an export trade almost as soon as the stills were first fired up.

Rum was thus unique among spirits in that it made productive and profitable use of a by-product rather than taking crops out of the food chain in near-subsistence economies. The large-scale production of the refined, white, "clayed" sugar drained off even more molasses, providing a lucrative opportunity for rum production, and molasses became extremely important in the later conflict between the Crown and the mainland colonies.

The Spirit That Could Clear-Cut Forests

The concentration on sugar and rum showed in more ways than socially or ethnically. Ligon, an aesthete who gloried in the scenery and the night sky and was no slouch at the culinary arts, records how stunningly green and wooded the island appeared on his approach by sea, from where he could view "high large and lofty trees, with their spreading branches and flourishing tops."[47] Although the coastal areas had been cleared for planting, he says, logs and stumps of felled trees still littered the fields when he first arrived. Ligon blames the stumps littering the ground for the reluctance of the planters to go bowling in the early days, when the plantations had not yet reached the interior. The deforestation raised the island's temperature, making things even harder for the mostly white workers who had originally clear-cut the forests, removed the stumps, and then tended the plantations.[48]

Once sugar mania had taken over, so quickly did they clear-cut the island across the interior that by 1667 coal had to be imported from Britain for the sugar boilers because there was no more wood to burn. Ligon himself recommended that shipmasters load sea-coal as ballast for the voyage out. Later the islanders used more ingenuity, maintaining one large fire under the first boiler, fueled by the *bagasse,* the crushed cane stalk that is left after the sugar is extracted, and then directing the heat to the other boilers through flues. The origins of this innovation are revealed by its name, "the Jamaican Train."[49]

The intensive development of the sugar crop in Barbados set the pattern for the rest of the islands. Sugar employed both land and labor too profitably to waste them on growing food. In temperate climes, growers of grain did so first to feed themselves and only then to sell their surplus or pay their taxes and rents. Sugar was pure liquid capital from beginning to end. It transformed the islands and made them hubs of commerce where even basic foodstuffs and necessities became commodities, and more and more basic foodstuffs were imported. From the beginning to the end of the slave–sugar connection, other French and English islands followed in the path of Barbados, where, by 1646, the settlers were "so intent upon planting sugar that they had rather buy foode at very dear rates than produce it by labour, so infinite is the profit of sugar workes after once accomplished."[50] These were the oil states of their time, sacrificing all to the production of an international trade commodity.

In his gourmet's guide to the island, Ligon also shows the beginning of one of the most notable ties between North American colonists, slavery, and the Caribbean: the food the New Englanders sent back to the islands, "pickl'd Herring and Macquerel, which we have from New England," and "most sorts of salt fish; as Ling, Haberdine, Cod, poor John . . . Sturgeon from New England."[51] Thus begun the division of savor that was to mark the next two hundred years. "The Negroes were allowed each man two Macquerels a week, and every woman one; which were given out to them on Saturday in the evening." Otherwise the slaves lived on "one large bunch, or two small ones" of plantains a week. This was supplemented by the "Skins, heads and intrails" of any cattle "dyed by mischance, or by any disease."The white servants, it seems, ate the flesh of these cattle, which may well have contributed to their rapid disappearance from the Barbados economy.

As well as changing the topology and climate of the island, sugar and rum also brought about a transformation of society. In 1645, there had been some forty thousand white settlers and only six thousand slaves, and as part of making themselves at home, the colonists brought their politics with them. Ligon says that their normal discourse included "English dogg, Scots dogg, Irish dogg, Tory, Cavalier or Roundhead."[52] As time went on, the Barbadian planters imported more and more slaves to replace the predominantly white workforce and middling yeomanry. Sugar and rum as commercial commodities completed the transformation of humans into an article of trade in an even more untrammeled way than selling the indentures of white servants.

Presumably, rum had a more stimulative than narcoleptic effect on some of them, since Ligon records that Austin's Bay in Barbados was named "not in commemoration of any Saint, but of a wild mad drunken fellow, whose lewd and extravagant carriage made him infamous in the island."[53] The planter in question was one Edward Austin, whose name transmuted to Oistins.

It was at Oistins in 1652 that an event took place that was hugely important for the island and for the whole

British maritime empire. Parliament sent out a small fleet under Sir George Ayscue to wrest the island from its Royalist governor, Lord Willoughby. The parliamentarian paper *Mercurius Politicus,* a pioneer in both political and yellow journalism, suggested that alcohol fueled the defiance of Lord Willoughby, the Royalist governor: "partly by the Brandywine wherewith we have furnisht him, the spirits of rombostion, which our men there make him, and other hopes we give him, he becomes very valiant."[54]

After some desultory fighting and feinting, the colonists secured an amicable deal that in a sense could be described as the opening shot of the American Revolution. In return for a pledge of loyalty to Parliament in London, the colonists secured their own Assembly—and the prescient right of no taxation without representation, a demand that echoed down the years. Equally indicative of the future, the island's black population was not represented. The negotiations took place in the Mermaid Tavern, where one feels sure that rum was served by the pint. By the eighteenth century, when George Washington visited the island, the head of the Barbadian Senate was known as the president, so we could say that rum and revolution had an early outing together long before the American Declaration of Independence.

Despite that outbreak, the freeholders who could vote and take an active part in politics seemed to concentrate on pragmatic moneymaking rather than issues of high principle. "A standing commission there was also, for punishing Adultery and Fornication, though rarely put in execution,"[55] Ligon comments. Above all, the proprietors seemed to be united in their indifference to the suffering of their indentured compatriots. Many of the white settlers took the hint. Those who had survived the grueling labor, the "West Indies *Dry Gripes*," the yellow fever, and the rum voted with their feet and headed for the Carolinas and even Philadelphia and New England. It did not help that in 1655 Admirals Penn and Venables, on their way to take Hispaniola from the Spanish, recruited many landless freemen and indentured servants for the enterprise, which failed totally. However, they picked up Jamaica as a consolation prize, thus offering many more opportunities to landless whites than on Barbados, where real estate values had soared in the face of the land hunger of the big sugar plantations.[56]

Twenty years after Ligon had prophesied it, the trees had gone—and so had many of the white settlers, who preferred the more congenial North American colonies, hence reversing the proportion of slaves to whites.

The Home of the Rum Shop

The Barbadian invention of rum established itself firmly at home before spreading throughout the burgeoning British Empire. The Barbadian Assembly had to ban the prototypes of the rum shops from selling anywhere near the highways, and when the island exported white settlers, they were not always welcome if they brought their habits with them. In 1671, the governor of Florida valued one English servant as worth two Barbadians, "for they are so much addicted to Rum that they will do little but while the bottle is at their nose."[57]

Rum's habit of eliding social divisions was also apparent. In the same year the Florida governor was grousing about Barbadians, a lieutenant in the garrison in Bridgetown was court-martialed because he not only married another man's wife but took to "her employment of selling Rum and other such pitiful things." It is interesting to note that selling rum wholesale by the grandees attracted no obloquy at all—but retail sales were frowned upon.[58]

By 1708, the drink had acquired more respectability, and even though John Oldmixon, the early historian of Barbados and North America, did not like the beverage, he was objective in his assessment of "the famous spirit known as Rum, which by some persons is preferred to Brandy," even if he was not one of them. "'Tis said to be very wholesome, and therefore it has lately supplied the Place of Brandy in Punch. Indeed, it is much better than Malt spirits and the sad Liquors sold by our distillers."[59] This rise in rum's status was not just because people had become accustomed to its taste; it was also because improvements in distillation techniques had reduced some of the stronger odors and flavors, as Oldmixon explains:

'Tis brought to such Perfection, that were it not for a certain Twang or Hogo that it receives from the Juice of the Cane, 'twould take place next to French Brandy; for 'tis certainly more wholesome, at least, in the Sugar-Islands; where it has been observed, that such as drink of the latter freely, do not live long, whereas the Rum-Drinkers hold it to a good old age.[60]

This wasn't just a matter of the British and the Barbadians being patriotic. According to French author Père Charlevoix, Barbadoes Waters were the best of all the sugarcane spirits because, unlike the French islands' production, they did not have the "taste of cane which gives it a quite disagreeable aftertaste." The use of the pot still had meant that by the beginning of the eighteenth century, Barbadoes Waters were renowned, only to be overtaken shortly by Jamaica rum, which was the standard for a long time afterward. From a "hot, hellish and terrible liquor" to elixir of life in half a century is not a bad transmutation for kill-devil.

The Barbadians gave their own invention and product the best recommendation of all—they drank it like fish. By the time of the American Revolution, they were drinking a third of their own substantial rum production. Pickled in every sense, the planters on the island thought, according to Governor Christopher Codrington in 1703, that the "the best way to make their strangers welcome is to murther them with drinking; the tenth part of that strong liquor which will scarce warme the blood of our West Indians, who have bodies like Egyptian mummys, must certainly dispatch a newcomer to the other world."[61]

However, just as the Trinity has Satan as an integral opposition, the trinity of rum, sugar, and molasses has a sordid counterpart for most of its history—slavery. One cannot help wondering if the early days in Barbados were not better than later, since Archbishop Tenison complains: "Black Women ... after those intollerable Works and Fatigues, you give them Rum, which at present is a little refreshing, yet you cannot but know it is distructive to Nature, wasting the vitals, and an Enemy of Propagation." He goes on to complain that the planters also plied the "Negroe Men" with this "destructive liquor: and that upon Sundays too, to very bad purpose." The purpose was to "perpetuate their Servetude," and encourage them into "venery" and "Polygamy" to breed.[62] In what was only the first of reams of sermon paper devoted to the iniquities of rum, he suggests that the social results were carried down the generations, since "no vigorous Issue can be expected," not because he had stumbled upon an early discovery of fetal alcohol syndrome but because of the "immoderate use of Venery" that rum provoked in the drinkers. And at no point did his concern for the moral welfare of the slaves extend to freeing them.

He was not alone. The equally pious Codrington bequeathed his plantations to the Society for the Propagation of the Gospel, and their efforts to enhance the spirituality of the Caribbean went in tandem with the prodigious and highly efficient production of spirits from his endowment. But because the absentee owners of the plantations expected to keep the full price of their sugar when it landed in Britain, as reported by Adam Smith, the managers were forced to boost rum production—which they did by skimming deeply in the pans, "robbing the sugar for the still— whose proceeds they retained on the islands." By the time of the American revolution in the British West Indies, the molasses had shifted from being the by-product to being the essential for rum production and the main source of finance for the operations of the plantations.

For its first two centuries, Barbados's position as the first port of call for ships to the other British colonies in the Western Hemisphere gave it an importance greater than its tiny size. Any "good" ideas that originated in the island, whether rum, sugar plantations, African slavery, or even the idea of calling the head of the local government the president, were sure to spread to all the British colonies, and in those early days these ideas were carried by the departing colonists. Some of them founded Charleston, where they left their marks on the names and habits of the Carolinian town and helped to establish a frequently forgotten connection between the Caribbean and the Eastern seaboard. Eleven of the first twenty-three governors of South Carolina came from the islands, seven of them from Barbados.[63] Henry Winthrop, son of John Winthrop, New England's first governor, put in three years in Barbados before moving north.[64]

While maintaining the trading connections that progressively expanded over the following century, the colonists took with them something far more pernicious than rum. Slavery had no basis in contemporary English law, and it took the autonomy of the Barbadian planters to codify it separately. The Barbadian slave code in 1661 was a legal breakthrough that was adopted by Antigua and Jamaica and then copied and emulated by South Carolina and Virginia, transforming the English legal idea of indentures for a fixed period into a state of perennial servitude for one group of people only. Whom the planters wished to enslave, they first insulted. "The Act for the Better Ordering and Governing of Africans and Negroes" began by referring to its subjects as "heathenish," "brutish," and a "dangerous kind of people."[65]

So, along with an aversion to taxation, the title of president, and rum, the codification of black slavery was

Barbados's contribution to the development of the North American colonies. Of Churchill's triptych on the navy, "rum, buggery, and the lash," two out of three were Barbadian exports to the mainland. Buggery was optional, one supposes.

Many other aspects of the economic and social structures of the Southern plantation system had a dry run in Barbados. Even at this early stage, Barbados had some amusing precursors of later stereotypical Southern lifestyles. Long before the Kentucky colonel's heyday, every planter or "gentleman" on the island was titled "Captain" or "Colonel." But there were more serious precursors in the persistent semifeudal politics setting poor whites as the first bulwark against the possibility of slave revolts. You could say that the fuse for the American Civil War fizzled its way north from Barbados, the sugar colony that rum made profitable and habitable.

Many of the founding fathers had family connections and current ties to the islands, ranging from George Washington's sojourn in Barbados to Alexander Hamilton's birth in Nevis and Thomas Jefferson's visit to Saint Kitts, where his grandfather had owned a plantation. There they had time to appreciate the model mix for the new republic, at least from the southern colonies' perspectives—slave owners' autonomy. Washington visited Barbados in 1751 and was almost tempted by his findings to stay—which could have started a whole new alternative history. He confided to his diary, "Canes is from 40 to 70 ton of sugar, each ton valued at 20 shillings out of which a third is deducted for expences, unless rum sells for 2/ and upwards pr Gallon than it is, though the sugar is near clean."[66]

Adam Smith put it more cogently than the founder of the United States, whose grammar and style improved over the years. "It is commonly said that a sugar planter expects that rum and molasses should defray the whole expense of his cultivation, and that his sugar should be all clear profit."[67] The presence of Washington in Barbados is testimony once again to the connections between the mainland colonies and the Caribbean.

However, it was not just the South but also New England that owed its heritage to the island. The rituals of two Indian slaves, John and Tituba, brought from Barbados to Salem by minister Samuel Parris, inspired the Salem witch-hunts, thus setting the precedent for the periodic paroxysms of intolerance that still beset the American mainland from time to time.[68] Barbados was everywhere—in spirit and in rum—throughout the new colonies. And the Barbadians also exported northward one of the more commercially lucrative ideas about what to do with their rum, an idea morally on a par with the "customs of the country." Soon emulated by Jamaica and the other islands, they took their rum to Africa to trade for slaves.

John Winthrop was a pioneer of the Barbadian–Boston connection. His journals record the first documented slave voyage from Boston in November 1644, a voyage that took staves for casks to Cape Verde Islands and traded them for slaves, whom they took to Barbados and exchanged for sugar and tobacco, eventually returning to Boston after a five-month round trip.

PART II
RUM IN THE AMERICAS:
THE SPRIT OF 1776

5. Early Settlers

In its early days in the mainland American colonies, rum was more likely to be drunk in a punch of some kind than as raw spirits. Indeed the ingenuity of the early settlers would bewilder most modern bartenders, although it is probably no coincidence that the historical memory of such concoctions should have made the United States the home of the cocktail, unlike Britain, where they simply added splashes of soda or tonic to their drinks. For example, *bombo,* or toddy, consisted of rum, sugar, water, and nutmeg, "which was made weak and kept cool" and was obviously one of the same species of drinks, ranging from punch to *mojhito* and *caipirinha,* that rum encouraged in the tropics.[69] A *julep* was similar but without the nutmeg and stronger.

Although rum soon became the top tipple, the American settlers generally attacked any keg in a drought. As a matter of routine, like their kin in the motherland, they drank alcoholic beverages in huge quantities—and vastly variable qualities. Of course, Darwinian selection was at work here. In those days, before sewage treatment plants and water filtration, water drinkers were at a strong dysenteric disadvantage. Clever survivors usually added alcohol in some degree to their H_2O intake. In 1623 the Virginia Assembly called for all new immigrants to bring malt so they could brew their own beer on arrival rather than be felled by the New World's water before they became accustomed to it.

The absence of malt was a recurrent theme for colonists from the very beginning, as shown by a letter from a thirsty Massachusetts Bay colonist to England in 1630:[70]

> *If Barley be wanting to make into malt,*
> *We must be content and think it no fault,*
> *For we can make liquor to sweeten our lips*
> *Of pumpkins and parsnips and walnut-tree chips.*

American literature has advanced a little since this Pilgrim protopoem, but it is revealing that alcohol inspired and fueled the Muses even at that early time.

When, as was often the case, barley was scarce, a substitute was made by mixing molasses in a wort with boiled spruce branches to make spruce beer. This was a reflection of desperate shortages—and fairly desperate thirsts as well. But it could get worse, and the list of brewing materials bespeaks many horrendously failed experiments, as desperate colonists sought substitutes by trial and error.

Governor William Berkeley of Virginia includes almost

everything except mare's milk in his description of offer-
ings the colonists laid at the altar of Bacchus, adding:

> The poorer sort brew their beer with molasses and
> bran, with Indian corn malted with drying in a
> stove: with persimmons dried in a cake and baked,
> with potatoes, with the small green stalks of Indian
> corn cut small and bruised, with pumpkins, with
> the Jerusalem artichoke, which some people plant
> purposely for that purpose, but this is the least
> esteemed.[71]

There are few limits to the technical imagination of
thirsty people anywhere in the world, but it would really
take Yankee ingenuity to top that artichoke brew, "boiled
with the scores of roots and herbs, with birch, spruce or
sassafras bark, with pumpkin and apple parings, with
sweetening of molasses or maple syrup, or beet tops and
other makeshifts."[72]

Faced with these concoctions, it is not surprising that
almost as soon as Barbados began to produce rum, the
New Englanders began to drink it. They developed a
ferocious thirst for it and, with Yankee ingenuity, soon
began making it on an industrial scale. They also began
distilling whiskey, although they called it brandy. Massachusetts whiskey was considered superior to the stuff
imported from London, and New York's first distillery
opened in 1640. However, if the colonists on the eastern
seaboard did not have the grain surplus to brew beer, then
it was even less sensible to use it to make whiskey. By
1660, three out of the five breweries in New York also

made whiskey. In a society that measured the cost of living by the price of bread, the distillers' demand for scarce grain not only raised the price of grain locally but made New York flour too expensive to compete in the Barbados market—where it was sold to buy rum, sugar, and molasses.[73] Eventually, it was more economical to ship grain to the Caribbean and get rum or molasses in return. So it was with both famine and profit in mind that in 1676, Edmund Andros, the governor of New York, simply banned distillation with grain unless the grain were too spoiled for milling into flour.[74]

In New England, cider was for a long time considered a potently acceptable beverage. The region's hot summers were even more conducive to apple growing—and hence cider cultivation—than most of England itself, where only the southwestern counties of England could consistently raise enough crop to make cider a regular drink. One Massachusetts village with only forty families was making three thousand barrels of cider a year in 1721, but apples could not compete in portability with molasses, and potent though it can be and doubtless was, cider could not compete in strength with rum.[75] New England cider manufacture may have been an early casualty of globalization Hanoverian-style. In an era when land transport in particular was not just expensive but intensely laborious and difficult, distilled drinks were a transportable and value-concentrated commodity, and molasses was the most portable of fermentable substances.

Rum-drinking did not supplant cider-drinking but was added to it, so that Americans drank even more than ever. For example, John Adams, while worrying about the

effect of rum and similar liquors on the morale of the
infant republic, quaffed a tankard of hard cider every
morning for breakfast.[76]

The technical obstacle to making rum in New England,
apart from the impossibility of growing sugarcane in such
a cold place, was the very property that had led to the invention of rum itself. Molasses is both bulky and prone to
spontaneous fermentation, which could have led to dire
and messy consequences on the voyage north as casks
exploded under pressure. It did not take long for producers
to discover how to concentrate the molasses to the point
that fermentation was impossible without diluting it, which
also reduced the bulk and hence shipping costs. A gallon of
this molasses produced a gallon of rum, and the value added
was considerable.

It made commercial sense to distill in New England,
with its superior technical and metalworking skills to
make the stills and its ample supply of timber for fuel and
cooperage. New England rum was like whiskey; it did not
have the color or the aroma of the West Indies rum, which
was why anyone who could afford it drank the Caribbean
import. Local rum's biggest advantage was that it was
much cheaper. For example, in 1740 in Philadelphia, the
local spirit cost one shilling and eight pence a gallon,
compared with two shillings and five pence a gallon for
West Indies rum. It was, as the saying has it, close enough
for government work—and for sale to Africans, Indians,
and people who were not concerned with the nose or the
palate.

Thus began the tradition of New England rum—
cheap and strong but not for connoisseurs—which was

to culminate in the Kennedy dynasty making its fortunes supplying Yankee thirsts during Prohibition.

Enter "Demon" Rum

Rum distillation soon became the colonies' biggest manu-facturing industry and a major export as well. The insa-tiable demand for molasses led the colonial merchants to venture far beyond the permissible boundaries of the mer-cantile system. Yankee trading ships docked in the harbors of the Dutch, French, and Spanish colonies to stuff their holds with the raw material for rum and the slave trade.

The new beverage spread like crack through a slum. By 1661, the General Court of Massachusetts in Boston had declared that the overproduction of rum was a menace to society. It also disapproved of the innkeepers' adulterating their beer with this "cheap sugar drink," although one can assume that many happy customers would think of these proto-boilermakers as fortification rather than adulteration.

In 1722 rum in Boston was three shillings and six pence a gallon.[77] But the pressure of production and increasing availability of molasses drove the price down. In 1727, the Connecticut authorities tried to ban rum distillation on the double grounds that the price of molasses was rising with the huge demand and that rum was "unusually unwholesome"—the ban lasted six months in the face of popular demand for the drink.[78] They were legislating against the laws of economics and, perhaps even more important, against a thirst that knew no bounds. The shift to rum continued. In the eighteenth century, colonists drank forty-four different kinds of beverages, and rum gave its kick to no less than eighteen of them.[79] Anticipating at least one American tradition unspoilt by Prohibition, recipes for punch contained immense amounts of calories as well as a potent kick.

In 1738, William Burck, a historian of the colonies, noted that New England rum cost only a little more than cider had cost a century before. By then Boston boasted eight distilleries, of whose product Burck comments, "The quantity of spirits which they distill in Boston, from the molasses which they import, is as surprising as the cheapness at which they sell it, which is under two shillings a gallon. But they are more famous for the quantity and the cheapness than for the excellency of their rum."[80]

Rum gained a further boost with the French wars that began with the accession of William of Orange to the British throne in 1688. Protestantism, protectionism, and patriotism together hindered the legal import of French brandy into Britain and its colonies. It inadvertently gave a big boost to distilling in Britain and the American colonies and led to a rapid appreciation of rum as a substitute. It must also be said that it led to a rapid rise in smuggling on both sides of the Atlantic. Partly in response to losing British markets for brandy, the French government in 1713 adopted its own protectionist policies and banned the import of rum even from its own colonies. It was a trade measure that would have massive unforeseen consequences, as we shall see.

New England rum did not sell well in Britain, despite the rapidly growing amounts distilled. It was all about the "excellency," and even the colonists, if they had money, preferred the rum from Jamaica, Antigua, and Barbados to their own local products. Jamaican rum, Benjamin Franklin's favorite, was much in demand in Britain and elsewhere, so it was the highest priced; demand was also high for Grenadian and Barbadian rum, which was also double distilled. The different colonies had their own preferences. New Yorkers liked Saint Croix rum, Philadelphians preferred Saint Kitts and Barbadian rum, while Virginians liked Antiguan rum and Marylanders preferred rum from Barbados.

6. THIRSTY SAINTS

The Pilgrim fathers were a bunch of weird cultists, rejected from their own country and perhaps overly devoted to things spiritual. Even before the Indians rescued them from their own incompetence on that first Thanksgiving, they had been dependent on sailors for their supplies. And their very first crisis was a beer shortage. Their own had run out on the way across the ocean in 1621 and had been eked out only by the occasional charity of the ship's company.

However, once the Puritans were cast off on this bleak shore, the crew, who did not share their fundamentalism, saw no reason to leave any beer behind when they had a voyage back to Europe ahead of them. Both sides were appalled at the prospect of a beer drought, and in the end the captain, with perhaps more Christian charity than the Pilgrims were ever to show, probably risked mutiny among his crew by leaving enough beer for pilgrims who were sick through the winter.

Strangely, although prohibitionists and temperance advocates would often be accused of puritanism, this was a calumny against the real Puritans. A Puritan, as H. L. Mencken says, is someone who has "the haunting fear that someone, somewhere, may be happy." That fear drove the Pilgrim fathers to drink, and as long as they managed to do so without breaking loose or falling over—or getting caught fornicating and committing adultery while their inhibitions were loosened—they escaped censure.

In the seventeenth century, the rambunctious and certainly non-Puritan Ned Ward was driven from old to New England by "Bishops, Bailiffs, and Bastards" but found the un-Episcopalian saints he found there equally unappetizing. He comprehensively condemns them:

> Many of the Leading Puritans may (without Injustice) be thus Characteris'd. They are Saints without Religion, Traders without Honesty, Christians without Charity, Magistrates without Mercy, subjects without Loyalty, Neighbours without Amity, Faithless Friends, Implacable Enemys, and Rich Men without Money.

Although he notes that the sailors who worked the ship that ferried him over depended on brandy and tobacco to fuel their labors, he contrasts that with the habits of the New World, where:

> Rum, alias Kill Devil, is as much ador'd by the American English as a dram of brandy is by an old

Billingsgate. 'Tis held as the comforter of their Souls, the Preserver of their bodys, the Remover of their Cares and Promoter of their Mirth; and is a Soveraign Remedy against the Grumbling of the Guts, a Kibe-heel or a Wounded Conscience, which are three Epi-demical Distempers that afflict the Country. [81]

He also alleges that "The Ground upon which Boston (The Metropolis of New-England) stands, was purchas'd from the natives, by the first English Proprietors, for a Bushel of Wampum-peag and a Bottle of Rum, being of an inconsiderable Value."

Validating Ward's low opinion of the pious pilgrims, Cotton Mather, the famed divine at the hub of the Puritan dynasty, shows how exclusive Christian charity could be in the following letter written during the period of Ward's visit; the letter also demonstrates the strong connections with Barbados and rum that the new colony had already built:

September 15, 1682
To Ye Aged and Beloved
Mr. John Higginson:

There is now at sea a ship called the *Welcome* which has on board an hundred or more of the heretics and malignants called Quakers, with W. Penn who is the chief scamp at the head of them.

The General Court has accordingly given secret orders to Master Malachi Huscott, of the Brig *Porpoise,* to waylay the said *Welcome,* slyly as near the Cape of Cod as may be, and make captive the said

Penn and his ungodly crew, so that the Lord may be glorified, and not mocked on the soil of this new country with the heathen worship of these people. Much spoil can be made by selling the whole lot to Barbados, where slaves fetch good prices in rum and sugar, and we shall not only do the Lord great service by punishing the wicked, but we shall make great good for his ministers and people.

Master Huscott feels hopeful, and I will set down the news when the ship comes back.

Yours in the Bowels of Christ.
Cotton Mather[82]

That about defines the level of practical morality of the godly merchants of the New England coast, whose descendents were impelled by taxes to raise the flag of revolution. Almost as good an example was the case of the captain of the Boston ship *Rainbow,* who was arrested and forced to return his cargo of slaves to Africa because someone informed on him—he had acquired them on a Sunday, when he should have been praying![83] But being sold as a slave in Barbados was more merciful than the fate that attended the Salem witches, whom Cotton Mather helped hang as part of the battle with Satan for the souls of New England.

Drinking in the early days was carefully distinguished from drunkenness. Increase Mather saw drink "as a good creature of God" while warning that a man "must not drink a Cup of Wine more than is good for him." He complained "That they that are poor and wicked too, can for a penny make themselves drunk." At contemporary rum prices, a penny would have provided over a quarter pint, which would have tested many a liver.

Increase's son, Cotton Mather, had also not reached the stage of his spiritual descendants, who saw rum as an agent of the Pope and the Devil. He also declared drink to be "a good creature of God"; however, he worried that "The Flood of RUM would overwhelm all good Order among us."[84] "Woe to drunkards," was the message of the learned divine's pamphlet. Charles Rorabaugh, a historian of American drinking, glosses that Mather was worried the ruling elite would lose social control in the meetinghouse and allow the tavern to become an alternative focus of power—and indeed, eventually a tavern was where the American Revolution was fomented.

One of the more ritualized forms of drinking that the Puritans often inveighed against was toasting. From the seventeenth century onward, failure to drink the health of every body present, not to mention the ladies, the governor, the king, or, later, Independence Day, was considered an offense ranging in severity from disrespect to petty treason. Indians cleverly took advantage of this custom, recognizing a good ritual when they saw one, to coax rounds of drinks from colonial officials. Cotton Mather elaborated long theological objections to this practice of drinking pledges: it was rowdy, subversive, and threatened to replace prayers to the Divinity.

However, as the decades and the hogsheads flowed by, rum began to acquire the roaring evangelical connotations that would take it to Prohibition and damnation. The (very) Puritan poet Edward Taylor went beyond mere pledge-drinking. In his late seventies, as he approached his maker, he prepared himself to say "Farewell to the Terraqueous Globe" and to its drinks, reserving special fervor for "that strong liquor calld damnable Rum":

> *Or otherwise Kill Divell as its nam'd,*
> *And for its mischiefe is greatly blaimd.*[85]

Not all agreed with his damnation of the "Kill Divell," and some embraced it even more closely, but perhaps none in so macabre a manner as the First Baptist Church in Providence, Rhode Island, which rented out its basement to local merchants for storage. One such entrepreneur was the local undertaker, who stored hogsheads of rum (presumably the cheaper New England version) for transport of the departed to faraway places. The bodies were squeezed into the barrels to begin their journey into eternity. Perhaps in those days Saint Peter did not mind if they turned up at the Pearly Gates with rum on their breath. It was sweeter than the arsenic or formaldehyde that later undertakers used to pack their cargo.

More lively in his spirits, Pastor Nathan Strong, Congregationalist minister of the First Church in Hartford, Connecticut, kept both holy and profane spirits in close proximity: his successful distillery was close to his church. But he must have been too busy writing hymns to one spirit to pay due attention to the other—his distillery went bankrupt. Maintaining the spiritual connection, the building of a church at Medford required several barrels of beer, twenty-four gallons of West Indian rum, thirty gallons of New England rum, thirty-five pounds of refined sugar, and 465 lemons.[86] Alice Earle, a historian of pious New England, notes that the results were not always what the architect may have wanted. "When the Medford people built their second meeting-house, they provided for the workmen and bystanders, five barrels of rum, one barrel of good brown sugar, a box of fine lemons, and two loaves of sugar. As a natural consequence, two thirds of the frame fell, and many were injured," she records.

It was not just voluntary work that was accompanied by drinking. Rum was essential for almost any form of work As a local rhymester put it:

> There's scarce a Tradesman in the Land
> That when from work is come
> But takes a touch, sometimes too much
> Of Brandy or of Rum.[87]

But most of them were drinking all day long.

The Puritans were puritanical about sex, Catholics, and Quakers, but not about drink. The early licenses for taverns specified that they be next to the meetinghouse. Indeed, in 1656 the Massachusetts General Court made it compulsory for every community to have a public house, or tavern. Connecticut had already passed similar legislation in 1644. However, some of the unholy spirits descended too much, and so the General Court of the Plymouth Colony in 1662 forbade tavern keepers from drawing wine or liquor, under penalty of a shilling fine, unless the customers were "faint and sick." It appeared that many of them became just that to get their shots, and so in 1674 the court had to repeat the strictures.

These were not the rollicking taverns of G. K. Chesterton

or Samuel Johnson. On the contrary, they were places where the law came down heavily on any manifestations of pleasure or enjoyment. No more than half a pint of wine per person. No more than half an hour at a time. No noise, music, or dancing. John Josselyn, an acerbic English visitor to Boston in 1663, records the long arm and the short measure of the nanny state:

> At any houses of entertainment into which a stranger went, he was presently followed by one appointed to that office, who would thrust himself into the company uninvited, and if he called for more drink than the officer thought in his judgment he could soberly bear away, he would presently countermand it, and appoint the proportion beyond which he could not get one drop.[88]

Indeed, in some colonies it was the duty of the innkeeper to report to the selectmen when any strangers arrived in the place!

Here we see the joyless beginnings of Prohibition. "Promulgating laws had already become an American remedy for the ills of society and the weaknesses of the flesh," the ever wise and urbane Taussig lamented.

7. The Spirit of Celebration

In agnostic, modern England, the joke is that most people attend church only for christenings, weddings, and funerals—the rituals of life that in New England, rum pervaded. In New England, strangely, the Puritans did not regard weddings or funerals as proper spheres for clergymen, and perhaps that led people to use rum to mark the occasions. In Londonderry, New Hampshire, the Scots-Irish, who were eventually to drink their way down the Appalachians, had dour divines with Dionysian overtones. It was alleged that they never gave up a point of doctrine nor a pint of rum.[89] Parishioners would assemble in parties at the homes of the bride and groom, firing muskets into the air. The groom's party then marched to the bride's house, firing a volley and getting one in return at each house. The parties would meet in the middle and select their champions to run for "a beribboned bottle of New England rum."[90] The ceremony culminated in the drinking of much more than one bottle.

Funerals were, naturally enough, the occasion for heavy spirits. In Londonderry, they would mount the equivalent of a wake, an *arval,* which would induce genuine tears in the eyes of any stereotypically economy-minded Scot. The rum bill for the funeral could leave a bereaved family financially crippled for years, not least since the drinking went on before and after the interment.[91]

Similar customs prevailed across New England. And to show that piety was not necessarily the enemy of social concern and communitarian endeavor that today's religious right would pretend, even a pauper funeral would include a few gallons of rum or a barrel of cider for the mourners— at the public expense in some towns.

The First Steps to Prohibition

Since people were obviously enjoying themselves too much at funerals, the Massachusetts General Court in 1742 forbade the use of rum and wine during these ceremonies, but as an edict it was doomed. Alice Earle lamented:

> It was a hard struggle against established customs and ideas of hospitality, and even of health, when the use of liquor at funerals was abolished. Old people sadly deplored the present and regretted the past. One worthy old gentleman said, with much bitterness, "Temperance has done for funerals.[92]

However, drinking on such a scale was not necessarily predicated on an absence of ministers from ceremonies. In fact, the booziest events in old Massachusetts were ordination ceremonies for new pastors, when, to celebrate the new connection to the Holy Spirit, all the local pastors would descend and down gallons of the unholy variety:

> Six hundred and sixty-six dollars were disbursed for the entertainment of the council at the ordination of Mr. Kilbourn, of Chesterfield; but the items were really few and the total amount of liquor was not great—thirty-eight mugs of flip at twelve dollars per mug; eleven gills of rum bitters at six dollars per gill, and two mugs of sling at twenty-four dollars per mug. That bar bill was a consequence of war time depreciation. The church in one town sent the Continental money in payment for the drinks of the church-council in a wheelbarrow to the tavern-keeper, and he was not very well paid either.[93]

Earle cites the bill for "keeping the ministers" at an ordination in Hartford in 1784:

To keeping Ministers	£0	2s	4d
2 Mugs tody	£0	5s	10d
5 Segars	£0	3s	0d
1 Pint wine	£0	0s	9d
3 lodgings	£0	9s	0d
3 bitters	£0	0s	9d
3 breakfasts	£0	3s	6d
15 boles Punch	£1	10s	0d
24 dinners	£1	16s	0d
11 bottles wine	£0	3s	6d
5 mugs flip	£0	5s	10d
3 boles punch	£0	6s	0d
3 boles tody	£0	3s	6d

The flip, the toddy, and the punch would all have been mostly rum, which was obviously indispensable for ensuring a smooth launch of the new minister's spiritual career.

But even so, in some less Calvinist jurisdictions there was a broader-minded communion with the spirits. In the South, as Taussig pithily puts it, "the Negroes did the hard work, and their masters the hard drinking." Saint Philips's Church in Charleston, South Carolina, was built in 1770 wholly upon the spirit tax of two pence per gallon levied on rum.[94] Indeed the salaries of ten ministers accounted for a quarter of the revenue raised by a 3 percent duty levied on rum, sugar, and slaves imported into South Carolina.[95]

The spirit moved in mysterious ways and motivated congregations as well as those who built the churches and those who preached in them. The wily old Benjamin Franklin, in his *Autobiography,* recounts how, as he led five hundred men against the French in the Seven Years War:

> We had for our chaplain a zealous Presbyterian minister, Mr. Beatty, who complained to me that the men did not generally attend his prayers and exhortations. When they enlisted, they were promised, besides pay and provisions, a gill of rum a day, which was punctually serv'd out to them, half in the morning, and the other half in the evening: and I observ'd that they were as punctual in attending to receive it: upon which I said to Mr. Beatty, "It is, perhaps, below the dignity of your profession to act as steward of the rum, but if you were to deal it out and only just after prayers, you would have them all about you."

He liked the tho't, undertook the office, and with the help of a few hands to measure out the liquor, executed it to satisfaction, and never were prayers more generally and punctually attended; so that I thought this method preferable to punishment inflicted by some military laws for non-attendance on divine service. [96]

Franklin, although an inveterate tippler himself, was not always so tolerantly worldly-wise. In 1736 he republished a British temperance article, hoping that: "Perhaps it may have as good an Effect in these Countries as it had in England. And there is as much necessity for such a publication here as there: for our RUM does the same Mischief in proportion as their GENEVA." *Geneva* was gin, the drink of the poor in England—who tended to drink as much of it as they could afford. It did not become popular in the United States until it was mixed with vermouth in the twentieth-century martini.

Franklin was probably being truer to his own character when, after escaping Boston for Philadelphia at a time when even Boston was escaping its Puritan past, he hymned rum punch and its convivial effects:

> *Boy, bring a bowl of China here*
> *Fill it with water cool and clear:*
> *Decanter with Jamaica right,*
> *And spoon of silver, clean and bright,*
> *Sugar twice-fin'd in pieces cut,*
> *Knife, sieve and glass in order put,*
> *Bring forth the fragrant fruit and then*
> *We're happy till the clock strikes ten.* [97]

Electoral High Spirits

As befitted a burgeoning democracy, the other occasion for high spirits in colonial America was an election. Rum played a large part in political life. Elections were fought and won in the taverns, which themselves laid down some amazingly persistent traits in American political behavior. Quasiprohibitionist sentiment from the religious restricted licenses for inns to one per district except at strategic junctions and similar places. However, local politicians needed the support of the taverners and drinkers to be elected, and they would support someone who was not scrupulous about how many licenses were issued.[98] So there were a lot of inns and taverns in which, fueled by punch and flip, people would discuss their grievances. As the struggle to raise revenue from the recalcitrant colonies grew tougher, and Parliament introduced more measures, the issue of representation became more tangible.

At the end of a meeting to discuss opposition to the Stamp Act at the Wolfe Tavern in Newburyport in 1765, the instigator, Dr. Joseph Stanwood, picked up a tab of fifty-nine pounds, seventeen shillings, and three pence— a round that would be respectable for a modern British pub. And Washington, while he was away fighting the French in 1758, won his seat to the Virginian House of Burgesses in the traditional way—by suborning three hundred and one voters with extraordinary quantities of booze, of which, needless to say, the bulk was rum, probably produced from molasses smuggled from the French islands.

The law in colonial Virginia prohibited treating voters to drinks and officially declared that any such election should be rendered null and void, but the father of the country that has ever since evaded all forms of control on campaign contributions paid the tab with hardly a murmur.[99]

His agent sent him an accounting of his election expenses:

Dinner for your Friends £3 0s 0d
13 gallons of Wine at 10/ £6 15s 0d
3 pts of brandy at 1/3 . . . . 4s 4d
13 gallons of Beer at 1/3 . . . . . 16s 3d
8 qts Cyder Royal at 1/6 . . . . . 12s 0d
30 gallons of strong beer at 8d. . £1 0s 0d
1 hhd and 1 barrell of Punch,
consisting of 26 gals. Best Barbados
rum at 5/ £6 10s 0d
12 lbs S. Refd. Sugar at 1/6. . . . 18s 9d
10 Bowls of Punch at 2/6 each . £1 5s 0d
9 half pints of rum at 7d each . . £0 5s 7d
1 pint of wine £0 1s 6d

If the Federal Election Commission were to be presented with such a bill now, it might react like Prince Hal when he saw Falstaff's bar bill: "What a monstrous deal of sack for two penn'orth of bread!" One £3 dinner and a river of rum floated the worthy member home to victory.

The colonial and early American militia also elected its officers, and since the usual mustering place was the tavern, there was less concern about men's rights to carry arms than about officers' financial ability to carry out their primary duty—to buy drinks. Anticipating the electorally successful inarticulacy of the Bush dynasty, one newly elected colonel responded to his elevation by announcing, "I can't make a speech, but what I lack in brains, I will try and make up in rum." [100] Ironically, in view of the Bush dynasty, Shrub, a pet name for President G. W. Bush, was a well-known rum punch.

Even auctions or *vendues* would not proceed without the rum flowing. One auction went through twenty gallons of rum for a mere £200 in sales, but the spirit often loosened the inhibitions of bidders, making the investment worthwhile for the sellers.

It would take a long time for the habit of drinking at almost every public event or ceremony to disappear completely. There was a lot of rum to drink.

8. THE FISHY SIDE OF RUM

The connection between rum, slavery, and the North American colonies was a fishy one. A huge industry grew from the fish that Ligon mentions the slaves being fed, and in memory of that industry, the codfish is the Massachusetts icon.

Soon after its arrival in New England from Barbados, rum became a driving force in the colonies' development, transforming them from enclaves of bitter sectarians clinging to the fringes of an inhospitable land to an independent economic force with large trading and manufacturing interests. As Taussig records, rum had "an astonishing influence on the history of the United States. Throughout our history, from Columbus to the Civil War, we are constantly confronted with rum or its social, political and economic by-products." [101] He also notes that rum was the "currency of the slave trade, which in turn was the backbone of New England commerce."

The colonists loved rum and drank like it like fish. In fact they also drank it like fishermen, since one of the main uses of the hugely important cod fishery off New England was to trade the catch for molasses. And although the folkways of those areas still include molasses in recipe books, the main attraction of the viscous black syrup was not its taste but its potential for distillation.

On the eve of independence in 1770, there were only 1.7 million colonists, but Patriots and Loyalists together managed to knock back 7.5 million gallons of rum a year and exported 1 million gallons a year. In addition, despite the sterling efforts of their molasses smugglers and domestic distillers, they still imported almost half the rum they drank, since most discerning colonial tipplers preferred the more expensive Caribbean rums to the home-distilled versions. When you discount the women and children from the population, these figures imply that the adult white males drank prodigious quantities of the stuff, amounting to three pints a week. Luckily, driving under the influence was neither technically nor legally possible at the time. But the effects of such heavy drinking on livers and tempers surely influenced the tone of political deliberations and certainly helped inflame the political discourse that led to the Revolution.

Even so, this heavy tippling was not necessarily a sign of depravity on the part of the pioneering settlers. Prohibitionist sentiment tends to discount alcohol as a food source, but rum was a potent source of calories and helped in more ways than one to give energy. In the frigid winters of New England, when fresh food was scarce and the work was hard, rum was liquid energy as well as a winter warmer. Captain Francis Wheler in 1684 said about the fisheries off the Grand Banks, "It would be impossible to continue in that trade for ten hours in the boats every day in the summer, and the intolerable cold in the winter makes living hard, without strong drink."[102]

Early governors and sailors also noticed a big advantage in the northern winter: the usual beer rations froze solid when the frosts came, but the rum stayed liquid and drinkable—and thawed the icicles round the heart with its taste of liquid sunshine. [103] Sometimes it was too successful. In 1711, Brigadier General John Hill complained that his troops had drunk "rumm to excess" in Boston, so instead of confronting the French in Quebec, 250 had deserted and others were in hospital.[104]

Possibly not since the days of Ancient Rome had human settlements been so dependent on imported foodstuffs for their survival as the Sugar Islands were. But while Rome and Athens exacted tribute from just across the Mediterranean, the Caribbean colonies were not imperial metropoles but outlying outposts that had to pay their own way. Their feeding depended on complex currents of trade across the globe and more specifically with the other outposts farther north. The mainland colonists and the Caribbean islands operated as an integral part of the trading system, and without each other neither would have become as prosperous as they did, and indeed, nor would Britain, which profited both ways.

The mainland colonies exported much more to the Caribbean than to the mother country. For example, In 1770 New England merchants sold some £70,000–worth of cooperage supplies. Pennsylvania provided some 23,449 tons of bread and flour to the islands, in comparison with a mere 263 tons sent to Britain.

To pay for the molasses that their distilleries were consuming so thirstily and the West Indian rum that the more affluent and discerning colonists drank, the colonies fished the Grand Banks. Just as the molasses was itself a by-product, it was paid for with the spoiled portion of the dried and salted cod, a cheap and portable protein that could fuel the energies of the slaves whose toil produced the sugar.

Four hundred cod-fishing vessels and two hundred mackerel fishers filled their holds during the summer. The fishermen were not motivated by any feelings of charity toward the slaves they were feeding.[105] As John Adams wrote, "One part (the low grade) of our fish went to the West Indies for rum, and molasses to be distilled into rum, which injured our health and our morals. The other part (the high grade) went to Spain and Portugal for gold and silver, almost the whole of which went to London."[106]

Cultural patterns built up in this way continue long after the original economic and historical ties. Just as they have enthusiastically forgiven rum its part in their historical tribulation, Caribbean people have adopted salt fish as part of their cuisine. And no one who has had salt fish with akee can blame them on culinary grounds. Similarly, salt cod's primacy in Portuguese cuisine owes its origins to the Yankee's desperate need for gold and silver from the southern Europeans.

The New England colonies also provided timber and rum to the more southerly mainland colonies in return for basic foodstuffs like grain, as well as providing this essential fuel, rum, to the huge and growing merchant fleet sailing out of the northern ports and to the fishing fleets that brought all that piscine silver to port.

It was complex trade with many eddies in the overall currents. While the fishermen would scarcely think of setting forth on their travels without the necessary rum rations, even their solid rations, the flour, salt pork, and other provender they needed were bought from the south with rum. For example, in 1755 the *Bathias* sailed from Philadelphia to Boston with one and a half tons of bar iron, 262 barrels of flour, 250 bushels of corn, 1500 staves (for barrel making), 10 empty barrels, 5 kegs of beer, and 397 pounds of bread. From there she sailed to the Newfoundland fishing grounds with the corn, staves, bread, and just over half the flour, but with the addition of 12 hogsheads and 2 barrels of rum and 6 hogsheads of molasses.[107]

"Rum was the moving agent in these various summer voyages," William Weeden concludes in his magisterial— and pre-Prohibition—economic history of New England. "In whatever branch of trade we find ourselves we are impressed by the immense prevalence and moving power of rum, Negroes, fish, vessels, lumber, intercolonial traffic in produce, all feel the initiative and moving impulse of rum."

By 1770 the colonies boasted anything up to 143 distilleries and produced 4.8 million gallons of rum a year. There were at least fifty distilleries in Massachusetts alone, producing over 2 million gallons of ersatz liquid sunshine for the denizens of the chilly North. Even so, the colonists were importing 3.78 million gallons of rum, worth £338,579, and of this, 90 percent came from the English colonies, 8.7 percent from the Danes, and only 1.3 percent from the French. Rum bound the otherwise separate and indeed disparate interests of the thirteen colonies, with their widely differing basic economies, into an integral trading system. It also prepared the way for a common grudge against anyone who interfered with the feedstock they needed—molasses.

However, while rum was an immensely important part of the colonies' role in that external trade system, we should not forget what the colonists did with most of the rum they made or imported. They drank it—at a rate equivalent to twent-one gallons a year for each free adult male.[108] Even allowing for some of that going to the Indians, the colonists were copious drinkers.[109] Only one gallon in eight was exported, and it made up four fifths of the export trade of New England—and almost all of that was for barter in the slave trade.[110]

Rum, Rapine, and Revolution—The Triangle

It was one thing selling dried fish to feed slaves and drinking the profits. But in the hands of the New England merchants, rum soon became a double enslaver, both depending on the toil of slaves to make and being the main trade item to buy slaves in West Africa. To get their drinks, from an early stage African coastal monarchs staged slave raids on their weaker neighbors. By 1679, French slave traders were already complaining that the brandy they had formerly used in trade for slaves in Africa had been flooded out by cheaper rum, and one recorded that a large bull was bought for one pint of spirit in 1697 in Senegal. The monarchs along the coast had a huge thirst, and in Gabon, they traded an elephant tusk for a measure of liquor—which they emptied before leaving the vessel.[111]

British histories always depicted the Triangle Trade as having its apex in Liverpool and Bristol. Manufactured goods left Britain for West Africa and were traded for slaves, who were taken to the Caribbean and the mainland colonies, where they were exchanged for sugar, molasses, and rum for the British home market. The New England colonies had a triangle all of their own, although it shared a base on the same gruesome Middle Passage. But its apex was across the Atlantic in New England, Boston, and Providence rather than Bristol and Liverpool. Regardless of whose "triangle" it was, reality does not always favor simple geometrical metaphors, and the so-called triangle was much more like a cat's cradle with multiple nodes. There was a lot of direct trade between the American colonies and the Caribbean and between both and Britain, not to mention the voyages carrying Grand Banks fish to southern Europe.

From a moral dimension, there was indeed a triangle, or rather a trinity, of disrepute: slaves, rum, and sugar. The rum that was made from the molasses that had been traded for cod was then bartered in West Africa for yet more slaves, who were taken to the Caribbean or southern mainland colonies. The resulting trade links connected the frozen seas of the northwest Atlantic to the torrid beaches of the Bight of Benin—with the keystone of the structure being the slave-worked sugar plantations of the Caribbean. The mainland colonies were "the key to the Indies without which Jamaica, Barbadoes and ye Charibby Islands are not able to subsist,"[112] one writer commented in 1661—and this became truer as the decades rolled by—and as the hogsheads of molasses and rum rolled into the holds of the trading fleets. But it also doubtful whether the mainland colonial economies would have taken off so quickly without the trade to the islands.

The movements of men, goods, and ships that rum impelled ensured that New England and the North American colonies were not like French Canada or the Spanish Main. The traditions of local autonomy and lively entrepreneurship ensured that they did not linger as a sleepy backwater, fossilized economically and socially at the time of the settlement, but became a major link in the global network with a vigorous and growing commercial and industrial life of their own.

The ships were built, supplied, and equipped locally in New England on a scale that matched the mother country's capabilities. Indeed their shipbuilding and navigation techniques overreached that of their more conservative transatlantic cousins. For example, Franklin remarked on British captains' refusal to take advantage of the extra speed offered by the Gulf Stream. Yankee skippers roamed the globe in emulation of the Viking example of seeking riches at sea that they assuredly could not cultivate in their cold and relatively infertile home.

However, the rum trade also distorted economic development. George Weeden concludes that "the substitution of rum for food affected the whole business of commercial exchange in this period. Between the derangement of an inflated currency, and the diversion of productive industry to distilling and its collateral slave importation, the building of vessels and the catch of fish fell off." While allowing for some effects from the wars with France, he concluded unequivocally, "the main cause in the decline in these important industries must be found in rum."[113] It did not take long for the New England traders to get in on the act. In the late seventeenth century, Taussig comments with bitter irony, the Yankee merchants' first battle for "Free Trade and Sailors' Rights" involved their petitioning Parliament, along with their English colleagues, to break the monopoly of the Royal Africa Company on the slave trade along the coast of Africa. They enthusiastically proposed export duties of 10 percent on goods leaving for Africa to defray the costs of the slave forts and factories along the coast. Their proposal was adopted; whether they paid the tax as scrupulously is another story.[114]

In the Treaty of Utrecht following the War of Spanish Succession in 1713, Britain secured, in addition to Gibraltar, Newfoundland, along with confirmation of the Royal Asiento, whereby British ships, in return for a large cash payment up front to Spain, were licensed to trade slaves to the Spanish colonies. "British" for these purposes included the British colonies, and the trade just grew and grew. By 1721 the factor for the British Royal Africa Company on the Slave Coast reported that rum had become the "chief barter" there even for gold, let alone slaves.

There was much more to show in the way of negative results for the people at the base of the triangle. In 1740, four out of every ten slaves bought by the Codrington Plantation in Barbados died within three years. We must not belabor the New England divines alone for their flexible ethics; they were drawing on an old tradition. Since the Codrington Plantation was owned by the Society for the Propagation of the Gospel, its overseers branded slaves on the chest with SOCIETY to remind them and others that these human chattels were doing the Lord's work. When James Oglethorpe founded Georgia, he tried to keep out both rum and slavery—with only very temporary success. The great evangelist George Whitefield sympathized with the colonists against John Oglethorpe, who, he complained, deprived them of rum and slaves.

The heartland of abolitionism, piety, and the Union in the Civil War and of prohibitionism afterward has not often been ecstatic about being reminded of its close connections to rum and the lash. So popular histories have tended, if anything, to minimize both. Even at the time, there were some mild signs of embarrassment about the business. For example, Captain David Lindsay of Newport called the vessels engaged in the trade "rum Ships" rather than slave ships, and another slaver captain referred to "us rum men." Even the rum for the slave trade was euphemized into "Guinea Rum." As Taussig puts the hypocrisy, "New Englanders in honesty referred to 'Missionaries on deck and rum in the hold.'"[115]

"Guinea Rum" was what we now call overproof. It was double or even triple distilled to save the cost of freight, and water would be added at the destination to get it to the appropriate and more drinkable strength. Champlin's trade book of the Rhode Island slaver, the sloop *Adventure,* records that it traded five hundred gallons of rum more than it had shipped, despite evaporation—which could have been sharp practice or just normal business.[116] As

Simeon Potter, who had himself made his fortune privateering, ordered his Captain Earle of the *King George* in 1764, "Make Yr Chief Trade with the Blacks and Little or none with the white people if possible to be avoided. Worter yr rum as much as possible and sell as much by short mesuer as you can."

One could say that Potter's political principles were just as flexible. Despite calling his ships the *Prince Charles* and the *King George,* he became a superpatriot at the time of the revolution and was appointed major general of the Rhode Island Colonial Forces. More consistently, he was as remiss at paying taxes to the revolutionary government as he had been to the royal government. He anticipated his successors in American politics by having his legal residence in the town of Swansey, Massachusetts, where the taxes were much lower than in Bristol, Rhode Island, where he made most of his money. Neither tax evasion nor slave trading stopped him finishing his days as a vestryman at Saint Michael's Church in Bristol. It was what Weeden calls "A casuistry of culture, combined with rude impassioned humanity—a commingled hash of Satanic civilization and simple savage nature" that enabled such to speak of the inalienable rights of man and liberty or death while either dealing in slaves or owning them.[117]

And what was the price of a soul? In 1764 it was £12, or 110 gallons of rum in the standard unit of exchange.[118] In 1755 the price was 799 gallons of rum, two barrels of beef, and one of pork for four men, three women, three girls, and one boy. Twenty years later, just before the Revolution, Rhode Islander Aaron Lopez was paying only 22 gallons a head.[119]

George Washington was perhaps the most outstanding example of weighing souls against spirits and the osmosis of deceit involved in the process. In 1766, while still a British officer and a gentleman, the future president shipped off a slave called Tom to the West Indies to be sold in exchange for, among other things, a hogshead of best Jamaican rum.[120] With no truth-in-advertising law to inhibit him, he did not tell prospective purchasers that Tom seemed to have nursed the spirit of independence and freedom that later canonized his master and was being sold because he was "unruly." Somehow, it seems more shocking that he actually sent Tom to sell himself. He sent him to the captain of a sloop bound for the Caribbean with a letter saying:

With this letter comes a negro (Tom) which I beg the favor of you to sell in any of the islands you may go to, for whatever he will fetch, and bring me in return for him,

> One hhd. of best molasses
> One ditto of best rum
> One barrel of lymes, if good & cheap
> One pot tamarinds, containing about 10 lbs.
> Two small ditto of mixed sweetmeats about 5 lbs each.
> And the residue, much or little in good old spirits.[121]

Setting the price of a human being in such tawdry trade goods rather than in coin of the realm appears more shocking even if the effect is the same. To sell one's own soul for a cask of rum is one thing, but to sell someone else's certainly tarnishes the halo of a founding father. Like most people of taste, Washington preferred the West Indian to the New England rum, just as he preferred the Virginian definition of freedom to that elaborated by Lord Mansfield in England in his famous declaration that slavery was illegal in Britain itself. "How is it that we hear the loudest yelps for liberty among the drivers of negroes?" Samuel Johnson asked, and has never been adequately answered.[122]

But one of the side effects of the revolution for freedom and liberty was that a critical shortage of New England rum affected all the slave traders along the coast. The locals had become habituated and were unhappy with the substitutes.

9. THE GREAT SPIRIT'S APPOINTED MEANS

Once it had started, the rum trade sloshed around not only the Atlantic seaboard but deep inland. If there was any group that got a rawer deal than the Africans brought in involuntarily to repopulate the New World colonies, it was of course those who were involuntarily "depopulated"—the indigenous population. And once again, rum was at the fore of the operation. Rum entangled Indians in the trade and wars of the Atlantic. It was a weapon in the struggles between the rum-boozing English and the French, whose attempts to seduce the Indians with Catholicism and temperance—laced with occasional splashes of brandy—eventually failed. Rum was a potent ethnic cleanser.

As a deeply desired commodity and a highly concentrated, portable, and profitable store of value, it was traded deep up-country by settlers and Indians alike. Rum had potent effects on the Indians. It was not just the effect of alcohol and binge drinking on the individuals, their families, and their societies that prepared for the spread of European settlement; by tying the Indians into the transatlantic trade system, rum helped transform and destroy their subsistence economies. It lubricated the move of the colonists westward and across the Appalachians.

Since we are referring to Native Americans of three centuries ago, who were quite happy to be called Indians, and were referred to as such in all contemporary accounts except those that called them "savages," we have referred to them as Indians throughout, while, of course, in no way detracting from the right of their descendants to use a more politically correct term.

In the backwoods, away from the coast, the insatiable European demand for furs, paid for with rum, exhausted the natural resources and led to a widening sphere of commercial hunting and trapping as Indians became part of the world economy. Benjamin Franklin himself, with his trademark beaver hat, not only symbolized the importance of this trade, but the demand for beaver that followed his popularization contributed to reducing the beaver population.

Almost from the beginning of the English settlements in North America, when they were just precarious enclaves on the coast, rum was a crucial part of the interface with the locals. As we have seen, the colonists resorted to desperate straits to make alcohol out of almost anything, but the happy coincidence of the early continental settlements with the development of sugar plantations and rum in the Caribbean soon drove out most competing forms of alcohol. Traditionally, as one Indian chief had sniffed, "you rot your grain in tubs," but grain was too expensive and scarce to compete with molasses and rum, and while the Indians may have been able to manage fermentation, distillation used technology that was beyond their reach.

Almost from the beginning, the colonists, despite their own thirsts and drinking rituals, decided that the Indians could not hold their drink and that rum had evil effects on them. To begin with, it was a normal part of the social interchange with, the tribes. Then the settlers increasingly saw it as a means for Indian moral and physical degeneration, which, depending on your point of view, was to be welcomed or deplored. The settlers adopted a two-pronged approach. One was to try to ban the rum trade. The other was to use it against the Indians or at least to take advantage of its effects on them. "Thou shalt not kill, but need'st not strive, officiously to keep alive," as the Victorian poet Arthur Hugh Clough rephrased the commandment.[123]

In 1837 an anonymous Boston poet was under no illusions about what had fueled Manifest Destiny:

> When our bold fathers cross'd the Atlantic wave,
> And here arrived—a weak defenceless band,
> Pray what became of all the tribes so brave—
> The rightful owners of this happy land?
> Were they headlong to the realms below,
> "By doom of battle?" friend, I answer no.
> Our Fathers were too wise to think of war:
> They knew the woodlands were not so quickly past:
> They might have met with many an ugly scar—
> Lost many a foretop—and been beat at last;

But Rum, assisted by his son Disease,
Perform'd the business with surprising ease.

In the middle of the eighteenth century, Benjamin Franklin had already chillingly put it in his *Autobiography* that "indeed if it be the design of Providence to extirpate these Savages in order to make room for cultivators of the earth, it seems not improbable that Rum may be the appointed means. It has already annihilated all the tribes who formerly inhabited the Sea-Coast."

Franklin was adept at rum's diplomatic use. His *Autobiography* also engagingly records his trip to Carlisle in Pennsylvania in 1753 to draw up a treaty with the Indians. He used the promise of rum after the negotiations as an inducement for them to sign—if they stayed sober for the duration of the talks. He may have been aware that in Indian lore, a man under the influence of alcohol, even one who murdered, was not held responsible for his actions. So presumably, from a Indian point of view, a treaty agreed by an intoxicated Indian would be disclaimable afterward, quite apart from the perils of hard bargaining with bands of warriors with gallons of rum under their belts. Indeed, land transfers made under the influence of rum were often also negated by British imperial officials.[124] Franklin records:

They kept their promise because they could get no liquor, and the treaty was conducted very orderly and concluded to mutual satisfaction. They then claimed and received the rum, this was in the afternoon. There were near one hundred men, women and children, and were lodged in temporary cabins built in the form of a square just without the town. In the evening, hearing a great Noise among them, the commissioners walked out to see what was the matter.

We found they had made a great bonfire in the middle of the square; they were all drunk, Men and Women, quarrelling and fighting. Their dark-colour'd Bodies, half naked, seen only by the gloomy Light of the Bonfire, running after and beating one another with Firebrands, accompanied by their horrid Yellings, formed a scene the most resembling our Ideas of Hell that could be imagin'd. There was no appeasing the tumult and we retired to our Lodgings. At midnight a number of them came thundering at our door demanding more rum, of which we took no notice.[125]

In the morning, the Indians explained that "the Great Spirit who made all things, made everything for some Use, and whatever the use he design'd anything for, that Use it should always be put to; Now, when he made rum, he said 'Let this be for the Indians to get drunk with.' And it must be so."

About the same time, North Carolina Governor Arthur Dobbs in 1754 kept open house with food and drinks for several days, as a result of which the Cherokees gave their title to "the lands they claimed towards the Mississippi" to the British crown.[126] Although this was perhaps slightly more expensive than the wampum that the Dutch allegedly paid for Manhattan, rum was still a bargain when came to negotiations.

Indeed, some historians maintain that the wampum, the shell beads that paid for Manhattan, soon suffered ruinous inflation. Before the colonists arrived, the coastal Indians made them when they needed them for trade with others farther inland, but the settlers, who used them more like a modern currency, spurred the Indian makers into productivity by offering rum for wampum. Understandably, perhaps, the quality suffered even as the quantity increased, since what had once been objects of religious value were transmuted into mere liquidity by the flood of omnipotent rum. Wampum devaluation was yet another consequence of rum!

That flood of rum even went across the Appalachians, despite the huge cost of overland transport across the mountains. The overland trade was in kegs, and a heavy undertaking it was, by manpower, canoes, and packhorses, often in more portable but still heavy kegs of around 10 gallons each.[127] In 1767, Fort Pitt had 6,700 gallons delivered and one trader alone, from the renowned Philadelphia firm of Baynton, Wharton and Morgan had 8,000 gallons, mostly of Caribbean rum, in stock in faraway Kakaskia, Illinois—where he was doubtless taking commercial advantage of the recent defeat of the French who had previously controlled the area. Detroit took delivery of 24,000 gallons.[128]

The ambivalence toward alcohol can be seen in the correspondence between the British governor of New York, Thomas Dongan, and the French expedition in the north of the state at the end of the seventeenth century, when rum was already a weapon of war. The French governor, Jacques-René de Brisay de Denonville, who was engaged in a ruthless campaign of extirpation against recalcitrant tribes around Lake Ontario, complained about English merchants selling rum to the Indians, "which converts the savages, as you ought to know, into Demons and their cabins into counterparts and theatres of Hell."[129] In the French colony, under the firm control of His Most Christian Majesty, the French missionaries tried to stop alcohol sales to the Indians as part of their efforts to convert them. But the governor also wanted to get a French monopoly of the fur trade, which was proving impossible in the face of the inducement offered by English merchants: rum.

Dongan protested his own deep desire to convert the Indians but obviously also had a patriotic attachment to the virtues of rum. He promised that "care would be taken to dissuade them from their drunken debouches, though certainly our rum does as little hurt as your brandy, and in the opinion of Christians is much more wholesome." Having satisfied the requirements of patriotism, he declared himself a premature antiprohibitionist. "To keep the Indians temperate and sober is a very good and Christian performance, but to prohibit them all strong liquors seems a little hard, and very Turkish," he said, with sympathy and a staunch feeling for human rights as he and the other colonists saw them at the time.

Expanding upon this concept of English liberties as opposed to the cruel Turk, some broad-minded settlers and traders not long afterward agitated the Housatonic Indians with the idea that banning rum sales to them was "an unreasonable Incroachment upon their Liberty; that those who abridg'd them of the Liberty of using Drink, would by and by incroach upon their other Liberties; that they were us'd worse than Slaves; were treated as if they were Dogs."[130]

Certainly the prohibitions against selling rum to the Indians seem to have been motivated by a sort of panic about what the inebriated Indians would do to the colonists as much as it was by any deep moral concern about the effects on Indian societies. In Middlesex County in Massachusetts, in the first half of the eighteenth century, only two cases involving drunken Indians went to the courts and both involved assaults on other Indians.[131] But the colonial archives are filled with apprehension about what the Indians *could* do under the influence.

Unlike some East Asians, Indians have no genetic metabolic syndrome that prevents them digesting alcohol, but it is certainly true that alcohol abuse has been a major social problem for four centuries of European-Indian contact. On the other hand, we don't need to invoke biochemistry. It is hardly surprising that people afflicted with successive fatal epidemics, ethnic cleansing from their homeland, and the consequent trashing of their societies and environments were driven to drink. But the most self-confident Indians seem to have taken binge drinking to extremes. They poured rum down their throats until there was none left or until they collapsed. Indeed some reports say that even when they collapsed, their colleagues sometimes continued pouring the liquor down them. This was clearly, if not exactly sacramental, some form of social catharsis.

The colonists' censure of Indians' drinking, even as they quaffed huge quantities themselves, was a predecessor of the snobbish attitude that excuses high-end coke snorting while penalizing low-class crack smokers. As Peter Mancall has pointed out, the fears of Indian drunkenness may have been exaggerated, with the colonists' cultural perceptions of the "savages" exaggerating their views of the susceptibility of their neighbors. Several defenders of the trade averred that the lower orders in general, even among Europeans, could not be trusted to drink—so why pick on Indians in general: While the behavior of the Indians may have been exaggerated, the description of the effects of the rum trade on their society may well be all too direly accurate. The introduction of such potent mood-altering substances into a society that was unused to them certainly led to equivalent patterns of behavior and social breakdown. Rum's effect on Indian tribes is reminiscent of the effects of sales of potent habit-forming drugs on the ghettos of modern America, enhancing already strong effects of exclusion and social breakdown.

William Penn, the Quaker founder of Pennsylvania, wrote to the Earl of Sutherland in 1683, "The Dutch, Sweed and English have by Brandy and Specially Rum, almost Debaucht the Indians all. When Drunk, the most Wretched of Spectacles. They have been very tractable, but rum is so dear to them." Jefferson, in his *Notes on Virginia,* showed that the Indian population had decreased by one third in the first six decades of the settlement, which he put down in equal measure to smallpox and liquor, although rum only became a factor in the years just before the 1669 census he was commenting on.

In short, while drunken Indians may not have posed as much a threat to the colonists as the latter thought, they certainly threatened their own families and societies. Because while the Indians had a drink problem, the problem, as the boozer's quip has it, was in paying for the stuff, not least at the high markups that the long inland trade routes imposed. It certainly disrupted the economy, leading them to neglect working for their basic subsistence in favor of the fur trade for rum and, later, whiskey.

John Adams also demonstrated that the traders cheated the Indians; he tells the story of an Indian who called on a tavern in Connecticut in the fall and paid two coppers for a dram. When he returned in spring, the landlord hit him up for three, so the Indian asked what had happened to up the price. The landlord claimed "It is as expensive to keep an Hogshead of Rum over Winter as a Horse." The Indian riposted that "He won't eat so much Hay—may he drink as much water."[132] The practice of cheating was clearly general—and unlikely to be based on concern for the Indians' livers. For example, the superintendent of Indian Affairs for the southern colonies added eighty-seven gallons of water to the thirty-three gallons of rum he sold the Indians, and one group of sailors in Mobile even added saltwater. Such tricks made 400 percent profits possible on selling rum to Indians.[133] This sharp practice, as much as the drunkenness, seems to have been the occasion for Franklin's report that the traders "by their own Intemperance, unfair dealings and Irregularities, will, it is to be feared, entirely estrange the Affections of the Indians from the English."

Frequent pleas from Indian leaders to ban the sale of rum across the frontier were unavailing. Before the war with France in 1754 that was to end in the freeing of the colonists from the French threat to the north and west, a major item on the agenda of the meeting between the colonial authorities and the allied chiefs of the Six Nations was the prohibition of rum sales in their territories. The spokesman for the chiefs declared, "Brethren: We are in great fears about this Rum, it may cause murder on both sides." However, he spoilt the effect by adding candidly, "We don't want it forbid to be sold to us in Albany, but that none may be brought to our castles." In short, they seem to be saying, don't let our lower orders get their hands on the stuff—but please continue to sell it to us chiefs and our entourages.

In the end, the pleas of the chiefs were as ineffective as those of the modern American administrations to the Colombians, Afghans, and others to stop the narcotics trade. Even more so since rum was a legitimate commodity—an essential one even on the European side of the highly porous frontier. The British colonization process was much more a question of individual enterprise than the state-controlled French effort. There were missionaries in the English colonies, but they were not usually state-sponsored. The Church of England was a means of making a living for younger sons rather than the exercise of any evangelical fervor.

The problem was, of course, how to reconcile prohibitionism for Indians with the essential role of drinking as a social sacrament in British culture, which, as we have seen, was, if anything, greater among the colonists. The Indians had a wry sense of humor and were happy to adopt the English custom of toasting, knowing that a proposal to drink the health of the king or the governor made it almost obligatory for government officials to provide the fixings for the toast. Numerous accounts suggest that they were happily taking the colonists for a ride by playing on the settler's customs, even as the settlers thought they were putting one over on the Indians.

One major reason against a prohibition on shipping rum into the west was the demand from the Europeans there. For example, William Byrd's surveying party demarcating the boundary between Virginia and North Carolina from 1728 to 1733 was offered fricassee of rum—a dinner of bacon marinated in rum. More importantly, the military garrisons would probably have mutinied if they did not get their rum rations. An amusingly revealing example of the equivalent leveling effect of the desperate thirsts of the Indians and the troops comes from a letter from the commissary of the Detroit post, James Sterling. He was anticipating an attack by Pontiac on the fort at Detroit at the tail end of the Seven Years War: "I believe the main Attack is design'd against the Rum Cags [kegs]" he wrote. He was confident that the garrison would fight ferociously, since "I'll be hang'd if ever one of them offers to come past them 'till the last Drop is expended," said the custodian of the fort's rum supplies.

One of the reasons for the attack was the British prohibition on selling rum to the Indians. When the attack came, it was repelled, and Major Henry Gladwin, who commanded the troops, recommended to General Jeffrey Amherst, "if yr Excellency still intends to punish them further for their barbarities, it might easily be done without any expense to the Crown, by permitting a free sale of rum, which will destroy them more effectually than fire and sword."[134]

There were always excuses to cover the naked greed of traders. For example, during the war, General Amherst tried to ban the rum trade in the west but had to contend with the opposition of traders, who thought that without the incentive of rum the Indians would become "lazy," since they could buy the trade goods they needed—clothing, tools, powder, and shot—with only half the skins they would bring for trade unless they knew that they would be paid in rum as well. Sir William Johnson, the superintendent of Indian Affairs, declared that "The Indians can purchase their cloathing with half the quantity of Skins, which will make them indolent and lessen the Fur Trade."

The other perennial excuse was that if the English traders did not provide rum, then the French would provide brandy or they could get liquor from the Spanish. This offered double jeopardy. The idea of Frenchmen profiting while British rum went unsold was too much for patriotic souls, not least since it also could have meant the alienation of affections. We tend to forget that the "savages" whom the Declaration of Independence accused the king of unleashing on the colonists were so recently before that the frontline warriors for the American colonists in the Seven Years War against the French.

Chief Pontiac himself later became a more direct casualty of rum. An English trader, whether out of patriotic fervor or for personal revenge, saw him near a village and offered another Indian from the Peoria tribe a barrel of rum to kill him. The thirsty Indian happily tomahawked him in the skull three times and presumably got out of his own skull in consuming the reward. Gladwin's prescription for ethnic cleansing worked in its own messy way, since Pontiac's friends took extensive revenge on the assassin's tribe.

The rummy repercussions continued. A veteran of the Pontiac war, Lieutenant George McDougall, stayed on and bought Belle Isle, off Detroit, for eight barrels of rum, setting in train a chain of protests by the citizenry of the settlement, who had treated it hitherto as common property.

With the successful end of that war came the end of era. Until then, the Indians in the north and near the Great Lakes had traded with the French mostly for brandy. In the far North, the English Hudson's Bay Company even used French brandy and then "English spirits" colored to look like it. Only after the defeat of the French did the Indians become accustomed to trading rum, and on the eve of the Revolution in 1776, while 120,000 gallons of rum a year were making their way toward the southeastern tribes, no less than three quarters of a million gallons were going to Quebec, presumably mostly for the fur trade.

By the end of the colonial period, the colonies of New York, Quebec, and Pennsylvania, freed as they were from the competitive threat of French brandy, prohibited the sale of rum to Indians but the law was a dead letter. Like frequent previous attempts at prohibition of liquor sales to Indians, the fur traders would not, in the long run, forgo such a useful and desired item of commerce in their endeavors to get the Indians to hunt. The marketplace for furs and rum was driven further away. A colonist in Philadelphia could face with equanimity the prospect of inebriated Indians over the Appalachians, not least when he could make money on both the rum going west and the furs going east. As the old Dartmouth College song remembered:

Eleazar Wheelock was a very pious man
He went into the wilderness to teach the Indian
With a Gradus ad Parnassum, a Bible and a drum,
Eleazar was the faculty, and the whole curriculum
Was five hundred gallons of New England rum.

The imperial authorities had as little success in stemming the flood of rum to the interior as they had in stopping the illicit trade in molasses with the French on the coast. The settlers who followed in the wake of the rum trade provided another self-interested issue for the Patriots other than the molasses and rum excise that the British tried to levy on the colonists: the question of honoring treaties with the Indians.

It was here that rum's various influences on the drive to independence came together. Rum had already softened up Indian tribes adjacent to the Pale of Settlement and made them ripe for the plucking, despite the well-meaning attempts of some imperial representatives to restrict the trade. Once the Seven Years War was over and the French threat removed, the expediency of respecting the claims of the former Indian allies in the face of colonial land-grabbers was a major issue. The colonists were annoyed by the sentimental attachment of His Britannic Majesty to his former allies in the war and his legalistic attachment to the guarantees he had made them. The Quebec Duty Act inflamed traders by making it illegal to import rum into the western territories except through Quebec—with duty paid. The Virginian House, even the Tories, thought this was more than Turkish—it was unfair. It meant that they could not take rum to the trading posts for the Indians, "and consequently can have no trade."[135] No rum, no trade. It was not for nothing that the Iroquois knew the fur traders as "rum carriers."

It was bad enough that the colonies' Westward–Ho march to manifest destiny should be stopped by legislative fiat in London, but to stop rum going west! That was too much! John Hancock railed against the Quebec Act, and the law nurtured grudges reflected in the Declaration of Independence: "Cutting off our trade with all parts of the world." To the east and to the west, rum raised the temperature and spirits of patriots as 1775 drew near.

10. THE CARIBBEAN, RUM, AND IMPERIAL LIQUIDITY

The fulcrum of most European imperial ventures during the formative years of the thirteen colonies was not the North American mainland but the Caribbean. From the Spanish Main that hems it to its polyglot islands, the one universal uniting factor for the Caribbean is rum—lots of it, as a living liquid memorial to the time when the lands bedecked around that perfect blue sea were not the tourist playground of North America and Europe but the cockpit of all their rivalries.

Once the conquistadors had discovered that there was no metallic treasure to be found in the beaches and mountains, they pretty much ignored the islands. As sugarcane cultivation spread across the islands that nature had made for it, their importance soared in the global scheme of things. By the end of the century, fortunes were being made and dynasties established from the happy conjunction between Europe's sweet tooth—or rather, carious stump, as soon became the dental norm—and its Caribbean possessions.

The rum-soaked image of the Caribbean was in the process of creation. The icons that we see on modern rum labels, from bearded conquistadors to longhaired buccaneers, thirsty tars, and happy black people working in the fields, all owe their origins to this period. Like all stereotypes, some have a grain of truth in them, albeit overlaid with a lot of fanciful stereotyping.

The period's great naval battles between the French and English occurred more often than not in and around the islands, and if it were not for an ingloriously hasty departure by the French admiral Villeneuve from the Caribbean in 1805 with Nelson hot on his tail, the Battle of Trafalgar would have been fought there.

The Europeans sent hundreds of thousands of troops and sailors to these islands, reckless of the rapidly filling hospitals and cemeteries. Equal-opportunity mosquitoes more than enemy muskets filled most of those graves, but London and Paris clearly felt that this was a price worth paying. Scottish naval surgeon James Lind, who had served in the West Indies, calculated that Jamaica had "until lately, buried to the amount of the whole number of its white inhabitants once in five years." He estimated that "nineteen in twenty have been cut off by fevers and fluxes; these being the prevailing and fatal diseases in unhealthy countries through all parts of the world."[136] The former surgeon-general in Jamaica, Benjamin Moseley, wrote during the War of Independence that the French, Spanish, and English all saw a "great part" of their West Indian forces "exterminated by the Bloody Flux."[137] Each corpse was collateral damage from sugar, molasses, and rum.

The islands' importance was such that London lost more troops in the Caribbean than died in the Peninsular War to chase the French out of Spain. Indeed, the British sent more troops to Haiti, then called Saint-Domingue, than they sent against the thirteen colonies during the American Revolution. This may seem foolish, but Jamaica's trade was worth five times as much to the British as the direct American mainland commerce, so to any Georgian accountant it made perfect sense.

From out of Sweetness Came Forth Strength

To put matters in a contemporary light, think of molasses as crude oil and the sugar plantations as oil wells, which puts the importance of the Caribbean into perspective. There are not many places in the world where sugar can be grown. The effect of the concentration of liquid capital, is reminiscent of oil's importance to modern economies. Sugar profits, just like petrodollars, were recycled back to the European countries rather than remaining in the islands for the benefit of the people who lived there. In Britain, profits from sugar produced a Parliament that was often shortsighted in its protection of sugar interests.

The wealth that the sales of sugar and molasses produced needed a home. By a happy coincidence, the flood of cash coincided with the invention that really built the British Empire. Through much of the eighteenth century, Britain's military and commercial success was based on the national debt as much as on the Royal Navy. By the late seventeenth century, the British had effectively removed the Dutch as a major rival, so from then onward, in what was almost almost a replay of the medieval Hundred Years War, Britain's major enemy was France.

Rather than a missile gap, there was a national debt gap between the British and the French, but after far-ranging reforms in tax collection, the British government could always lay its hands on money, the sinews of war, when its enemies were struggling. There was enough cash held by absentee sugar plantation owners and others for them to invest in government bonds, while British tax collection at home was efficient enough to guarantee repayment of principal and interest, giving the Bank of England its legendary stability.

Commodity imports offer governments unrivaled revenue -raising opportunities. It is much easier to tax goods and services at the ports than elsewhere, so sugar, rum, and molasses were readily taxable—just as oil usually is in contemporary industrialized countries. But smuggling molasses and rum by the hogshead was much more profitable and feasible than trying to spirit a supertanker past the Coast Guard. So when it comes to smuggling, think of molasses and rum as the cocaine and ganja of the age, a trade generating huge amounts of money that guaranteed political influence and certain local insouciance about the niceties of laws and governments, and you have some idea of the corrosive effects of the trade on North America. The importance of the customs and excise duties to the European governments was what made smuggling such a threat and explains why they took such an obsessive interest in where rum and molasses came from and went to.

While the North American mainland colonies were populous and were economic success stories in their own right, they did not have direct representation in the Houses of Parliament to match the sugar barons, many of whom either held or owned there. As in modern American government, money talked persuasively in the corridors of power.

11. BLAME THE FRENCH

So how did molasses and rum lead to what the British call the War of Independence and the Americans call the American Revolution? It was of course the fault of the French, which seems fitting, given that they were blamed for so much in the aftermath of the Iraq War of 2003.

Prevailing economic doctrine held that the colonies' allotted role in life was to provide raw commodities to the mother country and import finished goods from it. Beginning with Cromwell's measures aimed at the Dutch, the British Navigation Acts prohibited foreign ships from trading with the British colonies and allowed the colonies to trade with foreigners only through British ports. The French, Spanish, and other colonial powers generally assented to the principle. In 1686, King James II of England and Louis XIV of France agreed that their merchants would not trade with each others' colonies, but the mutual exigencies of life and economics made a dead letter of the agreement. From the American side, the rapidly growing merchant marine fleets from the near-autonomous colonies were much more difficult to control than British mainland vessels while the French colonies did not have such a huge resource nor such a degree of autonomy.

The colonies of the European powers were supposed to provide commodities for their mother countries that could not be provided at home. The North American colonies were useful only for the fur trade. But New England broke the rules. The local labor and capital involved in distilling and in manufacture of barrels on a huge scale for molasses and rum broke all the spirit of the imperial rule by developing a large value-added manufacturing business. The other big natural resource in North America, fish, was not that competitive a business, since Britain itself had much closer fishing waters.

Shipping the raw ingredients and the finished product provided a huge boost for colonial shipbuilding and shipping industries and inexorably shifted the center of economic gravity westward. Rum brought liquidity in every sense to the mainland colonies. As we have seen, it functioned almost as currency, being accepted and even demanded as part payment for work. However, there was little incentive for the British Caribbean planters to sell their molasses to the colonists and every reason for them distill it themselves for local consumption and sale. Adding more of the sugar content boosted the flavor, aroma, and alcohol content of the wash. And the West Indian rum aged in transit in the oak casks. Jamaica rum was shipped overproof at 67 percent alcohol, 134 U.S. proof, which made for a stronger punch in every sense.

However, help was at hand for Yankee distillers. As they did later during the Revolution, the French came to the aid of the Americans. In 1713, the brandy producers of France, a lobby even more potent than that of the sugar planters, prevailed upon the king to prohibit the importation of molasses and rum, even from French colonies. One of their excuses was that the British King William's ban on the import of brandy to Britain had harmed their sales. Paris at first banned its Caribbean colonies from exporting rum even to French Canada.

The French islands' rhum, made for local consumption, was not as good as the British islands' products, and with the ban on exports there was no incentive for the planters to improve the quality. That left the planters with vats of surplus molasses from their sugar production that they had no legal market for. As the free-market gospelers preach, it's all about supply and demand. Set a veritable sea of molasses just down the coast from the insatiable demands of the American colonial distilleries for molasses, and there was an inevitability about the consequences. The trade between New England the French West Indies was clearly based on mutual benefit. Each side thought it was pulling a fast one on the other. The French were getting rid of a near-worthless by-product, and the Yankees were getting rid of fish that they regarded as "damaged." The usual deal was for the Yankee traders to land with knocked-down staves to make into barrels and then to fill them from the great vats that the planters kept waiting for them.

The "waste" French molasses allowed New England to

make its rum more cheaply than the British and thus to outbid them in the slave trade on the African coast, where rum was as good as currency. French molasses in 1691 was, for example, 60 percent to 70 percent cheaper than its British competition.[138]

There were some technical problems. One was that for much of the century, the British and French were at war, and often the issue over which they fought was control of North America. The American settlers never challenged the Navigation Acts in principle. Rather, as naval historian Neil Stout laconically puts it:

> The American colonists supported British regulations that they found beneficial and ignored, wherever possible, those that they believed harmful . . . New England, after all, built a magnificent merchant fleet under the protection from foreign competition granted by the navigation acts, and the "staple colonies," producers of tobacco, rice, indigo and naval stores, enjoyed a monopoly of the British market for their produce.[139]

Whether or not the rum and molasses trade retarded the healthy overall industrial and economic development of the colonial economies, as some writers censoriously maintain, the insatiable demand for rum and molasses certainly distorted and eventually broke the ties with the mother country, since this demand pitted the patriotism of the colonists against their purses—and the latter won.

12. No Taxation!

The colonists' interests differed from the motherland, above all on rum and molasses and on relations with the Indian tribes to the west, the situation of which, as we have seen, was in part a consequence of the rum trade. Those divergences paved the way for the independence of the United States. Any restraints on such a vital article of trade went beyond the sumptuary taxation of luxuries that the heavy taxes on rum, molasses, and sugar represented back in Britain itself. Taxes on molasses and rum threatened the whole economic development of the colonies in a way the politicians in the homeland neither understood nor, in some cases, cared about overmuch, way beyond a mere tax on tippling. And there, fermenting away, was one of the major causes of the American Revolution.

In 1733, worried by competition from the French

islands, the British Parliament passed the Molasses Act, which may be considered one of the prime causes—or perhaps excuses—for the American Declaration of Independence. The Molasses Act imposed what the colonists called a "crushing" duty of nine pence a gallon on rum and six pence a gallon on molasses, not to mention five shillings a hundredweight on sugar if it was purchased from outside the empire.

Actually it may not have been that crushing; after all, the Gin Act of 1736 imposed a duty of twenty shillings a gallon on gin in Britain. In fairness, the constant shortage of ready cash in the colonies may have made the outlay somewhat overbearing, since so much trade was in credit—or rum. And the Gin Act in Britain produced Gin Riots to match! Although the Molasses Act was disguised as a revenue-raising measure, everyone knew it was a protective tariff designed by a special interest, the sugar barons in London, so smuggling was a victimless crime as far everyone was concerned—apart from the absentee Caribbean plantation owners in London. "Sugar! sugar! All *that* sugar?" King George III had exclaimed in an engagingly lucid moment upon seeing the elaborate carriage of a sugar baron whose equipage outclassed the royal vehicle.[140] It was a measure of their influence.

The molasses tariffs were opposed by lobbyists for the North American colonies, but thanks to the court interest, the seventy sugar lords triumphed. Their investment outweighed the northern colonies by ten to one. It was like legislators from Idaho trying to persuade Washington that a tax on potatoes, however spelled, would bring the sky falling down.

Not only did the sugar lobby in London hit at the colonists' sources of raw materials, but tariff barriers also penalized the product itself, reducing the Yankee rum's comparative advantage—its cheapness. After all, economic theory at the time was that colonies provided things that the mother country could not produce. The sugar lobby made sure that rums from Jamaica and Barbados were exempt from duty until sold, while New England rum paid duty on arrival at British ports. The sugar lobby was favored again in 1760, when Parliament added an additional duty of one penny a gallon on all rums except those coming from the West Indies. As a result, in England, Caribbean rum imports rose, while the sales of New England rum remained low, with only six hundred gallons officially imported to Britain in 1770. It is also true that New England rum was not as good as Jamaica or Barbados rum in the estimation of the colonists themselves, and if people in Britain wanted to blow their skulls with cheap hooch, then they had gin to do it with.

While the colonists certainly protested a little too much, it was also true that if the New England towns had enforced the Molasses Act rigorously, for many of them it would have been economic suicide—and not for the benefit of the empire but for a group, the sugar lobby in Britain, that was widely resented and distrusted across the empire. Since rum was the fuel and lubricant for the whole of New England's trading patterns, the Molasses Act put the colonists in direct conflict with the motherland. That the law was so clearly seen as a manifestation of special interests rather than general principles made it even harder to muster enthusiasm for effective enforcement.

One of the virtues of Anglo-Saxon political traditions as exported to the American colonies was that law enforcement was a local community responsibility. On both sides of the Atlantic, central government interference was not welcome. There was in general a quite surprising consensus on many issues, but when there was contention, then local feelings tended to mitigate strict application of unpopular central directives. Even in England at the time, administration of power was very devolved to local levels. Locally recruited juries balanced out even the king's judges, and magistrates and town councils who were charged to administer the law would temper it in the light of local prejudice. The system was of a national oligarchy tempered by local interests and mob action, or at least the threat of it.

Whether over the price of wheat, the activities of the press gang, or revenue, the representatives of central government were often defied and even manhandled. In 1775, for example, a seamen's riot in Liverpool against an attempt to reduce their wages led the mob of mutineers to control the town for several days and trundle cannon from their ships to lay siege to the town hall. The property owners of the town were rescued by the military in the absence of any effective police force. Interestingly, when Liverpool and Manchester then raised regiments, some of the centralists in London wanted to know by what authority they did so—doubtless looking at how the same power had been used across the Atlantic. But these were not militia; rather they were troops of the line, who were also to die on the altar of rum and sugar. Over eleven hundred of the Royal Liverpool Blues went to the

Caribbean to fight the French—and after the end of the American Revolutionary war in 1784, only eighty-four fever-ridden survivors returned.

So the violence in the colonies was not so extraordinary itself, although the direction in which matters were moving certainly was. The law became unenforced and unenforceable until the end of the Seven Years War in 1763.

It was clear that the colonists were averse to any taxation at all, crushing or otherwise. The connivance of locally appointed customs collectors meant that the export of products from French islands was much greater than the officially declared imports into the British colonies. Some French molasses was "naturalized" in the Caribbean, smuggled into British colonies there, and then brought to the north as British produce. But much continued to come in through the northern ports, and arrangements with the local customs officials ensured that only a fraction of the duty was paid. As Neil Stout acidly comments, "The only notable result of the act was to give the American colonists a reputation for smuggling and customs officials in America a reputation for venality."[141] But it has to be said that there was ample reason to give rise to this prejudice. A law that was actually not enforced for three decades loses some considerable force.

13. Seven Years That
Changed the World

The colonists could live with the Molasses Act as long as it was enforced by bulliable and bribable local officials—in effect, not enforced at all. Peter Faneuil, the Bostonian patriot and doer of good works in Boston, funded both his political and his eleemosynary efforts by trading in rum and slaves. But his correspondence shows that he was as unashamed about tax evasion and avoidance as any modern millionaire.[142] His letters include strict instructions to his captains on how to avoid the duties on all goods in their care.

What brought the issue to a head was the Seven Years War, from 1756 to 1763. While it was known in the colonies as the French and Indian War, globally it has often been recognized as the real First World War. Lord Macaulay, accurately but with little regard to twenty-first century political correctness, later wrote, "In order that he

(Frederick the Great) might rob a neighbour whom he had promised to defend, black men fought on the coast of Coromandel, and red men scalped each other by the Great Lakes of North America." However, local color aside, if there is one war that shaped the modern world, this was it.

The proximate cause of the war may have been Frederick the Great, but underlying it was the century-long battle for domination between France and Britain. Yet we can see in retrospect that the final shots on the Heights of Abraham, from where General James Wolfe took Quebec and thus Canada from the French, were an overture for the American War of Independence. Along with Wolfe, shot in the chest in his moment of victory, there died the military dependence of the American colonists on the mother country. Globally, even the later struggles with revolutionary and imperial France only served to confirm the disposition of the Seven Years War. The French in India were routed, providing an alternative empire to console the British for their eventual loss of the thirteen colonies.

What made all this possible was the debt that the British government owed to private investors who bought government securities. The national debt, reflecting the British government's relative financial and fiscal strength, allowed the country to defeat the much larger more populous and arguably much richer France in these wars.

The Yankee traders, open-minded as they were, managed in their minds to separate the French in Canada, who were bitter rivals in the fur trade and an actual existential threat to the colonies, from the French in the West Indies, who were indispensable trade partners.

At the outbreak of war, Parliament had forbidden the

export of any food except fish or rice outside the empire, let alone to the actual enemy. But even though many colonists, like George Washington, learned their military skills in the wars against the French, many others continued trading, either through neutral ports or under false flags of truce, which were officially issued only for the exchange of prisoners. Years of peacetime scofflawishness about the Molasses Act made it easier to carry on the trade during wartime. It was only a small step from smuggling during the century-long cold war between France and Britain and outright trading with the enemy during open hostilities. Above all, there was no way the British Caribbean islands could or would supply the molasses on the scale on which the voracious stills of New England and Philadelphia were consuming it.

The French, of course, appreciated the courtesy of the colonists, and ordered their navy and privateers not to interfere with American vessels engaged in the trade. They even issued passes. One New York master, William Carlisle of the sloop *Dove,* gave a new meaning to sailing by the seat of his pants; that was where the British officials found his French pass, sewn into a patch.[143] The governor of Saint-Domingue, the French part of Hispaniola, rewarded the American ships that brought in the deported Acadian French colonists from Canada by allowing them to export a hogshead of sugar for each Acadian passenger they brought in. Exporting sugar to the British was illegal under French law, and importing it into British territory was illegal under British law. But the British authorities wanted the French Acadians out, and the French wanted them in. An arrangement was inevitable.

Rather than keep prisoners of war taken from captured French ships at local expense, the colonial governments were eager to exchange them quickly, but it was for reasons of economics as well as economy. Hundreds of American ships were engaged in returning prisoners. Being a French prisoner of war was almost a career, since, for Yankee ships, having one or two prisoners aboard allowed a flag of truce with an easily bought pass from the local governor, and while they were dropping off the prisoners, they could trade at their ease. Commodore John Moore in Antigua complained to the Admiralty in London that his cruisers had taken the same prisoners four times in less than two months.

Certainly once a captain had a permit, it would be used until it fell apart. Governor Denny of Pennsylvania sold them to the highest bidder, but he issued so many of them that their price plummeted from $1600 to $20! Indeed, when General Amherst heard that provisions were being collected in Philadelphia for the French navy and army in the West Indies, Lieutenant-Governor James Hamilton gave instructions to the customs collector there that all ships in Philadelphia should be detained except for those specifically cleared with a special warrant. The usual suspects, it turned out, were everybody! Virginia was more expensive. Its governor was offered 400 guineas for a flag of truce and turned it down. At one point, in 1760, there were 85 flag-of-truce ships loading in the French part of Hispaniola and 132 in the neutral Spanish port of Monte Christi along the coast of Hispaniola, which is where American merchants went to trade with the enemy when they could not be bothered getting a flag of truce.

During the war, revolutionary rhetorician James Otis defected from being the paid lawyer for the customs service to defending merchants. His speeches against the customs collections were described afterward by John Adams as the beginning of independence. Otis fierily asserted that "if the King of Great Britain in person were encamped on Boston Common, at the head of 20,000 men, with his entire navy on our coast, he would not be able to execute these laws."[144] Celebrating the customary inattention to the Molasses Act, Otis estimated that the revenue on molasses alone should have raised £25,000 a year. Up to 1735 it raised £259 on all the commodities, and even from 1755 to 1761, with special assistance, it probably did not defray the costs of collection, with an annual average take of £1189. The reasons for this are illustrated by a letter from a Boston customs collector Samuel Curwin, who, in the course of personal feud with a Captain Ober, warned merchants not to put contraband on Ober's vessel because it would be seized. "I shall not concern myself about any other coaster, let 'em bring up what they will," he advised them so that they would not "think hard of me," for doing his duty in this one exceptional case![145]

When the Spanish joined the war on the French side, the ambiguously patriotic reaction of one New York merchant was to ask for permission to supply the Spanish garrison in Florida quickly before the official notification came. The acting New York governor endorsed the request as he passed it on to the British military commander, General Amherst— because both the merchant's family and the New York colony needed the money! Amherst, understandably, indignantly refused. Even in a society based on mutual back-scratching in the oligarchy, this was going a little far. As Taussig, the patriot who tried to establish America's claim to rum, had to admit, "Thus we find continued pursuance of the illegal rum trade, acting as a moral anesthetic, and the staunch colonists tolerating treason."[146]

Indeed, smuggling was almost a national sport in Britain itself, where the customs and excisemen were reviled for performing their duties. In America, the laxity of law enforcement could be regarded as a dry run for Prohibition. Alcohol and rum always find their purchasers, whatever governments say. The duty of nine pence a gallon on molasses was quite enough of an inducement to smuggling in its own right, and even naval officers tried to take part. Governor Cadwallader Colden of New York reported on the difficulties of his new posting in 1762: "So many people, I suspect have been concerned in this illicit trade from this place that it is very difficult to find persons to execute any orders, who have not connections with them, or not affrayed of their resentment."[147]

Some of the revolutionaries from the colonial oligarchy may have been nudged that way during this period. The merchants from New York whom Colden reported for trading with the enemy included some later luminaries such as Bache, Livingston, Van Solen, De Peyster, Tetard, and Cunningham. Perhaps it shows the ubiquity of this scofflaw attitude that the families the governor named split both ways on the revolution, with some of them becoming fervent Loyalists who fought for the king and went into exile and others becoming revolutionaries who were present at the signing of the Declaration of Independence.

The Caribbean Spirit of Subversion

Many of the founding fathers whose views were developing during this period of growing confrontation with the motherland were closely tied to the Caribbean trade— and therefore rum. Jefferson, Washington, and others from the South had been born in or worked in the Caribbean. The ties ran both ways. Perhaps archetypal was Alexander Hamilton, born in poor circumstances in Nevis, who worked as a clerk in the Danish colony of St. Croix for New York merchants, Cruger and Beekman, where, one can assume, his duties involved providing a false paper trail to evade the British tariffs. It is not surprising that when he came to the colony of New York, he did so much so fervently to change its status. In 1767, for example, the head office of Cruger and Beekman in New York wrote to their agents in Christiansted on Saint Croix:

> Rum we are afraid to venture at without an regular clearance from an English island, and yett we find other people successfully introduce it to this market via Connecticut. We should have no objection to your shipping us about forty hhds of rum in your own names by one or two of these people, addressed to the care of Mr. Legrand Canon at Stratford, or Mr. John Canon at Norwalk to be forwarded us with the usual certificate of clearance in the manner they practice.[148]

"The manner that they practiced" in the American customs houses was to charge five shillings for a clearance and

£10 for "our trouble and expenses." In other words the ship would put into port in Connecticut and, after an amicable arrangement with the local customs officials, would then sail on to New York, the cargo disguised as duty paid, British produce, or whatever the exigencies of the law demanded.

To put it into perspective, at a time when Rhode Island was importing 1 million gallons of molasses a year, the duty collected was equivalent to a mere 50,000 gallons of it. Saint Croix exported 539,000 gallons of rum to the colonies in 1770—every last tot of it illegally! Saint Croix did not export molasses but distilled the lot, even though their Danish suzerains did not care for the stuff in the slightest. In fact, in 1780, the *Aalborg and Jutland Intelligencer* described rum as "kill-devil, because it has killed many, especial new arrivals who drink it immoderately, and it is very intoxicating and unhealthy. However, when it has matured for a year or more it loses this harmful quality, and when it is a few years old it is a serviceable medicine."[149]

Apart from pirates and sea dogs in general, smuggling has a big role in rum's legend, not just in North America but around the world, and particularly in the British Isles—and not just the temptation for travelers to stash an extra bottle or two of duty-free spirits in their suitcases. No image of a smugglers' cove or clandestine nighttime landing would be complete without the barrels being rolled up the beach.

One account during the American war shows the scant respect for customs officers and their ships. In 1780, the *Hussar,* a revenue cruiser operating out of Whitehaven in England, met a "large buccaneering cutter" off the east coast of Scotland. Far from heaving to, as requested, the eighteen-gun buccaneer, still flying the British flag, shot away the *Hussar's* colors and main halyards, holing her sails and putting several shot into the mainmast. The *Hussar's* captain had "part of his hat and wig taken off by a ball." Outgunned, he had to comply with the orders of the smuggler to return home.[150] If this was what it was like in the homeland, across the Atlantic life was clearly tough for revenuers!

The incentive for smuggling was clear. A West Indian planter, J. G. Kemays, complained of the "Crushing Rum Duty of £36 5s the puncheon of 100 gallons, or 725 per cent on Rum at a shilling the gallon." Kemays claimed to have paid no less than £300,000 in duties on Rum and Sugar in his forty-eight years, and if his father and grandfather were added in, the family contribution to the Exchequer was £2 million.

Just as used to happen in the American colonies, British magistrates presumably worried about their personal safety in the face of strong and vindictive local smuggling gangs and used jurisdictional dubiety to wash their hands of the issues. The size and efficiency of the gangs were suggested by long clauses passed into law by Parliament forbidding "any Light, Fire or Blaze, or any Signal by Smoke or by Rockets, Fireworks, Flags, firing of Guns or other Fire Arms or any other contrivance" after sunset, all means of signaling smugglers. More laws tightened up on activities in the Isle of Man, although much of the legislation dwelled at length on the iniquities of the Channel Islands, which were a handy staging point for contraband from the French mainland. Anyone found on the vessels was to be taken to court—but could avoid that by accepting being pressed into the navy for at least five years. Resistance carried a sentence of seven-year transportation or three years' hard labor, unless the captives had shot at officials, in which case the penalty was death without benefit of clergy.[151] The threat of withholding a few pious platitudes by the local vicar at the scaffold seems to have done little to frighten the smugglers.

In the small, isolated, Gaelic Isle of Man, in the middle of the stormy Irish Sea, fishing and smuggling were the intertwined major industries and were enshrined in local legend. The Isle of Man still maintains its offshore status for those who do not want to overpay their taxes. As a part of the British Isles with certain independence in laws and administration, the island participated in a neat, circular trade. Rum was reexported from Scotland and port cities like Liverpool to Ireland, which had a separate customs jurisdiction. The ever-efficient customs and excise services then reimbursed any duty paid on first importation. And since the ships had to pass by the Isle of Man, they often stopped there en route, where the rum they dropped off was promptly smuggled back the mainland.

The sugar lobby thoroughly resented this ruse and forced the government to buy out the interests of the Earls of Derby, who were the Lords of Man, and after 1765, the Isle of Man officially became part of the same customs regime—but the wily Manxmen kept their reputation as smugglers. The government's actions against the Isle of Man were very much part of its offensive against American colonial smuggling, an offensive reinforced by the irate sugar lobby: "No Leeward Island rum is now imported into the Isle of Man, but coarse stinking North American rum drawn from French molasses."[152] Liverpool slavers picked up this Guinea rum from the Isle of by on their way to Africa. As part of the same package, it was ordered that rum exporters from the American colonies had to post a bond that their produce was not to be exported to the Isle of Man. It was no coincidence that two distilleries opened in Liverpool—which was already a major sugar-refining center—to supply rum for the slave trade.

On the English South Coast and Channel Islands, the proximity to France meant that there were equal nests of smugglers to contend with. Admiral Edward Vernon, who also introduced the grog ration to the navy, showed some of the fervor that demonstrated why the Royal Navy had such animus against the American colonists. Charged with securing the Channel coast against the ubiquitous smugglers, he complained in 1745 that "this smuggling has converted those employed in it, first from honest, industrious fishermen to lazy, drunken, and profligate smugglers, and now to dangerous spies on all our proceedings for the enemy's daily information." He cited lawyers who claimed that "such an intercourse with His Majesty's enemies is now by our laws high treason," and suggested treating them accordingly. The penalty for high treason—and for almost anything worse than jaywalking in eighteenth-century England—was death.[153]

On the other hand, to put colonial trading practices into perspective, any spirits could substitute for rum in navy rations, and until 1802, French merchants were contracted to provide brandy for the same navy that was simultaneously blockading the coast of France and seizing ships. Until Napoleon tried to embargo the nation of shopkeepers into surrender through economic warfare, it was a strange but oddly civilized world, where tourists went to French-occupied Europe to broaden their minds, and merchants supplied the enemy. As the colonial customs commissioners pointed out, Ireland, which was then a separate customs jurisdiction even though under the Crown, was happily supplying the French armies with beef to fight on. These things were considered differently in those days—Napoleon ordered a million pairs of boots from England for the Grand Army to march on Moscow.

Even so, in the case of the colonies, the defiance of the Navigation Acts compounded the sin in the eyes of the authorities, and the sugar interests in Britain were quick to charge that the gold and silver sent to pay and supply the troops fighting in the colonies to save them from the French in Canada and the West was being rapidly recycled to buy molasses from the French. And perhaps they had a point. While smuggling was an admittedly common exception to the rule for trade in Britain, in the colonies it was the rule. The sugar lobby singled out Connecticut and Rhode Island, charter colonies rather than under any modicum of control from London, as being particularly outrageous in their attitude.[154]

Prime Minister Pitt sent a circular to the governors telling them to stamp out this "illegal and most pernicious Trade." Governor Stephen Hopkins of Rhode Island argued that he had done all he could to stop the trade and had issued proclamations making it illegal—but implied that he had no heart for the task, by arguing that if they did not trade with the French islands, then they would have no

cash to buy British manufactured goods—a persistent
argument that showed that the colonists were not, at that
point, challenging the general mercantilist philosophy of
the Navigation Acts but upholding a pragmatic molasses
and rum exception.

The British in general, and the navy in particular, did
not accept such nice distinctions. French corsairs built and
provisioned with New England supplies raided British
commerce with the Caribbean. Royal Navy ships and privateers returned the courtesy and were successful in cap-
turing many French ships, but ironically, that compounded
the problems of the economic war. While the Royal Navy
ships based in Jamaica were unable to go to sea because
they did not have enough flour to provision themselves, as
the British Admiral Augustus Keppel pointed out, the
French ships and garrison in Hispaniola had no such difficulties because of "the large supplies they have lately
received from their good friends the New England flag of
truce vessels," which had more than halved the cost of
flour there compared with Jamaica.[155]

The navy men were clearly annoyed, and in the
Caribbean they decided to seize the American ships going
to Hispaniola anyway. It was a risky step, since Admiral
Charles Holmes in Jamaica, who ordered the seizures, had
not had explicit legal instructions to do so; the crews and
officers could make a lot of money from prizes—or they
could lose it all if the Admiralty courts ruled that they
were exceeding their instructions.

The Royal Navy operated in a strange free-enterprise
way. The ships were paid for with taxpayers' money, but as
an incentive bonus, after the government's share, a large

proportion of the value of the prizes taken by the navy went to the individual officers and men according to strictly laid-down principles. It was a Georgian version of stock options, not least since the senior officers won a disproportionate share of the prize money. There were sticks as well as carrots. This war had begun with Admiral John Byng being sent to intercept a French fleet supposedly sailing to North America; he was court-martialed and executed by firing squad for his failure—"To encourage the others," as Voltaire later suggested. However, before the prize money was paid, it was up to the admiralty courts to decide whether the prize was legitimately taken. The American Vice-Admiralty courts simply refused to allow their ships to be condemned as prizes, no matter how flagrant their smuggling, and of course the Yankee traders contested every seizure.

Admiral Holmes made sure that the prizes were taken to Jamaica, where the Vice-Admiralty court was much more amenable to the navy. But by seizing all the ships in Monte Christi, Holmes had trodden on the toes of important business interests in London. The insurers who would have to pay for the seized British ships, some of which had had customs clearance from London, applied pressure, and the Admiralty Court of Prize Appeals in London split the difference in its judgment. The court ordered the ships seized from the harbor at Monte Christi to be returned, while those caught with a flag of truce were "condemned"—sold, and the proceeds split between the government and the crews. Any temporary disappointment on the navy's part was tempered because the judgment stopped the flag-of-truce scam. The final fly in the treacle was in 1761 when the navy took over the job of prisoner exchange from the colonial merchant ships that had profited so well from its abuse.[156]

English privateers took no less than two hundred ships from Salem in the last three years of the war—adding a whole new dimension to friendly fire and certainly conducive to loosening the apron strings between the mother country and the increasingly unruly daughter colonies.

Despite the best efforts of the Yankee traders' efforts to feed and finance the enemy, by the end of the war British fleets and armies had conquered and occupied most of the French islands in the Caribbean. Ironically, that meant that—nominally, at least—the sugar and molasses that these islands produced was now temporarily British and legal and so flowed to the bubbling stills of New England just as they had earlier when they were French and illegal.

One lesson that London learned from the war was that while the entire customs establishment of colonial America was unable to stop smuggling, the navy had been relatively successful by the end of the war. In the West, it took several years for the British to occupy the tracts down the Mississippi that the French had handed over. And the French Indian allies were not quick to surrender either. Once again, rum, the Great Spirit's chosen spirit moved in its mysterious ways to help clear the country for the white hordes moving across the mountains.

14. AFTER THE WAR WAS OVER

The Seven Years War shaped much of the modern world. It presaged the birth of the British Empire, on which the sun never set—at least, not for a century or so. It heralded the eventual triumph of English and its dialects as a global language. It paved the way to American independence and eventual world hegemony. In the light of such momentous consequences, perhaps it is understandable that people overlook that the war brought about the triumph of rum, which glugged into parts of the globe hitherto unaccustomed to its distinctive flavor and which is even now the most produced and drunk spirit in the world.

The Seven Years War may have been the first world war, but even at the time, no one was Panglossianly optimistic enough to call it "the war to end all wars." The British knew that it was just the latest, albeit the biggest, round in

the century-long struggle with France. They were confident that as soon as the various parties had caught their
breath, the war would flare up again in one form or
another. Macaulay called it the "the most glorious war in
which England had ever been engaged," but the cost of the
fighting had been unprecedented. As utilitarian philosopher Jeremy Bentham was to comment:

> you may . . . prove to yourself that a way to make a
> man run the quicker is to cut one of his legs off. And
> true enough it is that a man who has had a leg cut
> off, and the stump healed, may hop faster than a man
> who lies in bed with both legs broke can walk. And
> thus you may prove that Britain was put into a better
> case by that glorious war, than if there had been no
> war, because France was put into a still worse.[157]

Britain's "better case" was greatly enhanced territory but
more responsibilities than ever before, not least of which
was a £140 million national debt. That debt had won the
war as surely as General Wolfe's armies and Admiral
Howe's sailors, but it amounted to the modern equivalent
of some $35 billion—and an even more grossly dispropor-
tionate amount of government spending and national
gross domestic product.

The peace brought extra drains on the exchequer.
The British defense budget was the largest in peacetime.
Victory meant that Canada and the former French-
dominated territories to the west had to be tamed and
garrisoned to deal with the Indian tribes that had sided with
the French, so the military force there was doubled to

eight thousand, and the North American Squadron of the navy, with twenty-six ships and more than three thousand in crew, became the largest unit of the navy outside home waters.

At the end of war, taxation amounted to 23 percent of per-capita income in Britain, as a relentlessly efficient taxation system ensured that almost every item of commerce paid excise duty to ensure the payments of interest and principle on the debt.[158] For the British government, paying down that debt quickly was a matter of life and death in preparing for the next round of the fight with France. Strapped for cash, London wanted to raise revenue, and the only direct revenue raised from North America was from customs dues. Since the war had in large part been fought to protect the colonies, and new garrisons at this stage had the same purpose, the British government felt, with some justice, that the colonies should defray some of the costs.

The North American colonies accepted as sort of vague principle that they should really help pay something, somehow, sometime—but after Lord Grenville's government gave them a year to come up with voluntary suggestions for payment of their own, and no money was forthcoming, London followed the Sugar Act with the Stamp Act. But, as we have seen and as John Otis had boasted, far from being a revenue source, the American customs service ran at a loss. The duty of nine pence a gallon on rum had been quite enough of an inducement to smuggling in its own right. Naïvely assuming gratitude on the part of the colonies for the French defeat, the British government took what was, on the face of it, an

enlightened act. It decided to reduce the duties on
molasses—but make the Americans actually pay them. In
the new 1763 Sugar Act, the duty on molasses was reduced
from six pence to three pence a gallon. The new measures
were designed to raise revenue, not as protective tariffs.

The act deemed all sugar, rum, and molasses contraband
unless the ship's master could produce a certificate from a
British justice of the peace enumerating it—in words to avoid
fraudulent alterations to the digits and certifying its origins.
The controls presumed smuggling until proven otherwise
and, based as they were on all the reports that had come from
navy, customs, and colonial officials, they took account of all
the myriad ways that rum and molasses had been smuggled
for decades. To colonial merchants used to paying nothing at
all in dues on smuggled goods, an efficiently collected three
pence was an increase, not a reduction, compared with an
uncollected six pence!

The most cunning British move was to drop the rate to
one penny a gallon in 1766, which made it almost un-
economic to smuggle—but habits die hard! Indeed, it was
the smuggling which added value to the product for the
merchant! Part of the underlying motivation for the government in London may well have been a touch of vindic-
tiveness for the colonies' persistence in carrying on their
"normal" illegal trade with the French colonies despite a
wartime embargo. This time, the laws would be more than
just scraps of paper. The government drew up a compre-
hensive plan to ensure their application. In a precursor of
civil service reform, the colonial customs positions were
changed from sinecures for people living in Europe and
paying local substitutes to active positions on-site in

America. Those holding these positions who did not go to America were fired. And those who did found their jobs much harder.

Local officials in places like Perth Amboy, New Jersey, were also unhappy, since they had made a regular income from issuing false papers to ships for their cargoes. According to Judge George Minot, the historian of the insurrection in Massachusetts, "the strongest apprehensions arose from the publication of the Molasses Act, which is said to have caused more apprehension than the taking of Fort William Henry in 1754."[159] Interestingly, he was actually referring to the Sugar Act but disclosed the real obsession of the colonists.

This comment really highlights the question. When the French took Fort William Henry in the early years of the war, for Americans it was the contemporary equivalent of the Srebrenica massacre in Bosnia. Its garrison and civilian entourage were massacred as they withdrew under flag of truce, sending tremors of apprehension through the colonies of their possible fate under a French victory. Yet some were more worried by the prospect of paying tax on molasses than about being driven from their settlements as their compatriots had done to the French in Acadia.

At this stage the military were there to protect the colonies from the Indians, the Spanish, and the French. The colonies had often complained in the past that the navy was not protecting them properly, and the colonists initially welcomed the reinforcement to the fleet. That would change quickly.

London gave the Royal Navy the responsibility for policing the customs and preventing smuggling. The government believed the navy had been effective in stopping the contraband by the end of the war. It had actually been less successful than the London government thought, but the complaints from the colonists and the crowings of navy commanders gave the opposite impression.

The legislation provoked a direct conflict between the navy and much of the local citizenry by declaring that any ships of less than fifty tons that were "loitering" within two leagues of the coast were deemed to be smugglers. Such ships were also prohibited from carrying cargo usually subject to tariffs, such as alcohol, tobacco, and tea. The regulations were finicky and infuriating to local merchants, since they did not allow for the (perhaps occasional) honest trader and the importance of the coastal trade to the colonies. Rigorous application of the regulations laid a dead hand on local commerce as well as on transoceanic shipping.

As a potent incentive to the navy, the officers and crew shared half the proceeds of any seizure, thus almost guaranteeing an excess of zeal on the part of hungry commanders, who were hardly trained to be sensitive to civilians in any case, and competition with the local customs officers, who thereby lost their customary one-third share. It was difficult to maintain the high moral ground against the local authorities when the Navy was often overtly chasing profits; Admiral Colville made it plain that he had "made this voyage" with rich pickings in mind. In an era whose spoils system, unreformed, is still visible in American governance even today, his protests were entirely understandable to his peers.

Historian George Bancroft, himself later the customs collector for the port of Boston, described it as "a curiously devised system, which should bribe the whole Navy of England to make war on colonial trade." But the local colonial governments were more concerned about losing their third than about the propriety of navy officers getting half. The locals marshaled all their traditional weaponry against the navy. Local courts simply refused to convict smugglers. Even in Britain at the time, policing went from the watchman to the militia in one quick step. But any navy, military, or customs officer who was too zealous could find himself sued in local colonial courts, where local prejudice and fear of mobs would ruin or imprison him. There was no impunity for Crown officials and especially not for the military.

Even in England, there were strong residual prejudices against having a standing military force, and to ensure that they were not the tools of kings or lord protectors, parliament renewed military law on an annual basis. In America, these citizens' rights were perhaps carried to extremes. The slightest fault in the paperwork from the navy would be enough to throw out a case. And *in extremis,* courts were quite capable of throwing out a case in the face of the plainest evidence. In one case, New York Vice-Admiralty Judge Morris actually took evidence from himself in court on the innocence of the suspect's intentions! The courts were much more likely to convict navy officers than smugglers. Arrests, court suits, huge court fees, delays, total lack of cooperation from local customs officials, which kept the navy sloops from sailing, while they safeguarded their prizes, in case they were "liberated" by the locals—all built up tensions with the naval officers.

The merchants were also frequently accused of aiding

and abetting the desertion of navy sailors, leaving the sloops too shorthanded to go to sea—in ports where the press gang had no legal authority and where any attempt to press seamen would lead to a riot. This was not just in the mainland colonies. In the West Indies, Admiral Richard Tyrell complained that in the three years before 1765, he had had to spend $10,000 of his own money on keeping his own officers out of local colonial jails; if the navy detained a ship for smuggling, the local courts not only had it released but had the navy officers arrested.[160]

In the end, however, the West Indian islands remained British because the French remained a threat to them. Like their co-hemispherists farther north, they were eager to have the navy around when it came to keeping the French threat at bay but less keen when the keel was on the other rock, as it were. The British government responded to each evasion and legal maneuver with countermoves that were often based on the sound experience of navy officers but also often insufficiently tempered by a sense of what was politically astute for winning hearts and minds in the colonies.

In response to the legal difficulties, in 1764, the Earl of Northumberland was appointed admiral for all America and William Spry was appointed judge of the Vice-Admiralty Court for all America, which was a very elastic expansion of such courts' traditional maritime responsibilities. To compound the disadvantages, the court was in Halifax, away from colonial influence. In 1768, customs enforcement was backed up with the appointment of five customs commissioners for America. To help them were "writs of assistance" issued by the superior court, which were search warrants allowing the king's officers to search any vessel, storehouse, or private building and which were mostly used in pursuit of molasses, rum, and sugar tariff evaders.[161]

Permeating London's decisions was the prejudice built up during the war that Americans were smugglers and disloyal scofflaws. This was actually true—but it was true of much of the British Empire, including the homeland itself. In a much reprinted speech to the House of Commons, Edmund Burke pointed out that even when no one disputed the legitimacy of the law, it was regularly flouted in Britain:

> Your right to give a monopoly to the East India Company, your right to lay immense duties on French brandy, are not disputed in England. You do not make this charge on any man. But you know that there is not a creek from Pentland Firth to the Isle of Wight, in which they do not smuggle immense quantities of teas, East India goods, and brandies.[162]

London was now imposing a heavy hand on people whose participation in the imperial system had hitherto been quite voluntary. The British armies and fleets had not so far been agents of imperial repression but tokens of the motherland's concern for the colonists' defense. The imperial British system, like the domestic one, had relied upon local aristocratic and middle-class interests to run the show by consent. Without an imperial parliament, there was no recognized forum to mediate, and so there were few gradations between happy consent and brute coercion. In Britain itself, London and the central government were much closer to the rest of the land and hence able to counterbalance local prejudices that might have built up in favor of smugglers, but the local authorities in America were much more hostage to local feeling because the central government was so far away.

The introduction of brute external authority, which violated what both colonists and native Britons thought of as their natural rights as freeborn citizens, brought together naked self-interest and a sense of infringement of rights in an inflammatory mix. The presumption of guilt by imperial officials was bad enough, as they seized ships and rifled warehouses, but the new legislation had swung the pendulum back the other way. While before navy officers could be and were imprisoned and sued in hostile colonial courts, now, even if they abused their authority, they were almost immune to legal remedy by their victims.

Before, there had been an element of gamesmanship. No one really disputed London's right to impose the tariffs, but, like modern income tax evasion, the law did not have the moral force of more basic assumptions. Neighbors may well try to stop a robbery or murder and apprehend the perpetrators. But few and foolhardy are those citizens who take individual action to stop tax or tariff evasion. But by mandating forms of enforcement that threatened everybody's rights, London had provided an issue on which the smugglers could invoke the support of the whole community on questions of principle: locals against outside interference, local government against arbitrary rule, and basic civilian rights against military power.

The intrusiveness of the ubiquitous navy vessels was, according to Benjamin Franklin, made worse because

"especially those of the lower Rank, executed their Com-
missions with great Rudeness and Insolence, all Trade and
Commerce, even the most legal, between Colony &
Colony, was harass'd, vex'd and Interrupted, by perpetual
Stoppings of Boats, Rummagings and Searchings,
Unlading & Detaining," and of course whisking off sus-
pect vessels to the court in Halifax.[163] The situation was
summed up by the New Yorker who asked in the Boston
Gazette: "Are the Gentlemen of the Navy judges of the
Nature of Commerce and the Liberty of the Subject?"[164]
By eliminating the direct French threat to the colonies
from Canada, the British forces had made themselves
redundant as far as the colonists were concerned. Their
presence was no longer worth the trouble.

Revenue raising was much more successful than ever
before—but it was still not enough to cover the cost of
enforcement, not to mention the political cost of ill will.
And the system was still very porous. American merchants
paid £8,200 in duties on foreign sugar for which the real
assessment was £122,000. One historian concludes that
for sugar alone, for the five years up to 1770, "the smuggling of Caribbean produce into the Continental Colonies
bilked the British Treasury of well over £570,000 in the
item of sugar alone."[165] In those five years, colonists smuggled almost one barrel of molasses for every two that was
declared—and this was a period when the duty was down
to a penny a gallon. Some 3,936,000 gallons were legally
imported, compared with a further 2 million gallons that
evaded levies of a penny a gallon. So the treasury lost
import duty of £11,200.[166]

In their "patriotic" evasion of imperial customs duties,

merchants also bilked their own colonial governments, whose customs duties raised much of their revenue through a 5 percent levy on imported rum. For example, the rum duty accounted for up to a fifth of the provincial exchequer in North Carolina.[167]

A grudge fight had developed, with the authorities so obsessed with molasses that, John McCusker, the pre-eminent scholar on the colonial molasses trade, suggested that wilier merchants were actually passing off sugar and rum, which had a much higher tariff, as molasses and paying the much lower duty on it. In their petitions, the colonies were already moving beyond their traditional arguments, which they based on the grounds of sound economy business principles. The inventiveness of American lawyers was already deeply ingrained, and they went beyond carping about the amounts or even the methods of collection to denying the right of the British Parliament to impose such taxes at all.

John Adams declared that John Otis's oration against writs of assistance "breathed into this nation the very breath of life." The old Barbadian slogan of "no taxation without representation," became current, and it has great validity in the British tradition that the colonists shared— even if there is more than a suspicion that it was the taxation per se that concerned them. Of course the proponents referred to the principles in their rhetoric rather than the sordid reality of molasses and rum smuggling and Parliament's attempts to raise revenue. You could say that both sides got on their high horses, with London wanting to maintain the principle that the imperial parliament had at least residual suzerainty over the whole empire, and the colonists refusing to accept it. There was no sustained attempt by the colonies to gain representation in the House of Commons in London (although Franklin tried at one point), which would, on the face of it, have been the logical conclusion of the slogan.

By eliminating the direct French threat to the colonies from Canada, the war had also removed the most potent aspect of self-interest that could have impelled the colonists to break with the lifelong habits of tax avoidance. As the crusty old Tory Dr. Johnson inveighed once the colonists had revolted:

> By letting them loose before the war, how many millions might have been saved. One wild proposal is best answered by another. Let us restore to the French what we have taken from them. We shall see our colonists at our feet, when they have an enemy so near them. Let us give the Indians arms, and teach them discipline, and encourage them, now and then, to plunder a plantation. Security and leisure are the parents of sedition.[168]

Putting a Stamp on Smuggling

The Sugar Act worked, up to a point, in making contraband slightly less common than legitimate duty-paid goods. It dealt with an area—overseas trade—over which most colonists would admit that the king and the navy had nominal official oversight. With the Stamp Act and the force used under it, the scofflaw attitude became righteously inflamed, since London was denying local pre-rogatives and doing it with the regular military as law enforcers, which British towns and cities would have equally resented.

Even in England at the time, mob action was so common as almost to be an institution. Whether over the price of corn, the activities of the press gang, or the revenue, repre-sentatives of central government were often defied and manhandled. So the violence in the colonies was not so extraordinary itself, although the direction in which it was moving certainly was, and the degree to which it was con-doned and instigated by many of the local worthies was certainly beyond any experience in Britain. In British mainland towns in times of riot, the local gentry would call out the militia, which was very much a middle-class insti-tution. In the colonies, the militia was much more demo-cratic in its recruiting, officially drawing in all able-bodied men—and in the last decade before the revolution, colonial authorities called it out as often to repel the regular forces of the Crown, and even the local guns were run out to stand off the British ships that a decade or so beforehand had been welcome defenders against the French.

Duties on goods of such common consumption as rum, sugar, and molasses gave every citizen an interest in eva-sion. When the sum of those self-interests could be expressed in a principle of "No taxation without repre-sentation," the potential of the movement, as we now know, was significant. Historian and biographer of Wash-ington, Rupert Hughes has suggested that "Liberty or Death" actually meant "Liberty from Debt" since many of the worthies of the colonies, especially in Virginia, owed considerable sums in London, which often provided the original capital for trade.

June 10, 1772, provided an egregious example of the heated opposition to the motherland's tariffs when nine longboats from Providence, Rhode Island, boarded and burnt His Majesty's armed schooner *Gaspee* after it had become stranded while chasing a rum smuggler. The crew was bound and put ashore, and the well-known perpetrators got away scot-free, since no one would bring any information to the authorities, despite a large reward.[169] Burning a king's ship was an escalation of the conflict that was in itself almost a declaration of war—it certainly insured that the navy, despite the Whig sympathies of many of its officers, would not look kindly on the rebels. The combination of fellow feeling and fear of the personal consequences in a situation where the royal authorities had clearly lost power were enough to overcome self-interest over the price on the head of the perpetrators.

Rhode Island was a revolutionary center precisely because it was a rum-producing, molasses-importing locality, where the local authorities were men of substance and their wealth was mostly derived from the trade. In Newport, Rhode Island, when the mob tore down government officials' homes and drove out the customs collector, John Robinson, he took refuge on *HMS Cygnet*—and closed the port.

Even many of the revolutionaries such as John Adams tried to distinguish between "popular commotions . . . in opposition to attacks upon the Constitution," and "these tarrings and featherings, this breaking open houses by rude and insolent rabble in resentment for private wrongs, or in pursuance of private prejudices and passions."[170] But collective punishment like that imposed by customs collector Robinson played into the hands of the diehard rebels, who were able to enlist the support of otherwise relatively law-abiding citizens.

Conscious or otherwise, the hardliners' tactics were extremely successful. The changeover in popular mood was fairly quick. In 1758, the British commander in Boston tolerantly complained about the state his troops got into because grateful Bostonians, overjoyed at the fall of the French fortress of Louisberg, plied the soldiery with rum: "The jubilation was so exuberant that I could not prevent the men from being quite filled with rum by the inhabitants."[171] In 1766 the citizenry of New York, grateful for their deliverance from the French, erected an equestrian statue of King George III at Bowling Green. In 1776 a mob pulled it down and melted it down to make bullets, no less than 42,088 of them. But half of the statue's fragments were apparently rescued by Tory loyalists and treasured like relics. The head was even smuggled to England.

While modern patriotic accounts state that the statue was erected by the "British," in reality the Colonial Assembly had voted £1000 to have the two-ton statue of gilded lead made in London and shipped over to commemorate the "eminent and singular Blessings received from him during his most auspicious Reign." They had already voted for £500 for a similar brass effigy of William Pitt, not only for the outcome of the Seven Years War but also for "many eminent Services done the Northern colonies," chief of which was the repeal of the Stamp Act.[172]

There was no referendum or plebiscite on independence, however, historians estimate that the Loyalists and the Patriots were each a third of the population, with a middle ground of genuine moderates who probably wished both sides would go away. On both sides there was ambivalence. Until almost the last moment, Benjamin Franklin treasured dreams of a transatlantic imperial partnership, while his son not only was a royal governor of New Jersey but went into exile as a British officer. John Otis's wife remained a loyalist. When push came to shove, even many of the colonial oligarchy, who had fought legally and illegally against the Stamp and Molasses acts, stuck with Britain. But the extremists on both sides increasingly hardened the battle lines—and the most potent aggravation was the smuggling of molasses and the attempts to prevent it.

15. Fast Run to Revolution: The Spirit of 1776

F ew wars would ever withstand a retrospective cost-benefit assessment. They are rarely if ever over by Christmas. Even so, by the time they end so much emotional capital has been invested in them, so many sacrifices, so much blood, that it is expecting far too much of the participants to say that it was not worth it. The war that began as trueborn Englishmen fighting for their rights, not least of which was an assured and cheap supply of molasses to make rum, ended up with an independence and an American patriotism that saw itself as a self-evidently desirable conclusion.

Although questions like the Stamp Act and the supremacy of the imperial Parliament are on the face of it more important than the right to smuggle molasses, history makes it clear that they were in fact causally derivative issues from that prime motivation. As one of the

more deservedly well-reputed conspirators, John Adams
declared:

> Wits may laugh at our fondness for molasses, and we
> all ought to join in the laugh with as much good
> humor as General Lincoln did. General Washington,
> however, always used to assert and proved that Vir-
> ginians loved molasses as well as New Englanders. I
> know not why we should blush to confess that
> Molasses was an essential ingredient in American
> independence.[173]

While Americans referred to their love of molasses, this
was not a case of assuaging an American hunger for treacle
tart. Molasses was shorthand for rum. Per-capita consumption of rum had reached horrendous heights—and annual
3.7 gallons per head by the time of the revolution. But
rum was unsuitable rallying cry for a rebellion. "Bread,
Peace and Land," "Liberty or Death" may have their reso-
nance, but as a slogan, "Cheap Rum for the Slave Trade
and Revolution" lacks a certain *je ne sais quoi*.

Even the Boston Tea Party, the iconic event of the revolution, was, like many iconic events sanctified by pious
retrospective patriotism, not quite the full shilling. It was
really all about rum. The tea party was not in protest
against taxation. In fact, the sneaky British had let the East
India Company import tea into the colonies *without* taxes.
That meant that all the huge stocks of tea smuggled into
the colonies by local merchants were now devalued.

It is clear that in the American colonies, the definition of
"merchant" included "smuggler." In the Darwinian struggle

for commercial survival, any merchant foolishly law-abiding enough to pay duty on a regular basis would soon go bankrupt in the face of competition from all the others who didn't. The biggest fear of the merchant patriots was that once the East India tea was imported, their co-citizens would, quite naturally, follow the same commercial principles they had applied hitherto and buy the cheaper tea, no matter how unpatriotic the gesture would be deemed.

Samuel Adams, brewer, distiller, longtime smuggler of molasses and tea—and later signatory of the Declaration of Independence—was not going to let that happen. His actions were on a small scale an archetype of how a small group of determined fanatics—one might almost say terrorists—can provoke the authorities into acting as their recruiting agents. On the cold, dark night of December 16, 1773, Adams led a gang thinly disguised as Mohawk Indians onto the *East Indiamen* at anchor, broke up the tea chests, and threw their contents over the side. Interestingly even the official U.S. Information Service version of the event says "Adams and his band of radicals doubted their countrymen's commitment to principle."[174] They did not want the patriotism of their fellow Bostonians to be tested in the marketplace. As the eminently patriotic Taussig says of the many such incidents:

> It is difficult, however, to judge whether or not this was a conscious or unconscious effort on the part of such patriots . . . to raise all the grievances of the colonists, commercial, economic and political, to the high level of abstract principle, and then reduce them to a concrete formula that would be the battle-cry of the populace.[175]

Small fanatical groups can terrorize larger sections of the population into at least passive acquiescence to, if not active participation in, their endeavors, not least when they can also invoke a shared sense of grievance, which, as we have seen, the actions of the London government had certainly provided. That led to a reluctance of the local authorities to bring the gang to justice—and then the collective punishment that London imposed in closing the port was something that would genuinely unite the indignation of Bostonians and other Americans—even if they had looked askance at the original incident.

Strangely enough, from the beginning, possibly a majority of the population in Britain supported the colonists in their fight with overbearing imperial authority. Even before the official Declaration of Independence in January 1775, up to four hundred merchants trading with North America assembled in London "to remonstrate against the violent proceedings of the government towards the colonists, and to petition for the repeal of all acts which had interfered with the friendly and commercial relations with America."[176] They were joined by the West India merchants, one of whom pointed out that the Americans consumed twenty thousand hogsheads of sugar and twenty-five thousand puncheons of rum a year from the Caribbean. However, unshaken, the government "plunged madly into war with the colonists."[177]

And equally unshaken, once the war began, American privateers, who more often than not had been in the smuggling business themselves, did not make any distinctions between pro- and antigovernment merchants when they began raiding the commerce of the motherland. While we hear from Hollywood only of the atrocities wreaked by the British, it is clear that the Patriot forces used what would later be justified as revolutionary violence against Loyalists—or even needy local farmers found guilty of supplying the enemy, which was of course more than a little ironic considering the Patriots' behavior during the Seven Years War. On the other hand, some of the most redoubtable and vindictive fighters were the American Loyalist troops.

Far from independence winning free access to molasses for the revolutionaries, by 1776, the British had hit back at the colonists with sanctions as dire to some as the effect of modern versions in Iraq. Starved of rum and molasses, both traders and drinkers suffered, and the effect on the economy was marked; William Pynchon of Salem reported that someone had bought a house for only four shillings more than a hogshead of rum.

In the background, rum kept popping out of the cooperage. John Adams's barber told him in 1774 that "all Toryism grows out of bribery," instancing the local parson, Lyman, who was swayed by "ten gallons of rum, two or three hundred of sugar, and ten gallons of wine, a barrel of flour etc." whenever Deacon Sayward's ship came in.[178]

At the Bar of History: Taverns and Revolution

Patriotism was also irrigated with a steady stream of rum. The American Revolution was hatched in taverns by tavern keepers like Sam Adams, distillers like John Adams and John Hancock, and merchants. The Continental Congress assembled at the City Tavern in Philadelphia, while Jefferson retired to the Indian Queen. Fraunces' Tavern in New York is one of the relics of the revolution—slightly more upscale than Montagne's Tavern, where the Sons of Liberty regularly fired up their rhetoric before frightening the local elite almost as much as they worried the British. The shot heard around the world was fired when the minutemen, who had assembled, as the militia usually did, at Buckman's Tavern in Lexington, confronted the British Redcoats on the green. Their preceding session in the tavern may explain why no one knows who actually fired that first shot, although everyone was very clear about the many shots from both sides that followed.

After the revolution, John Adams reminisced about the earlier years, half a century before, when:

> I was fired with a zeal, amounting to enthusiasm [which then meant hysteria rather than assiduity] against ardent spirits, the multiplication of taverns, retailers, dramhouses and tippling shops. Grieved to the heart to see the number of the idlers, thieves, sots and consumptive patients made for the use of physicians, in these infamous seminaries. . . . [he tried unsuccessfully to reduce the number of drinking dens] But the number of licensed houses was soon reinstated, drams, grog and sotting were not diminished, and remains to this day as deplorable as ever. You may as well preach to the Indians against rum as to our own people."[179]

Adams later regretted his attempts to curb the spread, for which he was ridiculed at the time. In more mature and urbane mode, he dropped his vision of them as sotting houses and now saw the taverns as "nurseries of our legislators" since the publicans and their customers were a majority of the electorate.

Historian of American drinking Rorabaugh summed up the case for the tavern:

> Whether or not taverns were "nurseries" of the legislators, they were certainly seed beds of the Revolution, the places where British tyranny was condemned, militiamen organized and independence plotted. Patriots viewed public houses as the nurseries of freedom, in front of which liberty poles were invariably erected. The British called them public nuisances and the hot beds of sedition. There is no doubt that the success of the Revolution increased the prestige of drinking houses. A second effect of independence was that Americans perceived liberty from the Crown as somehow related to the freedom to down a few glasses of rum.[180]

Perhaps appropriately, considering the issues of trade involved in the rupture with London, Jefferson and Washington plotted independence in Mount Vernon and Monticello in homes that had rum rooms and rum cellars, and as they were historic figures, their rum ledgers have been kept. Mount Vernon itself was named after the admiral who was immortalized for instituting the grog ration in the navy.

It was also rum that set Paul Revere a-roaring and riding. It appears that far from rousing the countryside, he was simply warning the militia to hide their arsenals before a redcoat raid. His first stop was with the owner of a rum distillery, Isaac Hall, captain of the Medford Minute Men, who rewarded the messenger with several stirrup cups that "would have made a rabbit bite a bulldog," and sent him bellowing on his way.[181]

It was also mostly rum that raised the famous "First Salute" in the Dutch island colony of Saint Eustatius on November 16, 1776, when the Dutch garrison at Fort Oranje fired an eleven-gun salute to the *Andrew Doria*, an American brig. This was the first official foreign recognition of the young nation's independence. The salute raised the ire of the British to the extent that the local Royal Navy commander eventually stormed and took the port, whose sole *raison d'être* was as an entrepôt for smugglers from England and France and their respective colonies. The island was conveniently sited for equal-opportunity contrabanding between Guadeloupe, Puerto Rico, and deep in the British Leewards, with the Danish islands not far away. It was not just the symbolism that irked the Royal Navy, although navy men did tend to be pernickety about such things. Rather it was that the Revolutionary armies drew so much of their supplies and munitions from this freebooting port.

Tots with Shots

Rum was not only the proximate cause of the war; it was also a weapon in it. Troops on both sides insisted on their daily four-ounce ration of rum and were very unhappy at the desperate substitutes, such as pumpkin beer or even wine, that they were reduced to. General Israel Putnam, "who was almost perforated with bullets, complained most of all that a shot had passed through his canteen and spilt all his rum."[182]

When the war began, it was clearly not a dry Republic they were fighting for. Indeed the first and most strategic stores the armies and navies fought to secure were the rum stashes, with the British, who controlled the seas and the distilleries, at a distinct advantage. American and British military doctrine alike held that you could not expect men to fight without regular supplies of fighting spirits—rum. In 1775 Abigail Adams wrote indignantly to her husband that the British General Gage in Boston has "ordered all the molasses to be distilled into rum for the soldiers: taken away all licenses, and given out others, obliging to a forfeiture of ten pounds if any rum is sold without written orders from the General."[183] Similarly, nothing excited the ire of the New Haven township more than the dreadful news that the evacuating British garrison had taken the town's rum with them.[184] The drought of rum to some extent brought the threat of famine, or least scarcity, as grain was diverted into the distilleries.

Not only did Washington shock the later fundamentalists and prohibitionists with his drinking, but he combined his debauched tastes with a predilection for state enterprise that would put him way to the left of modern Democrats. Faced with a severe shortage of rum, he wrote to Congress in 1777 suggesting "erecting Public Distilleries in different States." Suggesting that even then he anticipated some resistance, he went on to explain, "The benefits arising from the moderate use of strong Liquor, have been experienced in all Armies and are not to be disputed." He returned quickly to the subject with the commissary general. But it is interesting to see the beginning of the end for rum in America. He called upon Congress to get grain for the distilleries, since the British had (finally) managed to stop the colonists smuggling molasses. In the meantime, the precious strategic resources of rum were the subject of constant correspondence between him, the various departments, and the states, such as New Hampshire, which levied each town to provide enough gallons of molasses to make up ten thousand gallons of West India Rum.

In this case, as well indicating a vast military thirst, rum may have been at work in its function as currency. Indeed, there was even an exchange rate: New England rum could be substituted at one and half gallons to one of West Indies rum—an eccentric lack of patriotism for the revolutionary armies.[185] Dartmouth, from which Eleazar Wheelock set off with 500 gallons, only had to provide 6 gallons, while Portsmouth was hit for 209 gallons. Abigail Adams complained about the price of rum and molasses shooting up and chronicled the beginnings of the huge inflation of the paper currency, not least, she said, because "our gold and silver" was being shipped to the West Indies "to pay for the molasses, coffee, sugar etc."[186]

Later on in the war, as the French brought more and more supplies, Washington once again showed his solicitude for the men under his command, writing to John Hancock in 1781 to deplore General William Heath's distribution of wine to the soldiers instead of rum. Washington laid down firmly, "Wine cannot be distributed

the Soldiers instead of Rum, except the quantity is much
increased. I very much doubt whether a Gill of rum would
not be preferred to a pint of small wine." Hancock took
his commander in chief seriously and wrote to Major
General Benjamin Lincoln in Boston on August 15, 1781:

> As to Rum there hass been a quantity procur'd and
> sent to Springfield, and we have lately been affording
> assistance to Qu. Mr. Genl, to enable him to transport
> it to Camp. It is of such importance that the army
> should be fill'd up & regularly supplied, that you may
> depend no exertions of the Executive here shall be
> wanting to effect those purposes.[187]

In 1782 Washington ordered an extra gill of rum to be
served to everyone in the tenth Massachusetts Regiment
for their work on the fortifications and, even more surprisingly for a republican army whose commander in chief
had learned the art of war fighting the French, he ordered
the same for the whole army to celebrate the birth of the
Dauphin, the future Louis XVII of France—but not a very
long future, as it would transpire. It is all the more ironic
that General Washington thought so highly of the martial
virtues of rum, since one of his few outright military
victories in the field—over thirteen hundred Hessians at
Trenton on Christmas Day, 1776—was reputedly because
the enemy was overfortified with the Christmas spirit.

In the south, the British were also fighting hard on the
rum front. When Cornwallis began his unsuccessful last
offensive in the Carolinas, the most demoralizing event for
the troops was when he shed the baggage train to speed up

his chase of rebels. And despite his throwing his own baggage on the bonfire, the troops were horrified when he also torched the rum supplies.

In 1783, mutinous Continental soldiers from Pennsylvania who were owed huge amounts in back pay marched on the Pennsylvania statehouse to demand settlement of their claims. The president of Pennsylvania (soon to be relegated back to being a mere governor) downed a bottle of rum with the two sergeants who were acting as delegates for the mutineers. When he opened the second bottle, they were canny enough to complain that "We didn't come to get groggy."

After the Revolution

Ironically, after the war, the federal government found itself in the same straits as the British imperial government had after the Seven Years War. It had no money and so it emulated what London had done earlier with the imposition of an excise duty on stills and spirits. Many of the states and cities immediately reminded the new government that in 1774 the British excise law was "the horror of all free States."

James Madison warned Hamilton, the ex-revolutionary and main mover of this tax, that "an excise would be received with indignation in some parts of the Union, it is not for this government to disgust any of its citizens if it can be avoided." But the federal government took no notice. The locals in western Pennsylvania showed the same contempt for authority that the Bostonians, Newporters, and others had demonstrated against British tax

collectors. Mob action, tarrings and featherings, and a refusal of officials to take up their posts soon confirmed that
it really was the taxation, not the representation, that concerned many Americans. They did not even take any
notice when the new president, Washington, remonstrated
that the excise duties were needed to protect them, in an
unintentionally ironic replay of the arguments that King
George's ministers had made a mere decade or so before.

If the mainland colonies had brought the Caribbean
islands with them in their project, then they could, perhaps, have started business as usual right afterward. But
Jamaica, Barbados, and the other islands, although close in
sentiment to the mainland, had tiny white minorities with
large slave populations and were under continuous threat
from rival European powers. The war brought the French,
Spanish, and Dutch in on the side of the American
colonists, not so much for any love of liberty and the
Americans but in an attempt to rewrite the results of the
Seven Years War. While the Americans got what they
wanted, not least because at Yorktown the French fleet and
army cornered Cornwallis, the French did not regain
Canada and lost the naval battle for supremacy in the
Caribbean.

Indeed, one of the reasons for the British defeat had
been that the planners in London were never quite sure
which was more important—defending the sugar and rum
islands or regaining the molasses consumers' territory. Too
often for strategic sense, the sugar barons had the British
forces defending their investments in the Caribbean.

The British West Indian islands were cut off from American trade, and that had consequences, since the trade that the

Yankee ships had conducted with the Southern colonies—
food in return for Caribbean produce—fell apart. Their
trading partners now wanted cash, of which there was a dire
scarcity in the new Republic. American ships could no longer
count on markets in Canada, Britain, or even Africa, where,
after 1807, the British antislavery patrols challenged the very
purpose of the rum exports.

North of the border, the Canadians followed a familiar
path in response to such artificial impediments to trade.
They smuggled in molasses and distilled their own rum. The
northern trade was of particular importance to the New
Englanders because their rum exports to Canada were paid
for with cash, which had been a perennial problem for the
colonies in financing their imports from Britain.

The embargo that the federal government imposed on
trade with Britain in the run up to the War of 1812 almost
split the new, fragile Union as the northern states suffered
from the break in trade followed by the war itself. However, just as tea suffered from patriotic comparisons after
Boston, so did rum begin its slow fade from the bar
counter. By the second decade of the nineteenth century,
as the new country was still paying off the debts incurred
in the fight for tax-free molasses, only a fifth of spirits distilled in the new Republic were rum. Rum was eighteen
cents for two gills—while whiskey was twelve cents. This
was patriotism made manifest! By 1790, whiskey had
come from almost nowhere to account for one third of
consumption—and possibly much more if all the backwoods and backyard stills' production were to be counted.

The Celtic connection we hypothesized for the Barbadian invention of rum was incontrovertible in the West,

where the Scots-Irish had spread down the Appalachians and then across to the West, often taking their stills with them and certainly taking both skills and tastes. Their technology conspired against rum. The Scots had pioneered highly efficient flat stills that worked well with grain mash but led to caramelization and scorching of molasses washes, which needed a gentler, longer process. Once away from the coast, the cost of transport of either molasses or rum proved too much for effective competition with the whiskey makers. The intrepidly lawless Scots-Irish had found their way across the mountains into Kentucky, where they could grow far more corn and rye than they could eat or profitably carry to any market, and since distillation came naturally to them, that is what they did. A bushel of corn increased in value fivefold when distilled and was much more "fungible" as an economic unit.

The greater taxes on rum and molasses and the somewhat greater surety of their collection as they were landed at ports, compared to whiskey, led to an inexorable price advantage for the latter. After all, this was a government of ex-smugglers, and who should better know the tricks of the trade, which could no longer brandish the moral shield of patriotism? No one had ever drunk New England rum for its taste; it was its effect people wanted, so whiskey was equal in every respect for people trying for a quick fix. Rum could hold its own on the sea lanes of the coast, but the high cost of land cartage gave locally produced whiskey a huge advantage—close to the customer and far from the customs collectors.

The consumption of alcohol of all kinds rose to unprecedented heights. Even as whiskey production and consumption soared, in 1818, according to Senator Rufus King of New York, the United States imported 6 million gallons of West Indies rum and 7 million gallons of molasses, which were distilled into a further 7 million gallons of rum.[188] Washington himself maintained the predilection for rum that he had shown throughout the war. In 1787, Washington bought a still from his former British enemies in Bristol. By 1789 he had five stills going. One magnificent example of his pot stills was confiscated by the Bureau of Alcohol, Tobacco and Firearms (ATF) from the descendents of his slaves in 1939 and put on display at the bureau's museum. (The ATF always seemed hotter about stills than either of the other two subjects of their charter.)

Whiskey brought out the strong jingoistic element of the new country. The nationalism and sometimes rabid patriotism that led Noah Webster, for example, to try to create an American language reflected on rum. Its sources had now become "foreign" and hence dubious. Kentuckian contributions to the discourse of liberty included a pledge to "drink no other strong liquor than whiskey."[189] The author of *The Distiller* declared that it should be:

> the particular aim of the American distiller to make a spirit purely American, entirely the produce of our country: and if the pure unadulterated grain spirit can not be rendered sufficiently palatable to those tastes that are vitiated by the use of French brandy or Jamaica rum, let us search our own woods for an article to give it taste sufficiently pleasant for these depraved appetites.

4. Négres au Travail.

The roots of rum: Slave women plant sugarcane in early nineteenth-century Martinique.

(Left) Magic ingredient for naval success: A Magic Lantern slide shows the grog ration on *HMS Alexandria*, circa 1880.

(Below) The other naval connotation: Pirates sell rum!

There's plenty of Old St. Croix at your favorite store

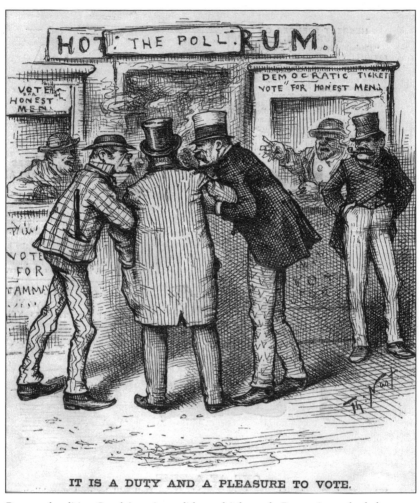

IT IS A DUTY AND A PLEASURE TO VOTE.

Rum and politics: Good Americans did not drink—only Romanists and rebels.

The end of an era: Franked postal cover to mark the last day of rum issue.

The History of Rum Making

The slurping continues: British Virgin Islands commemorative stamp pushes Pussers, the revived naval rum recipe.

The iconography of rum: The French wanted to show hot tropical connections to warm their spirits.

RHUM MOYETTA

L & B. — COGNAC

RHUM
JAMAÏQUE

Pedro Benito

RHUM
Vieux

RHUM

P. OUVIEZ & C° PARIS N° 1020   DÉPOSÉ

(*Left*) Old Havana Club postcard shows the name of the former owners dispossessed by Cuban Revolution.

(*Below*) The trademark that launched a thousand law suits: Modern Havana Club.

The spirit of the gods: Rum Barbancourt, Haiti's most successful industry.

BOUNCED!

Judge magazine (August 1894) celebrates the Roman Catholic Church turning on rum-sellers.

The visitor's entrance to the Bacardi distillery in Puerto Rico. Artificial cow, synthetic spirit?

Just what the doctor ordered: A Prohibition-era prescription form for those who could just not do without.

A more congenial Irish medical approach: It's good for you!

16. RUM AND THE DOCTORS

We have hinted at the rising tide of censorious temperance and prohibitionist sentiment. But before exploring that path, we should remember that once out of the fevered atmosphere of temperance halls and churches, our subject here has often been not "demon rum," but "rum the healer."

One recent winter, on my way to a friend's Christmas party in the Catskills, I stopped at the liquor store for some rum (of course) to take along. The owner lamented his poor stock: "I've had a run on it in the last week." When asked why, he responded as if it were self-evident: "It's been really cold the last week." The old tradition of rum as a specific remedy against the chill and a presumption of general restorative properties is still strong despite two centuries of bourbon-drinking. When William Byrd was surveying the boundary between North Carolina and

Virginia, he referred to rum as "that cordial for all dis-
tresses," and, apart from a few medical curmudgeons, folk
wisdom has usually regarded it as such.[190]

In the cold and damp of the northern climes, a tot of
rum does indeed seem to warm the body. In Germany and
Austria, they have *Jaeger-tee*, Hunter's Tea, which is ferociously overproof rum for just such purposes. They firmly
believe will help keep them warm and healthy. Certainly
in British and French folklore, rum was what the doctor
ordered for cold, flu, and other ailments. This may be
totally subjective, but it is difficult to disagree that rum is
indeed more "wholesome" than other spirits designed just
for drinking. People with colds would drink a rum and
blackcurrant in British pubs to help restore them, and at
home they may well have added a copious draft of liquid
sunshine to their hot tea.

Perversely, rum is also a beverage to see you through
the tropical heat. Richard Ligon thought that the rum was
necessary to help pale, cold northerners to survive the
tropic heart, despite the "costiveness and tortions of the
bowels" that overindulgence could bring. Such symptoms
could have been methanol poisoning from imperfectly
distilled spirit or even lead poisoning. Some of the symptoms Ligon described sound almost like malaria, "taking
cold through cold nights after coming home hot and
sweating in the evening," for which the cure was a dram.
It may not have cured, but it very likely made the pains
more bearable.

In the best traditions of eighteenth-century medicine,
the kind that bled patients to death or seared the insane
with hot irons to calm them, Hans Sloane regarded Madeira

and water as the drink of the gentry and rum the drink of
the plebs, claiming that in Barbados:

> no year passes without it having killed more than a
> thousand. When new immigrants start drinking it,
> they become very vulnerable, for this liquor heats the
> blood and soon sets up a fever which in a few hours
> sends you to your grave. It cannot be used with too
> much moderation. The best thing to do is abstain
> from drinking it altogether, at least until ones' body
> has got used to the air in this country.[191]

If this mortality rate were true in 1707, there would have
been few people left in Barbados. It is indeed likely that
new arrivals died in large numbers—from tropical diseases
to which they had no immunity. It is unlikely that even
badly distilled rum would have had quite such a rapidly
lethal effect.

Once the quality both of the rum and that of its customers improved, rum was not only considered a tonic to
keep at bay the lassitude of the tropics, it was also thought
to be medicinal. Robinson Crusoe in Defoe's story had the
good fortune to salvage three barrels of rum from the ship-
wreck. When he was hit by the fever, he infused tobacco in
rum and drank it, which sent him to sleep for two days and
nights, but he awoke recovered. It was given to sailors and
soldiers not out of charity but because it was assumed that
it made them fight harder. It was given to the slaves when
they were wet, not out of pity, but for fear that the damp
would bring on chills and fevers.

What rum taketh away, it sometimes also giveth. A man

called Andrews in Brunswick, Maine, was unloading a
barrel of rum when it fell and broke his leg; he was
inspired to verse:

> *By a sudden stroke my leg is broke,*
> *My heart is sore offended;*
> *The Doctor's come—let's have some rum,*
> *And then we'll have it mended.*[192]

It seems entirely possible that he had drunk rum before
the accident as well as in the instant anaesthetic dosage.
Navy surgeons had only rum as an anaesthetic as they
hacked limbs off their patients in the haste of battle.

Rum was seen as a healthy alternative to pernicious gin,
which had, apocryphally, been sold as "Drunk for Penny,
Blind Drunk for twopence, clean straw for nothing."[193] Of
course, no one has carried out double-blind trials of the
kind the Food and Drug Administration would now
demand for rum to be approved for pharmaceutical use,
but research of sorts was out there even three centuries
ago. *Short Animadversions on the Difference now Set up between
Gin and Rum* argued that laws against gin had made the
British return to being "sober, industrious, vigorous, hardy
brave and governable." They were saved from rottenness
and rags, since gin, taxed at a lower rate, was "vastly more
destructive to the Human Frame than Rum." Sounding
like a coy advertisement for Viagra, it claimed that rum,
which was "mild and balsamic, and benign," restores the
appetite and digestion and "recruits drooping nature."[194]

His point was echoed by a sugar planter, J. G. Kemays,
who wrote that rum is "none of your poor hungry

liquors" reviling the British retailers' habits of adulterating it with English spirits, and he complains that the government's taxation was hitting the bedrock of British security:

> Rums from which they draw such revenues, are too great a price to allow the Navy to be supplied with such wholesome spirit and . . . are doing what other Enemies cannot, destroying the brave English Tar, with poisonous British spirits. The Genuine Jamaica Rum, the most wholesome of all Spirituous Liquor, the most fragrant Cordial Balsam will, the more it is known, be the more in demand.[195]

Like drug-company-financed research, Robert Dossie's 1769 pamphlet, *An essay on Spiritous liquors with Regard to their effects on Health, in which the comparative wholesomeness of Rum and Brandy are particularly considered,* was paid for by the sugar interests and proved, entirely impartially, that rum was good for you and brandy not. Brandy was French, after all!

Rum was soon found to be a useful substance to keep the body warm in more northern climates. As early as 1663, John Josselyn described the effects of the stuff and showed that it was already a staple of commerce on the Atlantic seaboard. New England ships arrived at the fishing grounds with a "walking tavern" whose stock included "brandy, rhum, the strong water and tobacco." The New Englanders offered the fishermen free samples:

> which so charms them that, for no persuasion that their employers can use will they put to sea, although fair and reasonable weather for two or three days, nay

sometimes a whole week, till they are wearied with drinking, taking ashore two or three hogsheads of wine and rum to drink off when the merchant is gone.[196]

By then they were practically debt slaves to the merchants mortgaging their holdings, which was one of the facets fueling prohibitionist sentiment in the maritime provinces of Canada.

But voyagers, warriors, and civilians alike have contributed anecdotal evidence on a huge scale to the folk wisdom of rum. Warner Allen cites an eminent mountaineer who swore to the efficacy of rum in helping to conquer Kamet, a Himalayan peak of 25,447 feet, and who claimed: "Alcohol was found to aid digestion at high altitudes, and hot rum before turning in induced warmth and sleep."[197]

Even so eminent a scientist as Joshua Banks on Captain Cook's voyage testified that when he and several colleagues were collecting specimens in Tierra del Fuego, accompanied by a black servant, they were stuck in a freezing swamp by a heavy snowfall. "It was then found that a bottle of rum was in the knapsack of one of the men; the negro was roused by the spirit, but he and his companions drank too freely of it, and all but one of them succumbed to the frost." So despite its restorative properties, it was important not to exceed the stated dose.

During the First World War, rum was issued to all soldiers, but there are tales of doctors specifically prescribing it for gas poisoning and shell shock. One Australian veteran remembers:

The gas was phosgene, and we were all sick, choking, when the QM arrived with rum. We swallowed some and the fumes of the rum and gas made us horribly sick and we vomited most of the gas out. After a couple of hours we only had a bad headache and didn't go out of action. Rum is the best cure for phosgene gas, but no good for other kinds.[198]

At the end of the First World War, when the Spanish flu killed almost as many people as the war itself, the French government reacted by requisitioning all stocks of rum available for the hospitals and the troops, since it was seen as not only a cure but a preventative as well. In short, despite the lack of double-blind trials, rum's part in the popular *materia medica* is well assured.

The Spirit of Denial

It took about a century of hard work to move the image of rum from a health-giving elixir to Satan's tool for spreading moral weakness and ruining the physical and moral fiber of its imbibers. And then, as the previous anecdotes suggest, it was only partly successful. More people think rum is good for them than think it is from Satan's own cellar. At the end of the seventeenth century, for example, Captain Henry Morgan, the former buccaneer who became governor of Jamaica, died, allegedly of rum, only a year after Diarist and Secretary of the Royal Navy Samuel Pepys had suggested his rum experiment to the Royal Navy. But somehow one gets the impression that at this early stage, death by rum was a morally neutral mortality—unfortunate, like being killed in a car accident, but not necessarily an instant ticket to the Inferno. That would come later.

That older attitude toward drinking, an integral part of culture and machismo, can be seen a century after Morgan died in his cups, in the work of a Scottish judge, Lord Hermand, of whom it was fondly remembered that he had "great compassion for those who were unable to indulge in the pleasures of an old Scotch drinking, and an equal contempt for those who could but would not." He summarized one case in which he was arguing for transportation:

> We are told that there was no malice, and that the prisoner must have been in liquor. In liquor! Why, he was drunk! and yet he murdered the very man who had been drinking with him! They had been carousing the whole night; and yet he stabbed him! after drinking a whole bottle of rum with him! Good God, my lairds, if he will do this when he's drunk, what will he not do when he's sober?[199]

On the other hand, it was becoming obvious that drink had its toll. An American doctor, Thomas Cadwallader, was one of the founders of the temperance movement. In 1745, he determined that rum was the cause of the "West Indies Dry Gripes," otherwise known as the "Dry Bellyache," an agonizing and potentially fatal stomach disorder. His remedy, to stop drinking rum instead of using it as a medicine, was an effective cure, although its novelty with a population that usually thought rum was a panacea made it a hard sell.[200] After the revolution, in 1787, Dr. John Hunter wrote a paper on the cause of the "dry belly-ache" of the tropics. He applied the discovery of another doctor—that the lead in cider was the cause of "Devonshire colic"—to rum that had been distilled through a lead worm, citing observations by that inveterate scientific observer, Ben Franklin.

In those Caribbean days before Louis Pasteur, rum even took the blame for the tropical diseases, notably yellow fever, that devastated regiments and fleets based in the Caribbean. There was a significant if erroneous statistical correlation: all the soldiers and sailors drank lots of rum. And lots of them died of yellow fever. Hunter experimented with rum, which would have been fun—except all around people were dying. However, he proved to his own, possibly considerable satisfaction that it was not rum that was killing them directly. Indeed, he was ahead of his time; suggesting that when the military set up camps, they should pay close attention "to insects that breed in the marshes."[201] It was a century before doctors finally accepted that mosquitoes spread yellow fever and malaria.

But osmosing down from the chilly north were moral arguments far more persuasive than the merely medical. The two came together in the Quakers, whose anxieties about alcohol were often framed in utilitarian terms, set in the context of their lifestyle of moderation and avoidance of excess. The Philadelphia Quakers epitomized the Protestant work ethic and early in the eighteenth century eschewed the colonial habit of drinking the bottle passed around at auctions. Their morality was indeed outstanding, and they often had a rational reason for it, often with a proto-utilitarianism worthy of Jeremy Bentham. They realized that it was bad business practice to bid under the influence and additionally rationalized that since the rum had to be paid for, it added to the cost of the goods on sale.

Equally, while colonial funerals traditionally embalmed the memory of the dead in huge quantities of booze, the sober Quakers could not absolutely refrain, since it was inconceivable disrespect to the dead not to take a glass, but they restrained themselves to a politely respectful and respectable two drinks. As proto-Patrick O'Brien Captain Frederick Marryat found, even as late as the 1830s there was a dangerously sacramental character to American drinking. No matter how politely expressed, any demurral to a convivial glug from the bottle could result in the challenge: "Stranger, will you drink or fight?"

When the war began, the Friends in Philadelphia opposed their members' involvement in distillation because it raised grain prices and thus the cost of bread. It helped their arguments that they tied the rum and molasses trade to the slavery they opposed. The Quaker opposition moved onto a more openly moral point of view as the century went on, and by the end of the century they were calling on their members to abstain from the trade entirely, a process helped along considerably when Quaker Antony Benezet of Philadelphia published *The Mighty Destroyer Destroyed* in 1774 and overtly linked moral and medical arguments against drink. The Quakers, however, were tolerant in their temperance. They made rules for themselves and, unless it were by setting an example, did not lay down the law for others.

Farther north, where the Pilgrims had landed, there was no such indulgence. People had to be made to be good. This feeling emerges from Samuel Niles' appeals to the Massachusetts justices to cut back on tavern licenses in 1763. He inveighed against the:

> unnecessary Multiplication of *Taverns,* and Licensed Houses for *Retailing* Rum and other Strong Drink:— which by long and sad Experience has been found greatly prejudicial to any People, in Regard the Youth, as well as *elder Persons,* have thereby Places of Resort near at Hand, whither they are enticed and ensured often, to the Destruction of the Inhabitants, both in their Bodies and Souls; manifestly proved, particularly, when Heads of Families, not only spend their Time and Substance needlessly at Taverns and Tipling Houses, and by it bring their Families under pinching Wants, but also, in Part or in Whole, neglect the Religion of the Houshold, and by their Example draw their Children and Servants into the like irreligious, corrupt Practices; which will make them a Generation of evil Doers; a Consequence, to be dreaded by all that have the Fear of God before their Eyes, and that are Friends of our Zion![202]

He goes on to recall being:

> many Years past, in Conversation with the Reverend, and then very aged Mr. Keith, of *Bridgewater,* their first Minister, he told me, He supposed, that for the first *twenty* Years after his settling there, there was not

one single *Barrel* of *Rum* drank, in the whole Town, in a Year:—But *now,* said he, with great Lamentation, it comes *rolling* in; *Hogshead* after *Hogshead!* This he offered, bewailing it, as a manifest, Proof of the Growth of Corruption among that People, and consequently a dreadful Obstruction to the Success of the Gospel.

We cannot be sure whether he is objecting to the drinking of the rum or the location of the drinking. But it is quite clear that he distrusts the people, who have to be protected from their own baser interests.

Less evangelically, but equally strongly, Dr. Benjamin Rush, for a time surgeon general of the Continental Army, had views on rum at direct variance with what we have seen of his commander in chief's. The effective founder of the temperance movement, Rush approached his work with rationalism and was no teetotaler. He advocated the use of beer, wine, cider—and weak rum punch. He was in fact a pioneer of addiction studies and documented the effect of ardent spirits on the health of those who abused them. Even though he was, in what was a pejorative term at the time, an "enthusiast," his much republished *Moral & Physical Thermometer* was temperate in its approach to "cider, wine, perry, strong beer and porter," which equated to "Cheerfulness, Strength and Nourishment, when taken only at meals and in moderate quantities," but went a little over the top when it came to spirits, moving from "Obscenity, swindling, perjury and burglary," when drunk in the morning to murder and suicide morally, death medically, and the gallows socially if drunk at day and night.

From 1784 onward, Rush marshaled current scientific and medical opinion (which still included bleeding and hot irons as a cure) behind his case. In an uncanny prediction of Prohibition, this Nostradamus of the liver looked forward to a successful conclusion of the campaign so that by "1915 a drunkard . . . will be as infamous in society as a liar or a thief, and the use of spirits as uncommon in families as a drink made of a solution of arsenic or a decoction of hemlock."[203] Rush's work was widely published but listened to only by the upper classes, and even then, only by some of them, since, as we have seen, many of them based their superior social status on the wealth they made from importing, making, or selling liquor.

But Rush's more rational medical arguments added force to many antiliquor measures. In the Quaker spirit, Rush encouraged people to stop paying farmworkers in hard spirits. It was noticeable that such campaigns usually took on added fervor when the price of rum was high and the value of the currency low. With war against France looming, a meeting of Canadian farmers in Hants County in 1793 determined to pay cash and referred to the "Excessive use of spirituous liquors among the laboring poor." But they blunted their altruism with the comments that "present enormous price of rum will prove ruinous to farmers."[204] Similar resolutions came from Connecticut and other places across New England where rum was a significant part of the cost of labor.

Some of the revolutionaries like Rush had also seen independence as a means of rescuing the new Jerusalem from Babylonish Britain, the decadent mother country, which was indeed closely associated with rum, molasses,

and the other accouterments of hard liquor, as it was
mostly known. As an ardent patriot, Rush advocated what
he called "invaluable FEDERAL liquors," beer and cider,
as opposed to "Antifederal" rum and whiskey, "companions of those vices that are calculated to dishonor and
enslave our country." Similarly, those who wanted to raise
revenue for the struggling federal government used the
medical arguments that Rush had produced to help justify
tariffs on rum and molasses. The reformers had an eye to
excise duty, citing the success of the duty on gin in Britain,
which had anticipated modern tobacco taxes in cutting
consumption. It also seemed a good way to raise revenue
for the federal or, at the early stage, confederal government, but that overlooked the fact that aversion to taxes
and attachment to rum had been core factors in the revolt.
The states, unsurprisingly, refused to give their consent to
the excise proposed by Robert Morris in 1782. They were
no more eager to let the federal government tax them than
they had been to let London.

The rebellion brought out some of the same issues as
temperance and prohibition. In its aspect as a revolution,
coupled with the ungoverned move westward, independence had cultivated a resistance to upper-class controls on
a common man's drink imposed by people who drank more
refined beverages. It was a revolt against the paternalist
hegemony of the old elite who thought they knew best.
The elite may have engineered the revolution for their own
ends, but the mass of the people involved had taken up the
language of liberty and equality and did not see the end
result of their efforts as business as usual with London out
of the way. Once they had challenged the divine right of

kings, then it became inevitable that the divine right of local worthies to set standards was assailable as well. The same people who stood up to the revenuers would pretty much ignore the prohibition agents as well.

Despite his more urbane and, one might say, quite temperate attitude to temperance, Rush set in movement autochthonic forces beyond his imagination, which included the sides lining up over the Whiskey Rebellion. Realizing that the most effective distribution network for his ideas was the only institution that really crossed the new state boundaries—the clergy—Rush sent copies of his *Inquiry in to the Effects of Ardent Spirits in the Human Mind and Body* to them. His greatest coup was to send copies of his tracts to the Presbyterian National Assembly in 1811. They adopted it with gusto, and out erupted the other, less scientific current of American thought that was bubbling away just under the surface: the one that hanged witches and pilloried the independent-minded, that knew what was best for people.

Augmented by the rise of Methodism, fired by the Presbyterian intolerance of evil, temperance, in the sense of avoiding drunkenness, veered toward teetotalism and Prohibitionism.

America Takes Leave of Tom Paine—And Common Sense

The changed, postrevolutionary sensibility is inadvertently illustrated by the fate and reputation of Tom Paine, who, more than anyone else, had assembled the intellectual and moral arguments for the American Revolution. His pamphlet *Common Sense* inflamed and informed the Patriots with sound and ethical reasons for their actions—whether they had been the original motivations or not.

Himself a former exciseman in Britain, Paine was the first coiner of the name "United States of America" but was far too liberal in his views for the Revolutionaries. He tried to make a genuine American revolution out of what the British, perhaps more accurately, call the War of Independence. His freethinking views on religion and society led to him being denied the vote because, it was alleged, he was not a citizen of the country that he had in some measure invented and had certainly inhabited at the time of its birth. His enemies, in a sign of the changed times, accused him of drunkenness; in view of the prevalence of this state among his contemporaries, the objection may have been more to his tirades against religion while under the influence.

In Paris during the French Revolution, Paine was already fond of brandy—to the extent that his nose had turned red. When he returned to the United States, he turned to rum, at the rate of a pint a day. But that was scarcely exceptional by the standards of the times. However, the change in sensibilities allowed his many enemies to use the linkage of drunkenness with irreligiousness to slander the revolutionary who had lived past his sell-by date for the new rulers of the United States. The spiritual effects of rum, not the physical harm, now preoccupied the evangelical temperance movement.

In addition to being responsible for almost all social evils, rum apparently caused spontaneous combustion, in which living people suddenly burst into flames and autocremated. The phenomenon featured in numerous novels (Dicken's

Bleak House being the most famous, perhaps). Mary Clues, the first example of spontaneous combustion cited in all the pamphlets about the subject, was a heavy drinker, downing a quart of rum a day, and smoked a pipe. There is room to doubt the spontaneity of her ignition, but it was a potent example for temperance advocates and added a new dimension to fiery spirits.

Temperance societies suggested that parents frighten their children with "rum" along with hobgoblins or ghosts, and their publications certainly did their best to frighten everybody. The *American Temperance Spelling Book* of 1839 invited children to copy:

I once saw a little boy so drunk that he could not stand on his feet. He was very sick, and fell down on the floor. I have not seen him for a long time, but no doubt he is in the cold grave. But few boys, who learn drink beer, or gin, or rum when they are small, live to be old. Bad boys and bad men drink rum, which leads them to sin and death.[205]

Its author, Mr. Sovereign, obligingly defines rum as "A spirit distilled from cane juice or molasses: a general term used to denote all kinds of intoxicating drink." But it was much more than that. In cartoons, rum loomed as the alien other, invariably with a bottle neatly labeled "Rum," which was convenient for cartoonists short of space. They could have used "Gin," but most Americans didn't and hadn't, whereas rum was foreign and had a history. It represented Catholics, subhuman Irish, and similar nonnative breeds. At the time when most Americans were drinking whiskey, it was rum that was evoked most frequently. It was more patriotic than attacking whiskey overtly. It may also be that in the Puritan heartland of the reformers, abolitionists, and prohibitionists, rum retained its market dominance and hence its prominence in theories of immorality much more than inland, where it was the grain, not the cane, that drinkers increasingly turned to.

Its other virtue was its rhotic, rhyming uses; it could be combined with dislike of things foreign to roar out "Rum and Romanism" by the Protestantism that then dominated the country and later added *Rum Row, Rum Runners,* and *Rum and Rebellion* to the lexicon of American politics. As the 1837 Boston poet of "An Eulogium on Rum" declared:

> *"Hail mighty* Rum!—*and by this general name*
> *I call each species,*—Whiskey, Gin or Brandy:
> *(The kinds are various but effect the same;*
> *And so I chuse a name that's short and handy;*
> *For reader, know, it takes a deal of time*
> *To make a crooked word lie smooth in rhyme).*

His poem was dedicated to Rum "in Small and convenient quantities for Rich or Poor without distinction. Fifteen gallons or none. That the Rich may riot in luxury and poor laborer toil on, with cold water!" The temperance movement had taken some strange forms. Lobbying by the Massachusetts Temperance Union secured a law that forbade the sale of liquors in quantities of less than fifteen gallons. This rather perverse idea of enforced moderation (imagine the Drug Enforcement Agency demanding that crack be sold only in kilo packs) was easily evaded by tavern keepers; at the militia muster in Dedham, Massachusetts, an innkeeper exhibited a "freak striped pig," which he had painted in red-and-white strips, and charged four and a half pence for the privilege while offering an incidental free glass of rum on the side.[206]

Break the Chains, Empty the Bottle

The progression from temperance to abstinence to prohibition came in easy movements with an added dose of abolitionism. The good sense of Methodists and Quakers who could take a little rum punch for their stomachs' sakes was soon subsumed in the fires of Baptist and Presbyterian evangelism. In New England meetinghouses, rum and slavery aroused equal indignation. To a dangerous degree, the Puritan tradition was inclined toward legislating and prosecuting people into virtue.

The roots of abolitionism and prohibitionism reflected the inextricable ties of rum and slavery. In the decades leading to the American Revolution, reformers had began to see rum as a force of darkness, made by slaves and the very instrument of their initial bondage. The great Philadelphia abolitionist Anthony Benezet's pamphlet characterized rum and slavery as *The Potent Enemies of America*.[207] Somewhat more sympathetic than Dr. Johnson to those who demanded freedom while owning slaves, he recognized the hollowness of claims to "Liberty or Death" from the Virginian plantocracy and led the movement to free the slaves, who were still in servitude in Northern states at the time of the Revolution.

John Woolman, a New England Quaker and merchant, recounted in 1769 that "some years ago, I retailed rum, sugar, and molasses, the fruits of the labor of slaves, but had not then much concern about them, save only that the rum might be used in moderation."[208] After he had been "further informed of the oppressions too generally exercised in these islands, and thinking often on the dangers there are in connections of interest and fellowship with the works of darkness," he decided to spend his "small gain" from the trade in preaching, particularly in Barbados.

However, to get there he had to find a ship that was not in some way connected to the nefarious slave trade. And even it were not a slave ship itself, any vessel going to and from the Caribbean would be carrying either the produce of or the wherewithal for slavery. He wrestled with his conscience for a long time and even considered hiring a vessel in ballast or paying a higher fare than he was asked for so that he did not benefit from the relative cheapness of the fares on the lucrative West Indies trade boats. In the end he wrestled himself and conscience into immobility and never left the dock from New England, but he did exercise his conscience enough to stop using sugar because of its connections to rum, molasses, and slavery. Even if Woolman carried his conscience a little far, he was not alone. The poet William Cowper went along with many in wrestling with his conscience—and losing. As he wrote:

> I own I am shocked at the purchase of slaves;
> And fear those who buy them and sell them are knaves;
> What I hear of their hardships, their tortures and groans:
> Is almost enough to draw pity from stones.

I pity for them greatly, but I must be mum,
For how could we do without sugar and rum?
Especially sugar, so needful we see?
What? give up our desserts, our coffee and tea![209]

As the campaign against the slave trade developed, abolitionists introduced the then-novel weapon of the consumer boycott, admonishing that "A Family that uses 5lb
of Sugar per Week, will, by using East India instead of West
India, for 21 months, prevent the Slavery, or Murder, of
one Fellow Creature! Eight such Families in 19 years, will
prevent the Slavery of Murder of 100!" However, even here
the spirit of sordid commercialism interposed itself, since
this warning was used by Ms. B. Henderson of Peckham to
sell "An Assortment of Sugar basins, handsomely labeled in
Gold Letters: 'East India Sugar, not made by Slaves.'" [210]

William Lloyd Garrison fulminated that "Anti-slavery
wants her mouths for other uses than to be flues for besot-
ting tobacco-smoke. They may as well almost be rum-
ducts as tobacco-funnels. . . . Abolitionists are generally as
[determined] in regard to rum and tobacco as in regard to
slavery." In 1912, the luridly illustrated "Man that Rum
Made" also invoked tobacco—a graphic picture of a young
boy vomiting after a pipe and an older one with a cigar
behind whom the devil lurks. The caption warns:

This is the weed,
that sowed the seed,
making the man
That rum made.

The doggerel continues down to:

> *This is the nose that blossoms and grows*
> *On the face of the man that rum made.*[211]

Rum was no longer merely the lubricant in the great engine of commerce; it was evil in itself, to be purged from the body politic, a campaign that went along with the abolition of slavery. State after state, such as Maine, introduced forms of prohibition and claimed great social success. The first great federal victory for prohibition was the abolition of the grog ration in the U.S. Navy in 1862, at the height of the Civil War.

There was a culture clash going on here, and the broad lines were the reformers, who wanted abolition, prohibition, and everybody to be good, and the Democrats, who had a more latitudinarian outlook on sin in general and rum and drinking in particular. And, of course, on slavery for which they showed great tolerance. The New Yorkers who rioted against the draft during the war would almost certainly have burnt the place down completely if prohibition had been part of the package with abolition.

PART III
ROLLING AROUND
THE WORLD

17. HIGH SPIRITS

While we have been examining the dire effects of rum from slavery to drunkenness, subversion, prohibition, and splitting the Anglo-Saxon commonweal, we may have lost sight of an essential element of the story. Rum is heady, desirable stuff, which is why enough people wanted it to provoke all these effects. So we should really look at what makes it so attractive.

Under U.S. law and European Union regulations, rum is the distilled product of fermenting sugarcane juices or of the molasses that is left from sugar refining; different jurisdictions insist on different periods of aging, percentage of alcohol, and various forms of *appellation controllé*. When India complained to an EU commissioner that it was not allowed to export its whiskey to European Union territories, he replied that indeed they could—but only if they labeled it as rum, since it was made from sugarcane.

The French have been picky about rum for a long time, but not as long as the British. In 1789, the French author Charpentier de Cossigny distinguished between the *guildive,* made from the full juice of the cane, and the *tafia,* made from the molasses and other residues. *Le rome,* he pointed out, was simply rectified *tafia,* as the French call the first distillation, which was all that they had usually made on their islands. The big challenge for rum producers was to distill a product that kept the distinctive and desirable tastes and aromas while eliminating the potentially disagreeable ones. Before they could do so, there had to be some serious refinement in distilling, which the Barbadian and then the Jamaican planters had succeeded in doing.

The basic technology of distillation is the same for all spirits. You begin with a solution of sugars in water that the yeasts will feed on. The yeasts multiply and feed on the sugar, excreting alcohols and other organic compounds as by-products. Once the ferment reaches 15 percent alcohol, the yeast cells drown like drunkards in their own excretions. The resulting alcoholic wash is then gently heated so that the alcohol, which has a lower boiling point than water, rises and wafts along a tube, where it condenses.

If you are totally efficient in distillation, then it really does not matter what you start with. Dates were used to make arrack in the East, and in and around the Mediterranean, grapes could be used, as long as they had sugars. In America, apples were made into cider, which could be distilled into applejack. In the north and east of Europe, potatoes, rye, or wheat was used for the mash, while in Britain, malted barley was used for whiskey. If the fermented wash is distilled at exactly the right temperature, you will get pure ethanol—in effect, vodka. Dimitri Ivanovich Mendeleyev, the discoverer of the Periodic Table of the Elements that has decorated the wall of every school chemistry lab for over a century, is an important figure in the history of alcohol. Radioactive element number 101, mendelevium, was named after him, but he was responsible for a much more benign global glow. Czar Nicholas gave him the mission of establishing the standard for vodka. He laid down that vodka should be triple distilled and mixed with pure water to produce a 40 percent alcohol, 60 percent water mix, and this was patented in 1894 as "Moscow Special."

However, it is the stuff that comes with the ethanol that makes rum what it is. As rum connoisseur Warner Allen wrote seventy years ago, "Rum is remarkable for the colossal power of its esters, which in crude productions overpower the senses with a single whiff almost as effectively as ammonia or tear gas."[212] These heady organic compounds are what add flavor and smell to the alcohol. But vodka, the emperor's new spirit, emphasizes more than any other the role of marketing and suggestibility in the trade. If a spirit is actually made to Mendeleyev's formula, then, no matter how fancy the bottle, the label, or the backstory in the advertisements, it will be exactly the same liquid whether you pay $20 for a two-liter jug or $50 for a branded bottle. In effect, clairin, if distilled a little more carefully than Haitian cottage-industry standards usually demand, or medical alcohol would be indistinguishable from premium vodkas in the artistically decorated bottles.

The snobbish gullibility of spirits drinkers had a long history even before the wizardry of brand management

took off. Three centuries ago, John Steadman, who lived
and soldiered in what is now Surinam, recounted:

> On our passage we stopped at the estate Saardan, the
> proprietor of which . . . was our Lieutenant Colonel
> Des Borgnes. I found there an American sailor who
> came to load molasses, and having the inclination to
> try the will of a new planter (and his overseer) in
> rum, I desired the tar to colour a couple of gallons of
> *Kill-Devil* made at the same plantation, and bring
> them ashore as rum brought from Antigua. He did so,
> and they gave him in exchange for it a six gallon keg
> of the very same spirits, declaring it was so much
> better than their own, and then drank their contents
> in punch to my very great entertainment. . . . Such in
> all countries is the power of prejudice.[213]

And such, in modern times, is the power of branding.

Quality control with rum does have a long history
and was essential to its spread to become the world's
most widely consumed liquor. At first the science was
rudi mentary—for example, the old British definition of
proof spirit was 100 percent, being the concentration at
which gunpowder would ignite if the spirit were poured
over it. Another somewhat subjective measurement
involved agitating a glass tube of the spirit and scruti-
nizing the bubbles. If they were small and lingered, the
spirit was below proof. If they were big and dispersed
quickly, it was above. Adding olive oil to a small sample
was another test, a method used a bit like testing for
witches. If the oil sank, the rum was overproof; if it

floated on top, it was under. It was also assumed to be half water and half alcohol, and customs and excisemen estimated that a gallon of proof rum weighed seven and three-quarter pounds, compared to eight pounds for water. In the eighteenth century, the excise first used Clarke's hydrometer and then Sike's, enshrined in legislation to determine the alcoholic content of liquids.

But there was more to good rum than a high octane rating. Some discerning customers wanted agreeable flavor and aroma as well. Nowadays there is serious science in the rum. Many of the distillers I visited, even Barbancourt in beleaguered Haiti, whose telephone wire was regularly being stolen, use gas chromatography in their on-site labs and jealously check each others' products. But even the best-equipped lab needs to be supplemented with the more subtle, if less scientific, noses and palettes of their tasters.

From Kill-Devil to Lively Spirit

The drive for quality as opposed to kick began in the home of rum, Barbados, where the planters were faced with competition for their Barbadoes Waters. Fortunately for Barbados and unlike the French and Spanish colonies, at that time there was no large-scale commercial distilling industry in Britain, and the French and Spanish colonies were not allowed to export rum.

While other people also made spirits from sugar, the Barbadians made them palatable. The Barbadoes Waters held their own, as many contemporary references show. In

1723, Savary des Bruslons conceded its qualities in a spirit that was as rare for a Frenchman then as now: "Rum or tafia is one of the best branches of commerce of Barbados. It concedes almost nothing to the spirits of France. They consume considerable amounts in the English colonies in North America. People of the sea also use it a lot."[214]

Jamaica has a major place in the annals of rum for many reasons, not least being that after Cromwell's Roundheads took the island from Spain in 1655, Admiral Penn instituted the first rum ration in the Royal Navy—presumably drawing on supplies from Barbados. Thousands of sailors would soon be spreading the news about the quick fix offered by this new, strong drink. Jamaica also has the honor of the oldest surviving rum still, from 1680, discovered in excavations of Port Royal, the buccaneering capital of the Caribbean which was destroyed by an earthquake.

Over the years, Barbados lost its primacy in rum-making, which went to Jamaica, where the wash included the skimmings of the sugar boilers which were added to the molasses. Otherwise wasted, these skimmings also added to the distinctive flavor of Jamaica rum—but the key element was the double distillation, which produced a stronger, more concentrated, and possibly less toxic drink.[215] Certainly it was widely appreciated. Double distillation produced only 93.5 gallons of rum for each 100 gallons of molasses, while the old Barbados method gave 145 gallons—and almost certainly considerable hangovers to match. The Barbadians soon followed the Jamaican example. The flavorsome Jamaica rum was much favored for mixing and for punches, which were the main means of consumption. Toward the end of the eighteenth century,

Jamaica was supplying rum to Britain, the more affluent classes in the American colonies, and even nearby Spanish colonies. It also provided rum for ship's supplies and for the "Africa trade," as the slave trade was often euphemistically called.

By 1803, in the midst of the bruising trade wars between Napoleonic France and Britain, and despite his snootiness about genuine *guildive* compared with *tafia,* Charpentier de Cossigny complained that "It must be Jamaica Rum, or at least a liquor which passes for it. It is presumed that it alone can make punch. As a result of this preference, the trade of French tafia in Europe is as nothing, while Jamaica rum is in great vogue in Germany and the North."[216] The home market is always a good testing ground, and the product was certainly much appreciated by all Jamaicans involved in it. In 1770, white colonists each drank 26 gallons or so a year, free blacks and mulattos drank a temperate 14 gallons, and the slaves, a mere but much appreciated 2 gallons a year. In fact, between them, Jamaicans drank a quarter of their own production, amounting to almost a pint a day per adult male. The remaining three quarters were sold abroad, along with the sugar that made Jamaica what Dr. Samuel Johnson called "a place of great wealth, and dreadful wickedness, a den of tyrants, and a dungeon of slaves."[217]

Grenadian Rum took off after the British had finally seized the island from the French. Its planters and distillers learned from both Barbados and Jamaica, the former in terms of efficiency and the latter for double distillation. But while it was as strong as the Jamaica product, it lacked the full flavor and had to content itself with selling to the

American colonies rather than the more affluent and discerning motherland. Sadly, however, its growth curve in
sales was stopped by the American Revolution.

Across the Caribbean, slaves also had ways of boosting
their consumption. In addition to the regular allowance
that plantation workers were given from the moment of
rum's birth in Barbados, they could, for example, also win
a bottle of rum for every fifty dead rats they brought in.
The gallons of rum that the slaves in Jamaica drankshould
not be put down down to charity, it should be remembered that it was of execrable quality. As French distilling
researcher Jacques-Louis Demachy said in the eighteenth
century, it was "the worst drink . . . a liquor that the
colonists find all right to give to their blacks, because the
indifference to these unfortunate slaves goes all the way to
not thinking them fit to take decent drinks."[218]

Antigua was small but efficient in its sugar production
and made what was reckoned to be the best rum after the
Jamaican and Grenada double distillation. Antiguans were
careful in their techniques as well, producing more molasses
and even more rum with the addition of skimmings for the
wash. They produced 120 gallons of rum for every 100 gallons of molasses. Like Jamaican rum, it was a premium drink
appreciated in Britain and also in the northern colonies.[219]

Still Better Rum

On the Anglo-Saxon side, in the early nineteenth century
Robert Stein invented the continuous still. The pot still's
advantage is that it allows a lot of flavor and aroma to go

from the mash to the distillate. But it needs emptying and refilling, and the distillate needs at least one and sometimes more runs to eliminate the more toxic elements. The new continuous still could, as its name suggests, run without interruption and produce much purer alcohol. Stein's invention first began operation first in the 1820s in Cameron Bridge Distillery in Fife, Scotland, for John Haig, of that whiskey ilk, and one of Stein's stills was in operation as late as 1929. Maintaining the Celtic edge previously hypothesized, a Dublin exciseman, Andreas Coffey, came to see it in operation. Coffey ended up making further improvements and gave his name to the apparatus. Excisemen like him charged their taxes on the capacities of stills, and so they had to know the technology.

Coffey's still, also known as the column still, had many advantages. To gladden a canny Scotsman's heart, it was more fuel efficient than older models and allowed continuous production, with the alcohol being tapped from the second column without the more noxious admixtures. The drawback is that it loses much of the flavor, which is one reason why premium blends either use the pot still or blend the pot still output with the neutral spirit. It was not until almost the end of the nineteenth century before it was totally accepted that such blends could pass for whiskey. While most modern columns are made of stainless steel, the older ones were of copper, and many still masters will go to great lengths to keep their copper columns working, since they proclaim their superiority. Certainly throughout the Antilles, the small boutique producers still use the copper stills.

Whatever the wash or the still, aging has long been

accepted as the process indispensable for producing palatable rum. In particular, pot stills produce a whole hangoverish brew of chemicals that need aging in the wood to take the sharp edge off them. As Warner Allen notes, "Rums of age and pedigree combine therapeutic qualities with a real aesthetic appeal."[220] He recounts what must be the record in aged rums. Brought to England in 1805 by a governor general of the West Indies, "It was then sixty years old, being the choicest that he had been able to discover during his fourteen years tenure of office. It was confirmed and sealed by Lady Caroline Morrison and her housekeeper in 1837, the year that Victoria became Queen." As his host, her descendent, pointed out, that meant it was originally bottled in the year of the battles of Culloden and Fontenoy, when the British and French got stuck on the etiquette of who would fire first. Allen was invited to sample it almost two centuries later, in the late 1920s, when new and less courteous forms of warfare had taken hold and the empire was on the rocks, even if it did not yet know it.

He reminisces, "In such circumstances, a disappointment seemed inevitable. Spirits do not improve, but only lose their virtues in the bottle. It appeared impossible to hope for anything but a flat, watery liquid, which had lost all personality through age." However, instead of Alzheimered rum, he found, as he recounts in the finale to his eulogium to rum:

> As a matter of fact, that Rum was still strong enough (in vulgar parlance) to blow ones head off. It had certainly never seen a drop of water, since it was distilled

at strength fantastically aristocratic and benevolent in
its roundness. Such a Rum as that gave youth to the
old, health to the sick, even life to the dying.[221]

Roll out the Barrel

The original planters did not drink white rum as a fash-
ionable cocktail accessory. Thirsty as they were, they, like
many modern Caribbean consumers, did not keep their
rum around long enough to mature. The chances are
that the products of home-produced stills would be kept
in earthenware jugs at first. Wooden casks were the shipping containers of their day. Even items like crockery
were shipped in them, packed in straw or sawdust. They
are robust, durable, rollable, and hoistable. Even today,
Caribbean exiles sending packages home send them in
barrels, albeit steel ones.

Wooden, and specifically oak, casks have played an
important part in the development of modern "brown"
spirits. The early entrepreneurs of the intercontinental booze
trade discovered that as with many wines, such as Madeira,
the process of shipment seemed to improve rum remark-
ably. The raw and acrid spirit that was poured into the keg
emerged at the end of its journey mellowed and smoothed,
with interesting amber colors and more delicate fragrances.
Inadvertently, the very act of export created a higher-quality
product.

We often forget just how much the methods of packing
and preservation create tastes and desires in people. Retsina,
the Greek wine, does not taste of turpentine because some

unsung Hellenic oenologist thought it would be a wonderful flavor to add, but because in times past wine-makers
used pine resin to seal the containers, goatskins and
amphorae. People get used to tastes and aromas and then
grow to like and want them. We enjoy smoked salmon
because our ancestors developed a taste for it when it was
preserved that way. Fish was salted and pickled for preservation, not to pique the appetite. In fact, as part of our story,
salt fish, which was originally shipped to the Caribbean as
low-grade, cheap fuel to keep the slaves working in the
cane fields to make the sugar, rum, and molasses, is now a
local delicacy in many of the islands, found at five-star hotel
breakfast tables.

Habituation to the taste created by aging in oak created
a definite flavor expectation among consumers. Indeed,
even though many California wineries now use sterile
stainless-steel vats to make their red wines, they drop in
honeycombed pieces of oak to imbue the wine with the
tannin and vanillin undertones that wine drinkers demand
from their wines. The holes in the oak blocks expose more
surface area to the wine.

Admiral Rodney's personal physician Gilbert Blane
noted the difference between the locally bought rum and
that which had been reimported from Britain:

It is with reason that the new rum is accused of being
more unwholesome than what is old; for being long
kept, it only becomes weaker and more mellow by
part of the spirit exhaling, but time is allowed for the
evaporation of a certain nauseous empyrematic principle which comes over in the distillation, and which

is very offensive to the stomach; therefore, though this is the produce of the West India Islands, yet what is supplied there is inferior to that which is bought from England.[222]

The "empyrematic principle," was all those ketones, esters, and fusel oils that make "fresh rum" a taste acquired only by the brave and possibly shortlived.

Until the development of cork stoppers, bottles were not really viable containers and added too much bulk for the export market. Before the invention of the *bottscrew* or cork screw, the corks stuck out at the top. Even if some enterprising planter had thought of slapping a fancy label on a designer bottle, it could not be used for export. In its desperate attempts to prevent smuggling, Parliament legislated that spirits could not be imported in anything less than barrels of 100 gallons, and the usual measure was a puncheon, about 105 gallons. To save on shipping, the rum was usually double proof, and what Cognac makers call the "angels' share," the evaporation and leakage, was quite considerable. Merchants and customs officers alike assumed that one gallon in twenty would have gone by the time the rum reached North America, one in ten by British ports, and three gallons in twenty by the time it reached Africa. But the evaporation through the wood improves the flavor and doubtless made the holds interesting places for sailors to simply sit and sniff. Leakage was accentuated by the weight of the stacked barrels, which is why canny merchants preferred their consignments to be on the top.

Whatever the accidents of trade and technology that

produced the happy combination of oak and alcohol, in most serious rum-producing countries, the law mandates several years of maturation in those wooden barrels; the best rum stays in much longer than the law stipulates. And rum would not be the same without those casks, piled high as if waiting for smugglers or buccaneers to come and claim them.

Mount Gay Abandon

It seemed appropriate to go to the source of rum, Barbados, to check on what alchemy takes place there. At Mount Gay Distillery in Barbados, the blendmaster, Gerry Edwards, combines the art and the science of rum-making. He began as an organic chemist before sniffing his way into the enviable position of someone who has to taste and "nose" rum for a living. His laboratory bench in Bridgetown has rows of tall glasses in which samples are left for a few hours at room temperature with a filter paper cover to concentrate the aroma. Tasting is fun. A sniff at the concentrated vapors, rolling around of the amber contents in the glass, followed by a delicate sip and rolling it round the mouth to assess the feel of the drink—an important consideration.

When Mount Gay blends its barrels, which is done by broaching the appropriate selection over a trough to be run away for mixing, the product is given what Edwards calls the triangle test. Eight people are given three samples, two of which are the standard and the other the new blend. Of course, real tasters spit out the sip. But I was only sampling rum-tasting, so I did it in two rounds: the first in scientific and abstemious style, and then the second, knocking it back—since personally I think it is very important to test what the rum feels like as it rushes down the throat. It usually feels good.

Although what the French call *rhummeries* are being turned into tourist attractions, most of the work and the life cycle of rum are as exciting as watching grass grow. Rum casks stacked a dozen high simmer silently in dark warehouses shielded from the tropical sun, while all around is the heady, rich, organic aroma of the rum that evaporates continuously from the casks, in warehouses whose ambient temperature is much higher at twenty-six to twenty-eight degrees Celsius than those used for northern grape and grain spirits. Rum producers reckon that this means that the rum ages three times as fast as a whiskey matured in the damp and chilly warehouses of Scotland.

"Virtually all of the quality of the final product comes from the aging and blending," Edwards explains. Like many premium producers, Mount Gay uses two stills, the pot still, which is basically the same apparatus that was used three hundred years ago, and the Coffey still. The real mystery of distillation of premium spirits is in the pot still, what the French call the guildive in linguistic homage to kill-devil. Indeed the pot still is essentially an industrial-size version of the old alchemists' alembic and is almost as mysterious in its operations. When distillers have to replace a pot still, they often try to reproduce the dents and bumps, in case they helped produce the distinctive aroma and flavor. Luckily, since stills have no moving parts, they last for a long time, and some are in use for over a century.

When sugar is concentrated, it kills yeasts and bacteria, so the sugarcane juice or molasses is mixed with water to let the yeast get to work fermenting furiously to produce a wash of around 6 percent to 8 percent alcohol. Originally, Mount Gay relied on wild yeast, so it took longer to get the fermentation started at the beginning of the season, but then they used the previous wash as a starter culture for the following batches. The magic of distillation then depends on the simple fact that alcohol has a lower boiling point than water. So gentle heating of the fermented mixture boils off the alcohols, which in the old pot stills were led into the worm, the curled pipe, where they cooled down and condensed into liquid. Edwards failed to put me off the final product with his school lab explanation, "You get ethyl alcohol, methanol, quite poisonous but small quantities of propynol, butynol, isobutanol, and a host of other alcohols as well as aldehydes, esters, ketones, organic acids, and so on."

However, as Warner Allen, the poet laureate of rum, says, "The distiller . . . does not aim at scientific perfection. He does not want to produce alcohol in its absolute form, but a palatable and wholesome spirit."[223] So to produce brandy, whiskey, or rum with recognizable flavors, you want inefficient distillation that will bring over other organic chemicals to give it a distinct flavor. Enumerating the different factors that make a rum "palatable and wholesome," Edwards explains:

> It's first of all the wash, then the shape of the still, then how long and how you age it. Age is simply the length of time the rum has stood in the barrel, while

the maturity is a quality it has achieved in that time. Sometimes you can get a ten-year-old that has only really matured to a seven-year-old level, and of course it works the other way round, as well.

Edwards uses the special nosing vocabulary for rum, "People taste things like chocolate, banana, prunes, apricots, and so on in the rum, and some people ask if we add those fruits But it's just that some of the compounds produced are the same."

At Mount Gay and other places, the first rum comes over at 86 percent alcohol—172 percent proof on the pot still, and at 96 percent/192 proof from the Coffey still. Mount Gay dilutes its spirit to 73 percent alcohol, and the Coffey production and pot still production are aged in separate barrels to be blended later. Mount Gay's Eclipse brand is a blend of one- to five-year-old rum, and Extra Old mingles rums of between five and twenty-one years old and some up to twenty-five years and older.

Many rum producers add caramel to ensure that the color is consistent, which they measure by both eye and a photometer. "We don't want people to see a difference in color on the shelves," explains Edwards. To some purists such additives looks like adulteration, but, as one rum devotee countered, "Caramel flavors the Rum and its addition to the spirit has the virtue that nothing extraneous is added. Rum is made from sugar, and the addition of burnt sugar is in no way against nature."[224]

Some Jamaican producers actually try very hard to add some very strong smelling flavors and aromas, but there is a special purpose. They induce fermentation by adding *dunder*, the produce of previous fermentations with the yeast. The wash is then allowed to ferment for ten to twelve days, which encourages other organisms to flourish that produce acetic, butyric, and propionic acids and other substances. "A sniff of the flavoured Rum is a startling experience, for it is paralyzingly powerful,"[225] comments one observer of this special formulation, which is made to give essence of rum to neutral spirits.

The rougher edges of this biochemical brew are taken off in the casks. Edwards explains the science:

> Maturity is achieved during time of aging, and it has two factors, firstly, the extraction of materials from the wood: the tannins, vanillin, phenols, color, and other organic compounds. Then there is the chemical oxidation of many of those organic compounds produced during yeast fermentation, to compounds that give you more aromacity and more of the sweet aroma you'd expect from a well-matured rum, and these are mostly esters, sweet aromatic compounds which lend to the fruitiness and in some cases the spiciness of the rums.

Edwards justifies blending rums, since it produces better drinks:

> The longer you leave it in the barrel, the more the flavor of the wood you will get. We have no outer limits. But I do find if we have a rum that has been in a barrel for fifteen to twenty years without disturbance, it seems not to be able to mature much beyond

that, and if it does change, it tends to become very tannic, very bitter, very dark, heavy, woody, just like liquid oak. That's why we prefer to blend different ages to get the qualities you want. We will combine those rums to give a balance of aroma, of flavor, so we are able to get a consistent aroma and flavor and even a consistent feel in the mouth, smooth or aggressive.

Modern rum producers do not use new barrels. They are reassembled from the staves of casks that have already been used to mature bourbon. The coopers of America had enough clout a century ago to have legislation passed that bourbon has to use new, white, oak casks, and across the Caribbean and even in Scotland they are much in demand. The bourbon has already leached out the harshest oak elements from the wood, and the casks are usually flamed inside to give a layer of charcoal which, Edwards, scientific as ever, claims provides a "greater air-to-liquid surface content" to help the process of oxidation. For heavier, darker rum, you use the appropriate casks.

18. RUM, BUGGERY, AND THE LASH: THE NAVY AND RUM

I n 1931, H. Warner Allen, every bit as patriotic and with just as much or as little evidence as Taussig had for annexing the spirit for the United States, wrote:

> Rum is the Englishman's spirit, the true spirit of adventure. Whiskey belongs to Scotland and Ireland, Brandy to France, Gin to Holland, but Rum is essentially English, despite its tropical origin. The very word calls up heroic memories of the iron seamen who on the lawful and unlawful occasions built up the British Empire overseas, and if ever Rum were to disappear from navy rations, a great tradition would be tragically broken.[226]

There are plenty of myths about rum to go round, even if, like so many myths, there is a germ of truth in them. The intimate relationship of the navy and rum needs no invention but, like any old sailor's yarn, has had some artistic embellishment. One of the most pervasive tropes is "Nelson's blood." But the naval hero, contrary to legend, probably swam to his eternal home in a cask of Spanish brandy.

When he was based in the Caribbean, Nelson had reputedly asked that if he died, his body should be sent home in a barrel of rum. This was not necessarily an old sea dog's sentimental bow to the substance of the holy spirit issued daily but was probably more in deference to the pre-refrigeration practices of the undertaker's trade, where rum was indeed the only contemporary equivalent of embalmer's fluid. Various folklore versions have it that after Nelson's death at Trafalgar, his body was indeed shipped home in a cask of rum. The patriotic version has the mourning tars donating the stuff, and the more pragmatic naval version has it that the rum was actually siphoned out the cask and drunk by the same tars on the way home—who obviously meant no disrespect by it and were, in several senses, drinking his health. Clearly, rum would have killed any bacteria, even if the sailors were not to know this before Louis Pasteur made the connection.

It is true that Nelson's body was taken to Gibraltar, but contemporary accounts introduce an element of ambiguity. They say that the Spanish liquor, *aguardiente,* was actually used to take him home from there to Portsmouth, although the jury is out on whether he went from Trafalgar to Gibraltar in rum. And there is an additional layer of ambiguity—while *aguardiente* in Spain was brandy, in the Spanish Main, that was what they called their local rum production, and some of the Spanish fleet had just returned from the Caribbean, where they had accompanied Admiral Villeneuve's feint to get Nelson away from the English Channel.

The folklore has lots of parallels. Bodies were often shipped in rum, as the cheapest preservative around. And it was also a preservative that sailors liked. So, for example, Martiniquan planter Moïse Gradis willed that his body be transported home to Bordeaux in a cask ringed with iron and filled with strong rum. When his corpse arrived in a bad state, some sailors were accused of tapping the contents.[227] And as we have seen, New England undertakers kept the spirit at hand for helping the occasional homesick cadaver home, in addition to its more customary use in easing the shock of bereavement for the mourners.

Whatever its uses as embalming fluid, there is no doubt that rum was indeed a weapon of war. Napoleon may have thought that an army marched on its stomach; in the eighteenth century, the British and Americans knew that the army marched and the navy sailed on their livers as well. At the Battle of Waterloo in 1815, which finally finished off Napoleon's dreams, not only were the victorious troops issued rum to help them warm up for the battle, but when they captured the imperial coach, it was carrying a bottle of rum for the emperor—presumably, rum was already accepted by the French as a specific against cold mornings and the *grippe*.

Nelson's fate notwithstanding, up to the twentieth century the British relied on regular supplies of rum to keep their forces on land and sea fighting and fit. Rum was so essential that the regulations went far beyond the modern

Geneva Conventions, and during the wars with the French in the Caribbean, even prisoners of war were allowed a quarter-pint of rum a day, or "three pints of Small Punch made of good old Rum and good Moscovado sugar,"[228] which is a lot better treatment than modern POW camps in the Caribbean, such as Guantánamo Bay, manage.

If prisoners were getting a quarter of a pint, warriors needed much, much more. As we have seen, the American Revolutionary war was fought with hogsheads of rum on both sides, with particular attention to destroying—or drinking—the enemy's supplies, as when the British sixty-fourth Regiment of Foot destroyed no less than four hundred hogsheads of rum in Washington's stores on the Hudson. It must have taken superhuman discipline on their part, since, as we have seen, it was regarded as tantamount to sacrilege not to drink the stuff.

Strangely enough, despite the Treasure Island connotations of "Yo ho ho and a bottle of rum," the buccaneers, whose freebooting exploits were the foundation of the *Pirates of the Caribbean* mythology, did not pick up their flagons of rum until later. There is no mention of rum in any guise in Esquemeling's *Buccaneers of America,* 1678, nor the *Journal of Basil Ringrose,* 1686. Pirates went for Cognac and the finer things of life.[229] But that was early days, when the rum was rough and made sensitive drinkers green at the gills. Soon it was reported that the buccaneers chased wild cattle and smoked the meat, trading the food for slaves or rum. Sometimes, says Huetz de Lemp, they also traded rum for cattle with the Spanish colonies: "From buyers, they had become sellers of rum, while all the time remaining big consumers."

As soon as the quality improved, so did consumption. In 1720, the pirate John Rackham and his crew became so drunk on a shipload of rum that they had just captured that they weren't able to fight off the Royal Navy when it came for them. They were hanged for it, which is oblique but convincing testimony of the value they set by it.[230] Henry Morgan, the buccaneer who became a royal governor of Jamaica, was familiar enough with rum to die from drinking it. And by his time we had the beginnings of the quintessential military application of rum—the Royal Navy's grog ration, which, by sympathetic magic, was pretty much coterminous with Britannia's rule over the waves.

"Rum, buggery and the lash," as Winston Churchill said dismissively of the Royal Navy as he drank French Cognac with his Cuban cigars, but then he was an former army officer whose main involvement with the navy was as First Lord of the Admiralty, when he ordered British ships up the Dardanelles into the disastrous Gallipoli expedition.

Admiral Penn started the distribution of rum to the sailors in 1655, when he took Jamaica from the Spanish. It is worth noting that this happened during what Royalist revisionism has often implied was a joyless Puritan time. History is always seen through a prism of present prejudice. We ascribe modern nationalist sentiments to ancient feudal squabbles, and just as the role of rum and drink in both causing and effecting the American Revolution has been filtered out in a century of temperance agitation and the experiment of Prohibition, Cromwell's military victories and the reality of his era are obscured by the blinkers of a Royalist restoration and three centuries of professed monarchism.

With irony similar to that of the rum-based origins of
the American Revolution, which ended in the new government taxing alcohol, the English Revolution started
out with a parliamentary revolt against "ship money," taxes
to build the Royal Navy, and ended with the forerunner
of the professional and successful British Navy that was to
rule the seas for several centuries—and with the grog
ration. Since it was his fleets that defeated the Spanish and
conquered Jamaica in 1655, that makes the dour Oliver
Cromwell the great-godfather of grog, Bob Marley, big
spliffs, and the Jamaican bobsled team.

The Grog ration was based on the perennially dubious
qualities of water. While W. C. Fields may have avoided it
because of fish reproducing in it, seafarers found that all
sorts of what we now know as microbes fecundated in the
water tubs. The problems that landlubbers had with water
were compounded greatly at sea. Dubiously sweet at the
beginning of a voyage, it often presented a choice between
dehydration or dysentery after festering in the wooden
casks for a while. The Royal Navy's answer was the same
as that of the landlubbers—beer—and in 1590, the ration
was fixed at a gallon a day, distributed at meal times. The
alcohol and fermentation drove out the other bacteria and
parasites that could cause harm. However, until the invention of bottled India Pale for just such contingencies, a few
weeks at sea was also enough to see the beer too sour to
drink, and even in Elizabethan times, admirals noted that
sour beer led to sour attitudes from the crews.

So British ships in foreign parts were allowed to follow
local habits, which meant wine in the Mediterranean. On
the Atlantic route, the Canaries and the Azores provided

fortified wines, which, while they lasted the voyage, were expensive. The arrival of spirits solved the problem of preservation of the drink and of protecting the crew from dysentery from the foul water. After the beer had been drunk or had soured, the wine was tapped, and when the wine was gone, the spirits would be broached.

Brandy was the usual solution until Samuel Pepys took up Penn's previous experiment when, in 1688, as secretary of the navy, he dictated:

> Approval given to Mr. Waterhouse to supply King James' ships at Jamaica with Rumm instead of Brandy, he takeing care that the good or ill effects of this proof, with respect as well to the good husbandry thereof be carefully inquired into by you and reported to us within a year or two (or sooner if you find it necessary for our further satisfaction in the same).[231]

Pepys wrote his diaries in code, so neither his philandering ("and so to bed") nor his rum exploits received the contemporary praise they deserved.

The father of the grog ration is traditionally regarded as Admiral Edward Vernon, who became immensely popular with the fleet and the people back home after taking the massive Spanish fortress of Porto Bello with only six ships in the War of Jenkins' Ear, which had been whipped up by Jamaican merchants and the sugar lobby over Spanish attempts to restrain English smugglers. Jenkins' ear was as dubiously sourced a *casus belli* as Saddam Hussein's weapons of mass destruction, but any excuse will do when war fever grips, as we know to our cost through history.

With the grog ration, Vernon was building on what was already a long tradition. In addition to Pepys, Captain James Pack the historian of naval rum unearthed letters from a Captain Gascoigne in Jamaica who suggested to the Navy Board that the way to incentivize the workers toiling languidly on his ship in the tropical heat was to double the rum ration to a pint a day. In 1731, navy regulations stipulated that in the absence of the gallon-of-beer-a-day rations, a pint of wine or half a pint of "brandy, rum, or arrack" would suffice. But soon, regulations notwithstanding, only one drink would do. The navy agreed with the later sentiment of André Simon, the French wine critic who claimed, with more enthusiasm than accuracy, as is so often the case with rum aficionados:

> Rum is more satisfying, more comforting and possesses a greater food value than any other spirit; this is due to the fact that is usually distilled at a lower strength than most spirits, so that it contains less proof spirits per volume, but more "impurities" or by-products of the alcoholic mash from which it is distilled. It is to these by-products that Rum owes its distinctive characteristics, and as they are all primarily derived from sugar-cane juice, they are wholesome and nourishing. This is the reason why Rum is so excellent at sea and why it has long been and still is the staple spirit of the Royal Navy.[232]

Up to a point, M. Simon. Far from celebrating the pure spirit, in 1740, while commander of the West Indies stations,

Vice Admiral Vernon decreed the dilution of the pure spirit to produce "grog." Until then the sailors were issued half a pint of rum every day at noon in lieu of the quart of wine or gallon of beer that was their ration. Unsurprisingly, ships did not function well in the immediate aftermath of its distribution. As Vernon's officers reported back afterward, "the pernicious custom of the seamen drinking their allowance of rum in drams, and often at once, is attended with many fatal effects." It impaired their health, ruined their morals, and "made them slaves to every brutish passion."[233] The solution was grog. Vernon ordered the daily half a pint of rum diluted with a quart of water:

> To be mixed in a scuttled butt for that purpose and to be done upon the deck, and in the presence of the Lieutenant of the Watch who is to take particular care to see that the men are not defrauded in having their full allowance of rum . . . and let those that are good husbandmen receive extra lime juice and sugar that it be made more palatable to them.[234]

The allowance was split between two servings, one between ten and noon in the morning and one between four and six in the afternoon. Although the men may have looked at it as dilution of the rum, from another point of view, it was an enhancement of the water, since it had the incidental side effect of killing the bacteria in the water and making it much more palatable. The ritual, which also averted the common cheating of the seamen of their rations, became the center of shipboard life, the high point of the sailor's workday for crews for two centuries. It was not only the origin of the term scuttlebutt to describe the gossip that went on as the crew lined up for their rations, it was "perhaps the greatest improvement to discipline and efficiency ever produced by one stroke of the pen," comments the *Dictionary of National Biography* in its entry on Vernon.

The most common etymology for grog is from Vernon's nickname, "Old Grog," which owed its origins to his "grogram" cloak—a distinctive waterproofed garment of gummed wool and silk. And while the war itself was embarrassedly consigned to the memory holes, August 21, the date of the order for grog, was enshrined in British naval history.

Dr. Thomas Trotter, a deservedly overlooked poet in most respects, testifies to the etymology of grog in a poem "Written on board the *Berwick,* a few days before Admiral Parker's engagement with the Dutch fleet, on the 5th of August, 1781," that also maintains the noticeable historical connection between rum, poor rhymes, and mediocre verse:

>'Tis sung on proud Olympus' hill
>The Muses bear record,
>Ere half the gods had drank their fill
>The sacred nectar sour'd.
>At Neptune's toast the bumper stood,
>Britannia crown'd the cup;
>A thousand Nereids from the flood
>Attend to serve it up.
>"This nauseous juice," the monarch cries,
>"Thou darling child of fame,
>Tho' it each earthly clime denies,

> *Shall never bathe thy name.*
> *Ye azure tribes that rule the sea,*
> *And rise at my command,*
> *Bid Vernon mix a draught for me*
> *To toast his native land."*
> *Swift o'er the waves the Nereids flew,*
> *Where Vernon's flag appear'd;*
> *Around the shores they sung "True Blue,"*
> *And Britain's hero cheer'd.*
> *A mighty bowl on deck he drew,*
> *And filled it to the brink;*
> *Such drank the Burford's gallant crew,*
> *And such the gods shall drink.*
> *The sacred robe which Vernon wore*
> *Was drenched within the same;*
> *And hence his virtues guard our shore,*
> *And Grog derives its name.*[235]

By the Seven Years War, the Admiralty had incorporated Vernon's instructions into naval regulations, and Vice Admiral Vernon's recipe won the navy enough of the ensuing battles to justify the suggestion of the sea god's favor. But instead of prescribing the amount of water to be added, the regulations referred to "the usual proportion." Evidence suggests that this was a three-to-one mix, but some captains made it four to one, and Admiral Lord Keith made it five to one—and certainly would have won no naval popularity contest as a result.

Peacetime brought its own problems of discipline and efficiency. In his efforts to cut back the ration, Keith constantly referred to it in his letters to the Admiralty as

"a delicate point to interfere." No one wanted to provoke a mutiny on board the ships or, perhaps equally del-
icately, provoke legislation from the sugar lobby in
Parliament which doubtless appreciated the naval pur-
chases of rum. In fact, rum was not that delicate in its
effects. It was not just the fairly hefty daily dose of
alcohol in itself but all the opportunities for trading,
gaming, and hoarding the rum that led to serious medical and disciplinary problems.

After the Napoleonic wars, with the threat of mutiny
presumably muted, Sir John Phillimore, on his ship *HMS
Thetis,* won the consent of his crew for an experiment that
halved the half-pint ration to one gill while paying the men
the difference in cash. The experiment was judged a success, winning accolades from Lloyds of London, the
Gibraltar Merchants association, and the Admiralty itself,
which in July 1824 made it a navy-wide rule. Cheapskate as
it was, the Admiralty at first paid seamen at wholesale prices
for the forgone ration—or offered tea instead. The *Thetis*
and its crew were reviled by the rest of the navy for their
treachery and were known scornfully as the *Tea Chest.* An
old ballad offered the tar's philosophy:

> *While sailing once our captain,*
> *who was a jolly dog,*
> *One day served out to every mess*
> *a Double dose of Grog*
> *Ben Backstay, he got tipsy,*
> *all to his heart's content*
> *And being half seas over,*
> *why overboard he went.*

As a result the unfortunate Backstay lost his head in more ways than one, donating it to a hungry shark, and his headless ghost returned to share his conclusions with his former shipmates:

By drinking Grog I lost my life,
so lest my fate you meet,
Why, never mix your liquor, lads,
but always drink it neat.[236]

As part of its concern for the "delicacy" of the situation, the Admiralty tempered the blow by abolishing the "Banyan" days—when the sailors had to do without meat. It was a judicious balancing of entitlements to soften the blow. On the other hand, it also reduced the grog ration to one a day at around noon. The Admiralty, with an eye to costs, also ordered restrictions on "splicing the main brace," except for superhuman efforts—or with surgeon's orders! Splicing the mainbrace was the signal given for an extra issue of Grog, saved for victories, royal births, and royal weddings.

Ironically, parliament undid some of that good work by introducing the modern imperial pint, in 1826 which transatlantic drinkers will know is 20 percent bigger than the older American measure. They thus increased the grog ration, which led to the reintroduction of the twice daily ration again. Notoriously slow to react, in 1850 the Admiralty abolished the evening issue and thus halved the daily ration.[237]

Despite variations in the rations, the practices and customs of the grog issue became time-honored traditions that persisted even as the oak hulls became iron and then steel, and as the sails gave way to steam—indeed right up to the era when they added nuclear reactors to some of Her Majesty's ships.

Almost as perilous as shipping out with a shipful of fizzing uranium, carrying rum in wooden casks was a little like carrying gasoline in plastic buckets. This stuff was at proof, ready to burn, and could set a wooden ship aflame. So the Admiralty prescribed minutely the safety features to keep the spirit room safe. They were in fact modeled on the powder hold, with no naked lights allowed and as hermetically sealed containment as possible around it. If the rich aroma of the sealed room reported by sailors engaged in "Up Spirits," the order to decant the grog ration from the main casks in the secure spirit locker, was any gauge, the alcohol vapor in the room was indeed quite concentrated. The regulations prescribed "Centinels" whose job it was to keep candles and naked lights out—but there was an added danger to guard against. Few tars would see much gain in breaking into the powder room—but whole generations of them would and did exert their ingenuity to get access to the spirit locker.

Blood alcohol levels that would easily disqualify a modern driver were not really compatible with running along high yardarms in strong seas or dealing with the other complex issues of running a ship. Disciplinary problems abounded as sailors went to extraordinary lengths to obtain and drink the rum whenever they could find it, and since human resources management at the time all too often consisted of a flogging rather than a counseling session, the rum was a constant source of friction.

Transfusing Nelson's Blood

The navy was a huge enterprise, on shore as well as at sea. It made its own gunpowder, industrialized and mechanized the process for making ship's biscuit, salted pork and beef, and brewed its own beer. It did not distill its own rum but did buy the produce of the Caribbean and blend it to its own exacting standards.

The Victualling Department blended the navy rum at Deptford on the Thames, in the "Old Weevil." Conscious of status, perhaps, in 1858 they renamed it the Royal Victoria Yard, and it was not closed until 1961. By then, the blending was done by a private company in London, E. D. & F. Man, Ltd., for many years the navy's official rum broker. It was a solid foundation for a business that first got the contract in 1780 and still had it 190 years later. One former employee described the bidding process to me as somewhat truncated: the Admiralty would phone the broker once a year to say how much rum it would need.

The broker was in charge of blending to a formula that is still confidential but is reliably reported as being mostly Demerara rum from British Guiana, as it was then, with a substantial admixture of Trinidad rum and additions from other producers. Undoubtedly one of most sought after jobs in the Admiralty was to be on the frequent tasting panels to check that the formulation consistently met the exacting standards. Until 1961, when South Africa broke from the Commonwealth, one of the constituents was Natal rum, which may have served after maturing for five years in Deptford but did not get much approval when served "fresh" during the Second World War because Germany's

U-boats threatened the navy's jugular by sinking freighters full of rum. One navy ship in Colombo, in what is now Sri Lanka, returned a consignment of twenty-five gallons with the message, "Rum returned as it is the only drink ever received which made us wish we were teetotalers."[238]

Navy rum was 96 percent to 97 percent proof, so it was not surprising that over the years it was cut with more and more water. That may seem a formidable dose for both brain and liver, but like recent pronouncements on the beneficial effects of red wine, most doctors considered it all in a good medicinal cause, since it was thought that rum prevented scurvy—which it did when lemon juice was added. After all, it was the quinine in tonic water that kept down malaria—not the gin that British colonial officers took to make the medicine go down.

Despite the disciplinary problems, the whole ritual and vocabulary that grew up around the order to "Up Spirits" led to bonding of crews in the enclosed environment of the ship. The dispenser of the grog became Jack Dusty, transmuted from that eponym's previous task as the purser's assistant in the bread room, and his assistant became Tanky, after the former worthy who looked after the iron water tanks that replaced the old wooden casks at the beginning of the nineteenth century. A whole vocabulary grew to describe the various forms of trading that the tars did with their rations. "Sippers," "Gulpers," and so on became onboard currency to describe how much was due to each of the crew, whether for favors or for card losses, allowing various degrees of quaffing.

Once the grog was mixed with water, by common consent it became "flat" after three quarters of an hour or so because the alcohol mixed too well with the water, so it could not be left to stand. Once it had been mixed in the breaker, the *barricoe,* as the scuttlebutt had evolved into, and all rations had been served, the surplus was supposed to be tossed over the side, which was a challenge to the ingenuity of all concerned, whose ecological senses were outraged by the failure to recycle. It was a challenge repeatedly risen to. Petty officers and above did not have to dilute their rum—they could and did drink it straight, and in Nelsonian-era wardrooms, drinking healths was an important ritual. The navy was the only service allowed to drink the Loyal Toast without standing up, allegedly because otherwise they were prone to banging their heads on the ceiling.

As the war clouds loomed over Europe in 1938, the Admiralty held yet another meeting on rum rations. It reached the surprisingly enlightened conclusion that the three-to-one dilution did not do the rum justice and recommended a mix of two parts water to one part rum, which kept the flavor longer. Out of sight and out of mind, British submariners apparently took their own decision and invented a tradition of the one-to-one mixture, presumably safe from surprise inspections down in their octopus's gardens in the shade.

In 1970, the British Admiralty maintained that "in a highly sophisticated navy, no risk for margin or error which might be attributable to rum could be allowed." This may have been a coded reference to the nuclear depth charges and missiles then being carried in its vessels, but the Admiralty was too polite to say so. It even conducted a test of the newfangled Breathalyzer after the grog ration, and found, amazingly enough, that men who were considered fit to operate a nuclear submarine would have lost their driving licenses if they drove home from the dockyard immediately afterward. In a sentimental yet heated debate of the kind that the British do so well, if a trifle indiscriminately, the government stopped the grog ration. With all-volunteer armed forces, rising prosperity, and the sixties still swinging on shore, the Admiralty dealt with the abolition with genuine delicacy— certainly not as "Turkish," in Governor Dongan's old phrase, as the way the American prohibitionists had dealt with the U.S. Navy. The Royal Navy allowed the tars two cans of beer a day, and put £2.7 million into a fund for recreational facilities for sailors.

So it was with sentimental regret, but no mutinies, that the three-centuries-old tradition was killed. And fittingly, the burial was at sea, celebrated on bases and ships across the globe. The *HMS Fife* was the last British ship to serve the daily grog, on July 31, 1970, on the International Date Line in Pearl Harbor, where the final scuttled butt was brought out to the tune of the pipes and was then buried at sea with a twenty-one-gun salute in front of disbelieving American reporters. The Canadian Navy followed suit two years later, but the New Zealanders, always considered more British than the British, carried on piping "Up Spirits" until 1990. Despite the New Zealand example, the drive for temperance in the antipodes and indeed in the empire had been pioneered by one of the most unlikely forces for temperance—the Aussies. When the Royal Australian Navy was separated from Britain's in 1911, it defied its own large domestic rum production and never introduced a rum ration, although few Aussie sailors ever turned down the British rations if they were serving in a Royal Navy vessel.

The ghosts of the grog tradition are still maintained. The Royal Navy was more successful than the U.S. Navy in fending off Puritan boarders, and even now, if a British captain deems it medically necessary, a half-gill daily ration can be served, in addition to giving the order to splice the mainbrace to reward extraordinary effort.

The Czarist Russian Navy, deciding that rum was an essential part of being a real navy, imported rum for the fleet, but despite the legends, there was more to naval supremacy than grog rations, as the debacle of the Russian's crushing defeat in 1905 by the Japanese showed. The Indian Navy, which did not change its ensigns from the Saint George's cross until the turn of the millennium, still serves rum in its canteens, despite an official prohibitionist stance which at one point banned all liquor for civilians who could not produce a doctor's certificate of alcoholism. I discovered this when I shared a sleeping compartment on the Indian railways in 1985 with two Indian navy engineers and two bottles of rum. We had emptied the bottles by the time they had to be emptied off the train at their station. Even now, India's Old Monk Seven Year Old is not a rum to scorn.

Just as rum preserved the dead, naval rum had shades of Haiti: like a zombie, it came back from the tomb. Charles Tobias, an enterprising American based on the island of Tortola, negotiated with the Admiralty to market its rum blend as Pusser's and donate a sizable draught of the proceeds to naval charities, not least the recreational fund the

Admiralty had started in consolation for abolishing the rum ration on Black Tot Day in 1970. Working with the venerable E. D. & F. Man, Tobias revived the ancient formula for sale to the nostalgic, the thirsty, and the tasteful and launched the new product in 1980, ten years after the obsequies on Royal Navy ships everywhere.

The Dry Navy

In the United States Navy, it was a shorter voyage to dryness. In 1806, reasons of both economy and protectionism for home industries caused Congress to commute the rum ration to whiskey, which was apparently not entirely to the satisfaction of the fleet, although "Any Tot in a Storm" could have been its motto. The Navy Department claimed it had been "persuaded that it (whiskey) is a more wholesome drink." It was also locally produced and cheaper than rum.

The U.S. Navy insisted that the ration had to be drunk on the spot to avoid hoarding and binge drinking, while in the Royal Navy the grog was often drawn for each mess and taken with food, which probably covered for the deficiencies of the cuisine and may have helped the drinkers stand more firmly afterward. A prohibitionist, Assistant Navy Secretary Gustavus Fox, seized upon the temporary absence of the distinctly nontemperance Southern legislators in 1862 to abolish the grog ration in the navy. He found a compliant senator to move the abolition of the ration, and it was done. It would probably have been as difficult to pass abolition of slavery as it would Prohibition, even on this limited scale, if the U.S. Congress had not been split by the Civil War.

It may have been the disappearance of Southern ratings and officers that led to the report from Admiral Oscar Farenholt that more than half of the crew of the *USS Wabash* were taking cash instead of grog just before the abolition of the ration, or it could be that the spirit of temperance was really winning popular ground. Certainly, the vast majority of the Americans' British colleagues took the rum rather than the money right up to 1970. Although the actual ration went, the U.S. Navy itself did not go completely dry until 1914 when, with the sententiousness common to the temperance movement over the decades, Secretary of the Navy Josephus Daniels issued General Order 99, "convinced after a year's reflection that the cause of both temperance and democracy demanded it."[239] As befits a teetotaler, he totally banned all drink from bases and land facilities as well as onboard. He substituted grape juice, which was no substitute and has led many U.S. sailors to regard their sister navies mournfully during joint operations.

Richard Dana, author of *Two Years before the Mast,* speaks to the strong sense of entitlement that sailors had, both American and British, not least in the face of attempts to cut back and abolish the ration, some of which were soundly based on the incompatibility of complex machinery and a high blood level, others on religious fervor or prohibitionism. As temperance pressure built up in the United States, Dana had written that sailors "will never be convinced that rum is a dangerous thing, by taking it away from them and giving it to their officers; nor that temperance is their friend, which takes from them what they have always had, and gives them nothing in place of it."[240]

It is an interesting comment on social relations that

while the British Lords of the Admiralty in their deliberations were constantly aware of the friction that would be
caused by stopping ratings' drinks while allowing officers to
carry on imbibing, the prohibitionists of the United States
had no such sense of *noblesse oblige:* in 1900 Navy Secretary
John D. Long introduced prohibition for the ratings alone,
who nevertheless had to lug the booze supplies onboard for
the officers and then serve it in the wardrooms. The Royal
navy may have looked a tyrannical organization, but there
was a feudal element to the hierarchy, with the parties at
various levels having a strong sense of both duties and entitlement, customary and regulatory. It was clear that rum
was considered an essential part of a sailor's entitlement, yet
the temperance movement was not a tolerant one. It was
admonitory and based on a sense of the elite knowing what
was best for the lower orders. That may well have occasioned Daniel's invocation of democracy in General Order
Ninety-Nine, abolishing booze for everybody, but it was a
sour and leveling form of democracy—as much Bolshevik
as "Turkish!"

In contrast, when in 1850, the Royal Navy reduced the
ration to half of a gill per day, the Admiralty was careful to
cut it across the board for officers as well as ratings and in
the orders that preceded the reduction with a tactfully
effective announcement of increases in rations.

Jingo—By Rum

It is not only alcohol that induces amnesia—ultrapatriotism
does also. Contrasting with the more prevalent image of

demon rum in the United States, in Britain, Jolly Jack Tar
could do no wrong, and the iconography of the staunch
sailor defender carried with it favorable connotations for
rum. The freezing climate of the war in the Crimea, when
France and Britain attacked Russia, was countered by rum
rations for the troops on the ground and over-the-top
patriotism at home, which, in one of the archetypal jingoistic refrains, in true Orwellian fashion overlooked just
whom Nelson had been fighting:

> *Now the grog boys, the grog boys, bring hither*
> *And fill, fill up to the brim*
> *May the mem'ry of Nelson ne'er wither*
> *Nor the star of his glory grow dim*
> *May the French from the English ne'er sever*
> *But both to their colours prove true*
> *This Russian bear they must thrash now or never*
> *So three cheers for the Red White and Blue.*

Nelson would have been spinning in his grave—if he were
not already so dizzy with the spirits used to preserve him.

It was not only the navies of the world that relied on
rum to top up their belligerence; while the U.S. Army
reintroduced spirit supplies during the Civil War, it was,
of course, whiskey that got them fighting, although there
were temperance regiments such as those raised by the
governor of Maine. Lincoln was urbane on the issue, and
when there were complaints about General Ulysses
Grant's drinking, he suggested that he should ask "the
Quartermaster of the Army to lay in a large stock of the
same kind of liquor, and would direct him to furnish a

supply to some of my other generals who have never yet won a victory."[241]

The British Army never had to content with the do-gooding influence of temperance-inclined politicians. It continued issuing rum, especially in combat conditions. The cynical saw this as "Dutch courage." Men who had high blood alcohol levels would do things that no rational person would do, like marching over barbed wire waving a bayonet at murderous machine guns. As Warner Allen put it: "In the Great War both by land and sea, the rum ration proved itself at many a chilly dawn a valorous comforter and played its inspiring part in deeds of heroism."[242] Another writer cele-brated British open-mindedness: "It was most pleasant, during the late war, to read the unvarying testimony of all qualified and unprejudiced authorities to the invaluable serv-ices of the rum ration, which in defiance of fanaticism, and in compliance with common sense, was issued to our men."[243]

The official reason for the rum ration during the First World War was as a specific against the cold and damp, which even now many people associate with colds and flu. It was not supplied in the same copious quantities; it was delivered to the front in one-imperial-gallon earthenware jars, which were supposed to go around sixty-four people, which is half a gill each. The jars, which are still available on eBay, carried the mark SRD, for "Services, Rum, Diluted," which the Tommies interpreted as "Seldom Reaches Destination." There is a lot of anecdotal evidence that the rum was deeply appreciated, even if some may have been suspicious of the motivation for this kindness.

The Australian forces used rum not only as a remedy for poison gas but also for shell shock, and stories tell of how doctors would literally order young, abstinent troopers to knock back a shot. One of them, a trooper Robert Melloy, recalled later in his life: "I was fortunate that Doctor Thompson came from Bundaberg, the Queensland town famed for the growth of sugarcane and the production of dark rum. He was able to prescribe what was actually folk medicine. It worked and I am grateful."[244] This quasi-official blessing reinforced the belief in rum as a folk medicine; the French decided that *le rhum* was a prophylactic against the flu and sequestrated the entire national supply when the Spanish flu epidemic swept the barracks of the world.

Yo Ho Ho and Cap'n Bligh

Captain Bligh seems just the right person to conjoin military and naval rum, not least since he effectively completed sugar's circumnavigation of the globe and faced off two famous mutinies, in each of which rum played a major role. Captain Bligh's voyages to the South Pacific were not just for breadfruit to help feed the slaves. Sugarcane originally came from Papua New Guinea and the South Pacific; the Caribbean sugarcanes had come across Asia, Europe, Africa, and the Atlantic from their Southeast Asian home. Bligh and others brought varieties of cane from Tahiti and the South Pacific to the Caribbean.

Bligh provided a transoceanic bridge for rum as well. When he and his loyalist crew were put in an open boat by mutineers, one of the more softhearted of the latter also provided them with a cask with a gallon and a half of rum.

To reward the mutinous crew who stayed on board the *Bounty,* their leader, Fletcher Christian also issued a dram of rum each to fortify them in the face of the risks they were taking. Hanging from the yardarm was not just an old sea dog's figure of speech for mutineers in the Royal Navy.

When Bligh was cast off, the rations were seriously scanty, but Bligh navigated the open boat across thousands of miles of ocean, dishing out the rum by the spoonful with morsels of bread to keep the crew fueled. Bligh had political enemies and was much maligned. Yet all objective accounts, based on the log book and actual evidence, suggest that he used flogging much less than almost any other commander and that his care for the crew was shown in their perfect health after a ten-month voyage—except for the surgeon, who, in another connection with our subject, drank himself to death.

But this is almost in the way of an overture to the history of rum in Australia. For Bligh not only had political enemies, he had incredibly bad luck. After several voyages between the Pacific and the Caribbean, he was successful in getting breadfruit to the Caribbean islands, but as it turned out, the West Indians didn't actually like this Pacific version of Wonder Bread and, unlike salt cod, did not incorporate it into the local cuisine. On his return to Britain, Bligh was cajoled into becoming the governor of New South Wales (Britains new Australian Colony). Because of the revolt of the North American colonies, in some considerable part because of rum and its ramifications, the British government had a serious problem: it had nowhere to send its convicts. Following Captain Cook's voyages, Australia beckoned as a place to dump Britain's unwanted citizenry.

But in the colony that now developed, the problem was rum itself. It had become a currency, the standard of value for almost everything, as tobacco was in prisons before marijuana began to supplant it as the penal gold standard. The cane they planted in Australia was brought by the First Fleet from South Africa, even though Papua New Guinea, the original home of sugar, was just to the north. Bligh was called upon to restore some semblance of discipline, since, to a large extent, the convicts, or actually ex-convicts, were running the prison camp.

The New South Wales Corps had been raised to police the colony and defend it against the French or anyone else who would be irrational enough to try to seize it. For the first ten year or so, the corps practically ran the colony as a private enterprise for itself. It was eloquent testimony to the main business of the corps that it was known as the Rum Corps. "A more improper set of men could not be collected together," was the later verdict of the man who led them in mutiny against Bligh.[245]

The shortage of actual money in the colony, which was so far from the nearest mints and off the main trading routes, produced a liquidity crisis in every sense. No one since Croesus has ever actually been tempted to eat gold, whereas there was a strong temptation to glug down your savings account when rum was the monetary standard. And since it was not very good rum, it was hardly a standard for international trading. The Rum Corps bought up land, ran convicts into debt, and ruined economic growth while doing rather well for itself. Corps members bought up all the official rum supplies at cost price and resold them for huge profits. Their possession of stills and control of imports gave them a license to distill money.

The situation had been developing for fifteen years when Bligh took up the challenge. Once again, contrary to his draconian image, Bligh took steps to enfranchise the ex-convicts and reduce the power of the Rum Corps. He forbade the importation of stills, and when one of the leading rum monopolists nonetheless imported two and took them out of bond on the pretense that medicines had been stored in them, Bligh's officials seized them. In a manner reminiscent of the stacked courts of colonial New England, John MacArthur, who had tried to bring in the stills, successfully sued the officer who took possession of them. Later, he became a renowned founding father of the Australian colonies.

Under the command of Lieutenant-Colonel George Johnston, the Rum Corps, with what must have been a weary sense of déjà vu all over again for Governor Bligh, marched on Sydney in 1808 and imprisoned Bligh after he had refused an offer of a share in the rum distillery from one of the conspirators. As speedily as communications could allow, London sent the Eighty-Seventh Regiment of Foot under a new governor, Lachlan Macquarie, who disbanded the Rum Corps and sent them back to Britain. Macquarie forgave D'Arcy Wentworth, one of the Rum Corps rebels, and "loaded him with honours and emoluments outside of his various professional offices, making him director of the bank of New South Wales, and granting him with two others a 'spirit monopoly' for building the general hospital [hence popularly known as the 'Rum Hospital']."[246] The three entrepreneurs won the right to import sixty thousand gallons of rum over three years, which they bought at three shillings a gallon and sold at forty.[247]

Adding a new dimension to the term surgical spirits, Wentworth went on to become the surgeon in the hospital, and his son became known as the father of the Australian constitution. Ironically, in view of rum's early use as a monetary standard, in the mid-nineteenth century, the Rum Hospital became the Mint. The imposing edifice was widely seen as an unnecessary extravagance and highly unlikely to have been built if Bligh had remained.

More innocently, it is also casually recorded that Richard Johnson, the first Anglican cleric to arrive in Australia, came with the First Fleet and celebrated the first church service under "a great tree" at Sydney Cove on February 3, 1788. In 1793, he built a modest church, which he paid for in rum. It did not last long, burning down in 1798.

In 1796, the first theater opened in Australia with a convict cast. Admission was, of course, paid for in rum. Its first performance showed the sardonic humor that the continent has since made its own. George Barrington, "pickpocket and author," wrote the prologue for the first play to be produced in the theater, which was the tragedy, now totally forgotten, by Edward Young, *The Revenge*. While the play has been deservedly forgotten, Barrington's wry humor has made it part of Australian lore:

> *From distant climes, o'er widespread seas, we come,*
> *Though not with much éclat or beat of drum;*
> *True patriots we, for be it understood,*
> *We left our country for our country's good.*
> *No private views disgraced our generous zeal,*
> *What urged our travels was our country's weal;*
> *And none will doubt, but that our emigration*
> *Has proved most useful to the British nation.*

With this rum-soaked history and despite Australia at one time having some of the most restricted pub opening hours this side of Prohibition, rum has always been a very popular part of Australian tradition, with Bundaberg and Beenleigh rum being almost national icons. In 1961, Bundaberg adopted the polar bear as its trademark, which—despite the dubious connection of a denizen of the frozen Arctic to the last hot bit of land before you hit Antarctica—is now one of the country's most recognized brands. It has also responded to demand for higher-end premium rums with specially aged Bundaberg Black.

The first official still in Australia was opened in 1868. But the *SS Walrus,* a riverboat that ran between the various sugar mills, ran an illegal still as part of its steam engine until, according to legend, having evaded the troopers for so many years, the boat foundered near the Beenleigh homestead. The still was moved ashore along with the boat's enterprising bosun, who knew how to operate it.

Strangely, although the Royal Australian Navy never adopted the grog ration, Bundaberg proudly records that rum production was deemed an essential war industry during the Second World War and all its production was committed to the military. Indeed, rum is still a big drink in Australia, and demand rose so quickly in the 1980s that Bundaberg had to ration supplies. Getting Antipodeans legless is yet another role of rum in world history. Who but an Aussie would *boast* of being a "rum pig?"

19. RUM AROUND THE WORLD

Having made it from the Caribbean to Australia via both the Cape and the Horn, we should perhaps fill in the gaps in the globe between them for rum's world tour.

Rum was developed, refined, and made popular in the British colonies, and in keeping with imperial preferences, in the British domestic market rum became popular rapidly, if not as quickly as in the New England colonies, where, without grain or grapes to spare, there were few alternatives, whether beer, wine, or gin to compete with it. In Britain there was more grain, but the rum from Jamaica and Barbados was good, much more flavorsome than the French colonial stuff that had upset Père Labat so much. From Britain, rum moved by osmosis across Europe and became popular in Germany and the Austro-Hungarian Empire.

The British Parliament introduced high duties on spirits from foreign countries. The duties originally favored the production of gin in England, where the arrival of William of Orange had brought in a taste for Dutch treats, and for whiskey in Scotland and Ireland. But rising population, consequent demand for grain for food, and the dire effects of cheap gin led to the increasingly popularity of rum—often, as in America, in the form of punch.

There was some domestic production of rum from the molasses left from sugar refining, but this rum was mostly used to fill in for grain shortages when other refineries were lacking. English rum could not compete with the West Indian product. In the first years of the eighteenth century, old Jamaica rum weighed in at 15 shillings a gallon, compared with 10 shillings for Holland gin but less than brandy at 20 shillings. Much of this price, which you will note was way above American levels, was a result of the excise duties, whose application was the rule in Britain rather than, as in the colonies, the exception.

Even so, rum took off slowly in Britain. It accounted for only 3 percent of spirits drunk in the first few decades of the eighteenth century, compared with British spirit production, which accounted for 80 percent of local drinking, mostly of gin, with scotch whisky at 5 percent and French brandy at 10 percent. By the last quarter of the century, that had changed. Rum accounted for 24.5 percent, while English spirits production had dropped to 44 percent, and scotch to a mere 1.7 percent. It is possible that the amounts of both rum and brandy were understated, since they were the subject of wholesale smuggling throughout the period. It was much easier to land a ship without the customs being aware of it than it was to build a distillery without the excisemen noticing. Officially, 2.25 million gallons of rum were imported into England annually between 1770 and 1775.

It is worth recording that the close connection between rum and bad verse that we have inadvertently testified to in these pages was not invariable. Despite the subsequent fond connection made at Burns suppers across the world between haggis, scotch, and Rabbie Burns, he was in fact an exciseman, whose job was to hunt down distillers and smugglers. Part of the income that kept his muse aflame and his liver afire was the proceeds of the sale of seized smuggled rum.

As possible inventors of the stuff in Barbados, the Irish held up their own by importing and drinking prodigious quantities of rum, possibly attracted by its reputed medicinal qualities against colds and chills. From 1770 to 1775, Ireland imported over 1.6 million gallons of rum a year. It seemed, according to one commentator, that local production of whiskey was "insufficient to staunch the inextinguishable thirst" of the Irish. But even though they drank a lot in their own right, some of it could also have been smuggled to England, which was a separate customs jurisdiction.

Rum was not only smuggled; it was stolen. The arrival of 240 West Indian ships between July and October 1790 imposed heavy delays of up to six to eight weeks in unloading. The costs included 75,000 gallons of rum looted from the ships by the denizens of London's docklands. It was at the request of the merchants that the special "West India Docks" were put in service by 1806 to keep the thirsty locals at a safer distance from the quayside. Increasingly a lot of that rum was reexported to Europe. However, another port played a role more like that of its transatlantic North American partners. Liverpool was by now the world's largest slaving port. It was also the entrepôt for European trade and helped popularize rum on the Continent, to the extent that "By the end of the century there was a veritable enthusiasm for rum in Germany and the Nordic lands."[248]

Once the British exports helped create the taste, local enterprise was not slow to fill the gaps. Flensburg, which then belonged to Denmark, became the rum capital of the north, based in part on the Danish Virgin Islands production after 1755. Since the Prussian annexation of the province in 1864, the originally Danish company Potts has been not only a German company but one of Germany's predominant rum producers. Flensburg itself hosts a rum museum in tribute to the thirty rum companies that operated there at the end of the twentieth century. Frederick II of Prussia, not known for reticence in his opinions, thought that rum was "horrible" and preferred schnapps made from potatoes, which first appeared by that name in 1770. His historical legacy and triumph is the *rumverschnitt,* which could be regarded as rum-flavored schnapps.

Some years ago, in a bar in Prague, deep in a medieval cellar, I was explaining my rum book project to a friend when I espied some rum behind the counter. I asked the bartender what he had, and he became excited as he rushed into the back of the bar. He wanted me to try his own special favorite, Tuzemsky Rum. "The best," he declared. As I traveled across the chilly plains of Bohemia and Moravia, I had not noticed any fields of waving sugarcane, so I asked, "What's it made from?" He looked at me as though I were a natural-born idiot. "Made from? Potatoes of course!" In a country that, as a former part of the Holy Roman Empire, has very strict rules about what can be called, or at least sold as, beer, rum had come too late for the Nuremberg laws on beer quality. The latest incarnation of the Holy Roman Empire, the European Union, has taken the issue in hand. Rum has to be made from sugarcane extracts.

In 2004, with the Czech Republic's accession to the European Union looming, the distillers of Tuzemsky Rum, even though they were selling 5 million liters a year of their "rum," announced that the product would in future be called simply Tuzemak, meaning "domestic." The Czech Republic did not have the clout of the Germans to get the rules bent—and the country that staunchly holds to the name Budweiser for its beer is not in a position to resist truth-in-advertising regulations, although the producers invoked the traditions of the Austro-Hungarian empire for their abuse of the term *rum*.

Still, rum has quite a pedigree there. Sales of Czech "rum" were 25 percent of the market, only 1 percent less than vodka in 2005 when the changeover was enforced. And as I remember, it was rum that fortified the Czech Good Soldier Svejk in Jaroslav Hasek's classic novel, in his roamings across the Eastern Front of the First World War as he tried to get out of the Imperial Army. So to placate those who wanted to see the name rum on the label, the company introduced a "Key Rum White," made from blended Caribbean rums, but they expect that for most Czechs, the potatoes will do nicely, thank you.

There's an Awful Lot of . . . Something . . . in Brazil

Ironically, the country that probably makes more rum than any other does not use the word. Almost alone among the major rum-producing nations, the Brazilians did not take the word from the English. Nonetheless, Brazilians take their rum very, very seriously. They run their cars on it. As a means of reducing oil imports, they use alcohol distilled from sugarcane to fill their tanks, and no less than 25 percent of their auto fuel comes from it. But then, their drinking rum, *cachaca,* is often so raw that the product may be better off in a metal carburetor than in a mere flesh-and-blood throat.

In some ways this is strange. Neighboring Venezuela makes some excellent rums, and there are tantalizing hints that while the Barbadians may have been the first to mention rum in writing, the Portuguese in Brazil may have been the first to distill sugar products. Certainly it has been suggested that the slaves in Brazil began by fermenting the froth from the sugar boilers, which is what was originally called cachaca, and it was fed to the oxen and donkeys on the sugar plantations before its other uses were discovered by the observant slave workers. The ferment they discovered also took the name cachaca, and when they began to distill rum proper, in the seventeenth century, they called it *aguardente,* similar to the Spanish.

Records from the middle of the seventeenth century show that plantations had a stillmaster, an *aguardentro,* on their books. But protectionist decrees in favor of Portuguese wine producers banned production for sale, so it was, officially at least, made for the slaves, specifically for medicinal use.[249] The bans were lifted when wine supplies fell short of the copious Brazilian thirsts, and by the eighteenth century, distilleries were flourishing and cachaca was flowing to the local throats. The Portuguese also vied with the Americans in bartering their rum for African slaves, for which they used the production from around Rio de Janeiro. Slavery remained legal in Brazil until 1888, after the American Civil War, and Portuguese and Brazilian slave traders continued to thwart the anti-slavery patrols of the Royal Navy for many years.

The market conditions in Brazil, like those of New England rum, did not lead to excellence in savor or aroma, but at least the Brazilians never adopted prohibition and so could keep up their skills and tastes for rum. Although it is mostly intended as the active ingredient of the Brazilian equivalent of a rum punch, a *caipirinha,* some makers of cachaca have been trying to add sophistication, distilling it in small batches in pot stills. Their marketing speaks of aging it in oak barrels for a whole eighteen months. However, that is still less than the minimum that many Caribbean countries insist on for their cheapest rums, so it remains to be seen whether they can really penetrate global markets with it.

French Mystique

Perhaps the French are the most jealous about claiming rum as their own. Modern French distillers invented *rhum agricole,* made with the full sugarcane juice, and persuaded themselves that this is the only real rum, dismissing the Anglo-Saxon stuff made from molasses as *rhum industriel.* It was very clever branding. "The distinction stays fundamental," declares one didactic French rum expert, keen to maintain French supremacy.[250] Of course it does. In one stroke of snobbery they have converted every other rum in the world to mere industrial alcohol.

In 1996 the rums from the French Caribbean territories came under the same system of *appellation contrôlée* as Champagne and Cognac because of European Union rules. These rums must be made from the full juice of sugarcane grown in their own locality and fermented and distilled there.

The French, of course, were for centuries the major rivals of the English in every way—commercially, militarily, politically. And the history of rum in France and its Caribbean territories has become another front for an action replay of Agincourt and Waterloo; this is a history to rival the story of rum in the Anglo-Saxon world.

When it came to rum, the French started off with many advantages, not least some of the most productive sugar plantations, but they consistently fell behind. If you read some of the histories of the distilleries in the French Caribbean you could easily confuse the desperate attempts by eighteenth-century French reformers to bring their rum quality to match the British islands' production with an actual invention of the stuff. Indeed they called British West Indian rum *rome anglois,* and preferred it to the French versions.[251] The modern rhummeries of the French Antilles evoke a spurious antiquity for their techniques and locations, such as invoking Père Labat as the "Father of Rum," thereby ignoring the anonymously sozzled anglophone Barbadian entrepreneurs who took the first, doubtless very faltering steps after they had launched their product on a waiting Caribbean.

In reality, the rum habit had spread quickly across the Caribbean—from Barbados. At one time Martinique was the French equivalent of Barbados, an island that the Spanish had not bothered to occupy and to which colonists came for agriculture rather than gold-mining. As with Barbados, sugar cultivation technology on Martinique improved with the arrival of Portuguese Jewish refugees expelled from Brazil along with the Dutch. Unlike Barbados, however, the island was still inhabited, and the Caribs were not defeated until 1658, after twenty-five years of resistance to the incoming French colonists. By 1690, the island had 207 mills, and in 1689 the royal ban on refining sugar in the island, once again in defense of domestic French distilleries, provoked a real crisis, since the planters had taken to producing the more refined "clayed" sugar, which was put in clay pots to let more of the molasses drain out.

In 1667, Père du Tertre, in his *Histoire General des Antilles,* describing his various visits to the islands, says the molasses left after the sugar had been crystallized was kept to make *eau de vie* for the slaves. When the father of French rum-making, Père Jean Labat, came to the Antilles at the beginning of the eighteenth century, he recorded: "The Savages and the Blacks call it 'tafia' . . . it is very strong and of a disagreeable odor and has a sharpness which is a little like grain spirits, which can scarcely be removed."[252] With commendable pastoral concern, Père Labat sermonized in 1722, "The Savages, the blacks, the ordinary people and the tradesmen do not search any farther for their intemperance than this unspeakable stuff: it is enough for them that it is strong, violent and cheap. It didn't matter to them that it was crude and disagreeable."[253] More tolerantly, Père Charlevoix declared that the "poor have yet a great resource for drinking in the spirit made from sugar cane, which has double advantage over France in that it is less dear and more healthy."

The French planters, however, seem to have considered drinking rum to be beneath them, although even low-quality rum could be disguised in a punch. But rum was considered essential to maintain slave productivity. While du Tertre pictured the slaves making tafia from "Anything that ran off the slope of the boilers,"[254] the plantations of Guadeloupe were in the habit of giving their slaves a glass of rum in the morning, in the evening, and every time they were soaked by the rain. But in 1685 an ordinance forbade the distribution of guildive to slaves in place of the subsistence that the planters should furnish them each month. In French Trinidad, the slaves got a quart of rum per week.

Labat was savvy enough to point out how lucrative the trade could be—and how much it was being neglected. In effect, he was trying to get the French planters to adopt the same commercial practices as the English had. For forty-five weeks' work a year, Labat noted, "this would produce 60 barrels of the spirit that they make, of which they could sell at least 54, consuming the rest in the household: then 54 barrels of 120 pots each could make more than 6,000 crowns which would be enough to pay for the clothes, food, tools and other necessities, for a gang of 120 negroes." However, the French government did not agree with Labat's commercial proposition. The colonists were forbidden to trade with foreigners by the Colonial Pact, which was the French equivalent of the British Navigation Acts. Perhaps most devastatingly, the French Royal Decree of 1713, which banned the importation of molasses and rum, was a setback for the development of quality control in the French Antilles that took a century to remedy.

So in contrast to the British planters, who could use the by-product of their sugar production as a revenue source almost as lucrative as the sugar itself, the French colonies generated tons of molasses that they had no conceivable legal use for. The Creole planters were on the verge of drowning in a proto-European Union treacle lake. The first thing to do with it was to make rum, but even the prodigious local thirsts could not cope with this sea of spirit, and since they could not sell it, there was little incentive to improve the production process. The most cunning effect of this most cunning of French plots was to flood the West Atlantic market with cheap molasses for which the French islands had no call, thus encouraging wholesale smuggling by the American colonists, their resistance to taxes, and their revolution against the British crown. The British molasses tariffs had already led to a robust disrespect for the law in the British American colonies, indeed, in Britain itself, and so smuggling French rum and molasses was scarcely a jot or tittle worse.

Earlier, some was exported to the Spanish territories and some to French Canada, which took 350,000 gallons of rum a year, provoking even more complaints from the

French brandy and wine producers. In 1759, the corporation of La Rochelle, one of France's major trading ports,
petitioned the government in protest—they complained
that a pint of rum sold for 7 or 8 sols a pint in Quebec,
while wine went at 15 or 16 sols a pint. "It deprived
France of the consumption of its brandy, it made commerce unprofitable and caused losses. This trade must be
forbidden or the Nation will harm itself. It gives to the
colonies their own trade, it enriches them at its own
expense and it sacrifices for them its own agriculture, the
work of the people."[255]

However, the Anglo-American traders were doing so
well in Africa and with the Indians that the merchants of
Bordeaux challenged the law in 1752 by importing forty-
six hogsheads of colonial rum into a bonded warehouse, and
eventually the government backed down—a little—and per-
mitted rum for reexport to Africa to enter France and also to
allow rum to go directly to the colonies. Since the slave
traders of all the European powers sent their worst rum to
Africa, the poor quality of the French Caribbean production did not inhibit them from sending 900,000 gallons to
France for reexport to Africa out of a production of 2.5
million gallons. And, as today, the locals themselves drank a
lot—1.3 million gallons.

Eventually Paris saw sense and lifted export duties on
rum and molasses. By 1776, in another revolutionary move,
the French government encouraged the construction of
guildiveries, exempting the slaves working in them from the
poll tax. However, even as French sugar production went
up, France was denied the benefits of liquid sunshine. It
was not until 1777 that imports of "sirops of tafia" were

authorized, if only for reexport. The sight of all those English enjoying themselves so much must have had an influence, perhaps along with the alliance with the American colonists.

Despite Père Labat's efforts, as recounted in all the rhummeries of the modern French Antilles, France sent Charpentier de Cossigny to improve rum and sugar production at the end of the eighteenth century, and the process he described so unflatteringly is the same one still used today in Haiti to make clairin, essentially moonshine. The molasses is added to water and allowed to ferment for a few days, then heated in the alembic. De Cossigny records that the first run, the *petite eau,* was "a spirit of mediocre degree and disagreeable taste." Sometimes, at the end of the week they redistilled the accumulated products, but "although this rendered the product less disagreeable, it still left much to be desired."[256] As de Cossigny said, with as much tact as patriotism could muster, "This is perhaps to some extent the fault of our colonists who do not pay quite as much attention to the preparation of their spirits," although he also pointed out that "since 1789, the vogue for this liquor has become much favored and spread. In Paris they consume rum punch in all the cafés." It was also, he reported, much in demand in ports and on ships.

In France, as in the United States, rum had a heady, revolutionary aroma to it. In 1793, a revolutionary mob was about to loot a grocer's store and arrest the owner when they discovered barrels of rum. Instead of leading him off, they drank his health.[257] By the turn of the century, the affluent regularly included rum in their cellar inventories.

Napoleon's government allowed rum imported from its

colonies on payment of 10 francs duty per 26 gallons. Foreign rums were still officially forbidden. The decree was of
little efficacy, since within a year the Peace of Amiens was
broken, and imports from the colonies were difficult to get
past the British blockade, while the colonies themselves
were either taken by the British, blockaded, or torn in
rebellion by former slaves who had no intention of coop-
erating with Napoleon's plans for them to sweat away their
lives in the cane fields.

More effective, perhaps, in meeting the growing French
demand were the regulations that allowed the legal import
of rum seized from prizes by the navy or privateers on
payment of a duty of 40 percent. This encouraged the constant depravations of the privateers, the corsairs, who, more
than the singularly ineffective French navy of the period,
waited on the seaways from the West Indies to Britain to
raid the convoys of British ships.

As many have observed, the French Revolution and
Napoleon introduced many of the distinctive features of
our modern world. Metrification and commercial warfare
were two major innovations. However that second innovation was also eventually responsible for ending the
supremacy of sugarcane and its West Indian host islands,
which had been the focus of two centuries of Anglo-
French rivalry. Realizing that British finance and the Bank
of England were as much a threat as Nelson and
Wellington, Napoleon knew that the sinews of war, in the
British case, were spun from strands of sugar. So when
Napoleon imposed a Europe-wide embargo against trade
with Britain, he ordered a crash research project into
sugarcane substitutes. By 1811, Benjamin Delessert had a

pilot plant working, staffed by Spanish prisoners of war who were experienced in sugar refining. When the emperor turned up to inspect the plant with a troop of horse guards, he pinned a Legion d'Honneur medal on Delessert's chest and ordered the wholesale expansion of sugar-beet production, not to mention an embargo on sugar from the "two Indies," East and West, to take effect from 1813.[258]

Luckily for rum, however, sugar beet offered no serious competition. In fact, sugar is still a strategic crop. With three tons per acre from beet compared with six tons of sugar from cane, it has taken political intervention, tariff walls, and subsidies to keep beet production competitive with cane sugar, just as in the modern United States Florida sugarcane and high-fructose corn syrup both depend on subsidies and tariffs to compete with Caribbean sugar. But apart from the aberration, in all senses, of *rumverschnitt,* sugar beet does not make rum, so while demand for colonial sugar may have been hit by the beet production, the taste for rum grew, and that could only be met from the Caribbean or from Indian island territories such as Reunion in the Indian Ocean. The French colonies, which no longer included Haiti, rose to meet the occasion and also to rescue France from a phylloxera epidemic that devastated its vineyards and distilleries from 1872 to 1892. While North American root stock rescued the vineyards, colonial rum rescued and comforted the former wine and Cognac drinkers, so rum exports shot up.

In 1902, Martiniquan rum production encountered a rather large hiccup posed by Mount Pelée blowing up and destroying the town of Saint Pierre, along with dozens of distilleries. Rum was also inadvertently responsible for saving the life of one of the two survivors, Auguste Ciparis, whom the local gendarmes had locked up in the stout centuries-old holding cell for consuming too much of the local production. It is perhaps good that France did not have Protestant temperance reformers to frighten people with the diabolical results of demon rum. Ciparis came round from a complete stupor to see the red flames and smell the sulfur, while the temperature inside the cell rose steadily as the volcanic effluvia built up around it. Scarred more physically than mentally, he was recruited by Barnum & Bailey to tell of his ordeal, but one cannot help suspecting the prohibitionists would have made a better offer for him to retail his tale of the mother of all mornings after.

During the First World War, distribution to the troops not only boosted consumption but also popularized the drink immensely, to the extent that after the war French domestic liquor interests once again managed to secure the imposition of a quota on colonial alcohol imports. Ironically, the Second World War cut off the colonies from Europe, and sugar production languished. But the rum that was stockpiled while waiting for the end of the war was aging magnificently, which led to a black market and much-appreciated consumption, although whiskey gradually began to edge out rum from the markets. In the teeth of continuing quotas, the rum producers of Martinique finally, after a twenty-year struggle, obtained in 1996 the cherished *appellation d'origine contrôlée* for their rums and tried to make up in quality what they could not in quantity.

20. VOODOO SPIRIT: HAITI

When the French Revolution came, it liberated more than rum drinkers in the mother country; it also emancipated the slaves in the French colonies. For a decade, during which French naval weakness left the colonies almost completely unreinforced, the British were kept from the sugar islands by armies whose ranks were filled with and eventually commanded by ex-slaves. Their determination not to revert to servitude made them intrepid opponents. The British alone lost some eighty thousand troops in these wars against freed slaves, most notably Toussaint L'Ouverture, the liberator of Haiti.

A combination of prejudice, family influence from his Creole wife Josephine, and commercial pressure from the merchants and sugar traders led to one of the most shameful episodes of Napoleon's career. After the Treaty of Amiens in 1803, the very year when the last restrictions on rum imports were removed, he conspired to reenslave the very people whose courage and tenacity, along with, it must be said, epidemics of yellow fever, had kept the British out of the islands. One wonders if the soon-to-be Empress Josephine, born in Martinique, had a benign influence on the decree opening French markets to rum to counter her malign influence on the reimposition of slavery in her native Martinique, for which even now her statue in the island's capital Fort de France is regularly decapitated and soaked in ghoulish red paint.

The battles and casualties were horrifying, involving at once heroism and horror, as the action began to smack of an outright race war. L'Ouverture, a hero of the French Revolution, was tricked and kidnapped, to die imprisoned in France. In Guadeloupe, France won, but only after an epic incident in 1802, when a regiment of mixed blacks, mulattos, and white *sans-culottes* sent from France a decade before along with their wives and children, under the command of Martiniquan Colonel Louis Delgres, blew themselves up at Matouba rather than succumb to the counterrevolution.

It is perhaps a testimony to the revisionism of history that the French rum historian Huetz de Lemp describes what happened in Guadeloupe: "The French revolution in the island translated itself into a slave insurrection and 'black terror.' Most of the planters disappeared: order was reestablished by Bonaparte then by the English in 1814."[259] So the centuries of kidnapping, branding, executions, and floggings that constituted slavery were not a "white terror" but a neutral "order" which was reestablished by Napoleon.

The French troops carried out bloody massacres of the

slaves to force them back into bondage. In the French islands, the demands of the planters and their allies in the motherland retained slavery intact right up to 1848. In Saint-Domingue, however, even after L'Ouverture was betrayed, the former slaves fought on and in 1804 declared the second independent republic in the Western Hemisphere and the first black republic in the world. They showed their solidarity with the oppressed by giving their new republic the name that the extinct Caribs had used: Haiti.

A haven for French pirates in the early seventeenth century, Saint-Domingue had soon become a place where those of other, equally unethical trades could amass treasure. By the time of the French Revolution, Saint-Domingue was growing more sugar than all the British Caribbean islands together. However, Saint-Domingue rum production was barely passable in quality, even by the relaxed standards of the American colonists, who preferred to make their own bad rum. Less than one in ten of Saint-Domingue plantations ran a still on the premises.

On the eve of the French Revolution, which was to domino into the Haitian Revolution, Saint-Domingue boasted 793 sugar mills. Twenty years later, Napoleon's efforts to "reestablish order" led to the virtual end of production in what had been the world's most productive sugar island at the end of the eighteenth century. The economic and social scars of the struggle still contrive to make Haiti the poorest place in the Americas and one of the poorest in the world. The French eventually accepted Haitian independence only after imposing huge reparations, and pressure in Washington from the Southern states meant that Haiti, the second independent republic of the New World, was not recognized until during the American Civil War—and was scarcely independent of the United States afterward!

Throughout the Caribbean, people have appropriated as their very own the instruments and objects of their ancestors' enslavement. The slaves on one Martiniquan plantation, for example, celebrated their emancipation by rioting and destroying the rum hogsheads, which they then drained into a pond. Then they realized that they had erred, so they drank the pond, treating it like a natural punch bowl. Much as they liked the product, the Haitian regimes could not keep them down on the farm, or rather, the plantation. Commercial sugar and rum production all but disappeared. A British traveler, James Franklin, recorded that the only rum under production in 1828 was distilled by an enterprising Jamaican planter called Towning; the rest was *clairin* "of an acrid quality and fetid smell."[260]

The former slaves of Haiti had voted with their feet and machetes against attempts to restart the massive sugar plantations that fed the former French distilleries. As Victor Shoelcher, the French antislavery campaigner, wrote in 1843, "The fields of Haiti are dead. There, where slavery produced thousands of tons of sugar, no one makes anything but food and some syrup to make tafia. The perennial Bayahonda trees cover the cane fields with their thorns."[261] In fact, the Bayahonda trees themselves have now mostly been cut down to make into charcoal for fuel. Even so, one of the finer experiences in Port-au-Prince, Haiti's capital, is to sit on the wooden balcony of the Hotel

Oloffson, where Graham Greene once sat overlooking the fountain where the Tonton Macoute dumped their victims, and sip the fifteen-year-old Barbancourt Special Estate Reserve rum. The hotel is one of the few institutions that have persistently functioned in Haiti. Sitting there, Greene was inspired to write *The Comedians*. I was inspired to visit the Barbancourt Distillery, the only other viable commercial enterprise in the country.

It was evening as I made my way along the traffic-clogged Route Nationale Une. To the usual dust, potholes, and chaotic traffic were added another problem. Funerals take place toward sunset, and on this evening, three separate corteges held up the traffic. One hearse had broken down and was being pushed; another was creaking along just behind; while in the economy funeral bringing up the rear the pink-painted coffin was being born on the heads of the mourners, who did not seem to mind that the shroud was poking out from under the ill-secured lid. This did not bode well for the Haitian concept of quality control.

However, down a side road, past the goats grazing at the roadside and the pigs wallowing in the ditch, I suddenly came upon the best piece of paved road in Haiti. This road is for the heavy trucks that bring in two hundred tons of sugarcane a day to the home of Rhum Barbancourt, as well as for the oxcarts that bring in some of the crop from small farms. The cane has to be milled within twenty-four hours, and a ton of it gives about seventy bottles of rum— anything up to fifteen years after it is ground. There, sur-rounded by the cane fields that supply it, the plant distills, ages, and bottles what many people consider the best rum in the world, Barbancourt Estate Réserve, aged in oak for fifteen years to give it what its maker, Thierry Gardère, calls a "particularity" that makes it comparable to an old Cognac or single malt. Almost as good, and more easily available, is Barbancourt's Five Star mere eight-year-old rum. Connoisseurs would like to think that anyone who put coke in this rum would suffer the terrible wrath of the whole Voodoo pantheon. The Three Star, aged four years, could at a pinch be mixed without sacrilege, but not the eight- or fifteen-year-old.

Among Barbancourt's dedicated consumers are the Voodoo gods of Haiti, whose upper-class priests spray a mouthful into the air before pouring a libation on the ground. And then the priests drink the stuff themselves— straight, of course. Even those who provide only clairin will disguise it in a Barbancourt bottle, often decorated with gaudy beadwork as if to hide from the visiting spirits that the spirit is not of the top quality.

M. Gardère sniffed when I made at comparisons with a better-known rum. "Bacardi is very clever," he said, "they do not want you to drink their rums without a mixer to hide the taste." Barbancourt, a premium rhum agricole, has picked up gold medals galore for its qualities, since the company has been outward-looking enough to send its products to the fairs and expositions of the world, especially in Paris. It goes without saying that Barbancourt is un rhum agricole. Gardère also explains that the star on the label is, coincidentally, red, the color associated with the war god, Ogou. M. Gardère is not a devotee of Voodoo, but it is little short of a daily miracle that his factory survives at all in a country with a two-hundred-year-old history of political upheavals, and where the telephones and power lines work only occasionally. Barbancourt can sell everything it produces —if it can actually receive the orders. When I contacted its American importer before setting off, he sighed that the only way they could maintain supplies was by keeping a big inventory. The telephones do not usually work.

Dupré Barbancourt started the company when he opened his distillery in 1862. The Barbancourts had moved from the Cognac-producing areas of France to Haiti in the eighteenth century, and local legend has it that it was the quality of the rum the family made that preserved them from the massacres that accompanied the various slave uprisings, invasions, and civil wars in the aftermath of the French Revolution. When Dupré Barbancourt died without children, his widow, Nathalie Gardère Barbancourt, brought in her nephew, Paul Gardère, to help her run the rhummerie.

Now the fourth-generation keeper of the flame under the still is Thierry Gardère, the great-great-nephew of the original Barbancourt. The company is officially a partnership with five other family members, but they seem happy to leave him in charge to maintain the ancient traditions. Those are a rhum agricole, triple-distilled and aged in white-oak vats built with timber and carpenters both imported from the Limousin region of France that supplies the Cognac industry. The oak is from stand-alone trees whose large pores allow in more air to engender the mysterious alchemy of aging and maturation. Many rum producers use barrels that have been used for aging bourbon. The Barbancourt fifteen-year-old spends its last five years in old Cognac barrels.

Given that the family came from France, there have

been Balzacian family feuds, as when a branch of the Barbancourt family tried to sell rum under its own name.
Gardère's father sued, and Thierry chuckles when he
recounts the tale. When the Gardère advocate cited the rel-
evant laws, the judge declared that the law did not apply
since, he declared, "this is the Duvalierist revolution." He
asked for a bribe, and when it was refused, sent Gardère's
father and his lawyer to prison. Even Papa Doc thought
this was little too much, and ordered their release. As one
of the few legitimately profitable businesses in Haiti, the
company again attracted the attention of Papa Doc, who
wanted to nationalize it. It was saved when Duvalier's advi-
sors speculated about how much damage Haitian civil
servants could do to a product that depended on rigorous
quality control.

It was around that time that the company became a
near-monopoly anyway, but not as a result of Voodoo
politics or anything else. "It was ice," explains Gardère.
"When you put water in some spirits, it brings out the
fusel oil taste. You don't smell it at higher proofs, so
when they put ice in the other rums, it gave them a bad
taste." he explains. Before 1949, the company bought
the local hooch and then refined it again to eliminate
the more noxious hangover-inducing alcohols. Then it
began to make its own fresh from the *vesous,* the fermented
sugarcane juice. Indeed the original copper-column still
bubbles away even now, siphoning off the less-drinkable
condensate. As a measure of its potency, Barbancourt
donated the condensate to local hospitals for surgical
spirit after a recent hurricane.

Now the rum is distilled in three columns, and the final

product comes out as a highly volatile 90 percent alcohol, to which some 50 percent water is added before aging in oak vats. Gardère says, "We've modernized a lot, but we are trying not to do so too quickly. We want to go step by step so we do not lose too much of the original product. We want to go with the evolution of people's taste."

Although they add yeast, the local cane, slightly thinner than usual, has its own natural ferments, and the company is taking steps to buy more land to safeguard its supply, which is threatened by the spreading slums and sprawl of Port-au-Prince. However, Barbancourt cannot totally protect itself from the infrastructural chaos of the poorest country in the hemisphere. Jean-Mark Ewald, an engineer at the plant, comments sadly about this struggle against disentrepreneurial entropy: "There's no way we can go 'Just In Time' when it comes to equipment and material that we need. We never know how much time it will take." Recently, he says, they received a batch of chemicals for the labs that they had ordered a year before, most of which were stuck in customs for a year: "Some of them were already out of date."

Commenting on the difficulty of running a modern business without a telephone, Gardère smiles, "People keep stealing the lines. But thank God you don't need a telephone for distillation." However, you do need to tie up a lot of capital if you are going to keep spirits aging and unsold. For example, four years of embargo by the United Nations cut off the 40 percent sales that would normally go to export between 1991 and 1995, but Gardère is philosophical: "We are not so desperate, because it meant that we have more aged rum to sell! So in the end we can have better sales."

The secret of Barbancourt's success over more artisan spirits is the dedication to quality control. Just on the other side of the wall from the neighborhood's grazing goats are its labs, with gas and liquid chromatography facilities. The company has recently installed a cold filtration plant to anticipate another problem: when the rum moves from its tropical home to colder northern markets, the tannins in the rum precipitate out. "No one's complained about it yet, but we don't like it," says Ewald. In a country where even safe drinking water is rare, the plant uses osmosis and ozonization to ensure that it has soft, bacteria-free water for both fermentation and dilution of the heady firewater that comes off the stills.

Gardère hopes that his sixteen-year-old daughter will one day become involved in the business, but he senses a need for changes:

> We want to expand the export market, which is why we need more aged rum, and so we need more cap-ital. We have another problem, what I call a positive problem; more people want to buy than we can sell. I'm not sure that the family will put so much in it, so we may have to look for new partners for finance.

Meanwhile, as Barbancourt markets itself worldwide, taking advantage of globalization, the local clairin has been suffering. Christian preachers may well have inveighed against demon rum, but the local spirits like their local spirits. All the ances-tral African deities of Voodoo, Santeria, and Obeah acquired a taste for rum on their way across the Atlantic. Rum is a sacramental drink, a libation to the spirits and an inspiration to the worshippers. While Barbancourt is preferred, the cheaper sort of houngans use clairin to summon the gods of theVoodoo pantheon, and the ordinary sort of Haitians use it for escaping this world in other ways. In fact, in the archaeology of alcohol, you can probably recreate the taste of the old kill-devil by taking a drink of clairin.

You can get some sense of its subtlety from the protests by Haitian peasant farmers a few years ago about unfair competition from imported medical ethanol, surgical spirit, a flask of which they symbolically buried next to the Route Nationale. Unscrupulous importers had been bringing it in to the country to make *faux clairin,* under the banner of free trade and globalization. Like the native zombies, one cannot but suspect that its time interred would be short! It is probably significant that one of the traditional uses of clairin is washing down the dead. There is as yet no export market for it and one could not be sure that the Food and Drug Administration would favor its import into the United States.

In contrast to Barbancourt's solitary success in rum exports, the Dominican Republic, which was occupied for decades by the Haitians, has a flourishing rum export business. Since for so much of the time the republic was run as an American client state, its sugar was allowed preferential entry to the United States, and as a far-off former colony of Spain, its rum was also allowed into the European Union. The Dominicans, like the Puerto Ricans, appreciate their rum and have spent a lot time making some very fine specimens but have not really moved world history one way or the other. But it does raise the question of when the Spanish-speaking world picked up on *el ron.*

21. Cuba Libre!

Although the Spanish brought both sugar cultivation and the slave trade to the Caribbean, their
centrally controlled empire lacked the entrepre-
neurial urges of the British and even lagged behind the
French. The Spanish Crown was far more interested in
American silver and gold to fight its dynastic wars in Europe
than it was in the promotion of trade.

Even more so than Paris and Lisbon, Madrid tried to
inhibit any rum production that would interfere with
spirit production at home—to the extent of banning colonial production for local consumption. Spanish sugar production lagged and rum production remained modest
throughout the seventeenth and eighteenth centuries. On
the Spanish Main, they distinguished between *aguardiente
de canas,* made from cane, and *chinguirito,* made from
molasses. In general, the Spanish colonial authorities, on

both protectionist and moral, sumptuary grounds, tried to stop both.

To make chinguirito, the fearless colonists, in the true spirit of the intrepid conquistadors, fermented the molasses with water in a vessel of calfskin for two weeks and then distilled it in a pot still.[262] No one records whether the calfskin gave an extra kick to the drink, but it was unlikely to add a refined flavor. Clearly the product had limited export potential. The contrast between the French western half of Hispaniola, now Haiti, and the Spanish east, now the Dominican Republic, is instructive. The colonists of Spanish Hispaniola were reduced to buying contraband rum from their neighbors or, as in Puerto Rico, making local moonshine, *aguardiente de cana,* for local use. There was a certainly a demand. The Spanish imperial attempts at prohibition had pretty much the effect that prohibition often does. Penalties increase as deference to the law decreases.

The desperate measures enacted in Mexico for rum producers included the confiscation of all the offender's goods, two hundred lashes, and six months in the galleys. If these temporal pains did not deter offenders, the bishops added excommunication to the secular penalties.[263] However, this merely showed that the thirst was enough to quench the flames of eternal hellfire. Mexican doctors weighed in with a convenient opinion that rum was much less noxious than brandy because the latter contained "Lots of sulfuric acid and bitterness which made it acidic and corrosive, bad in every respect for the human organism."[264]

In Venezuela, despite prohibitions, rum was imported from the Dutch and the French, and later from Cuba. The governor of Venezuela destroyed no less than four hundred stills, but even so, thirty remained in Caracas alone in 1775.[265] One priest who caused particular scandal haunted the taverns all morning and afternoon, and gave himself over to games with "Negros y zambos," "as if there weren't whites with whom he could divert himself." Rum thus enslaves and democratizes.

However, the persistence of rum drinkers and makers pays off. The Spanish Main now produces some prizewinning rums from Venezuela through to Guatemala, Nicaragua, and Honduras, and Cuba has persuaded itself that it is not just the home of the big cigar but of fine rum as well.

The British occupation of Cuba during the Seven Years War—still attested to by British cannon as street bollards around the cathedral in Havana—transformed the sleepy sugar production of the Spanish colony and helped pave the way to a relaxation of the Spanish embargo on rum production. The influx of slaves brought by the British, the introduction of new cane-growing and refining techniques, and the opening to foreign trade, all put the island on the road to the monoculture that marked the twentieth century. A consequence of the increased sugar production across the empire was the production of lots of molasses and the commercial pressure led to the issue of the Spanish Royal Decree of March 16, 1796, the Queen's birthday, which finally authorized the production of chinguirito under license. And to show that the decree was serious, an amnesty was declared for all who had been condemned under the earlier quasiprohibition.

Cuba Libre

Cuba became the rum producer for neighboring Spanish realms, exporting to Cartagena, New Orleans, Florida, and the Yucatan. But it did not export to the thirteen colonies or, later, the United States, since the quality was abysmal. However, the events in the French colonies and the difficulties of maintaining relations with the former British islands after independence had left the Americans gasping for molasses, and Cuba filled the gap. In 1790, Cuba exported to the United States a puny 250,000 gallons of molasses and some 100,000 gallons of rum; by the end of the decade, exports to the United States were 2 million gallons of molasses and 1.2 million gallons respectively.[266] Production was boosted and techniques improved by an influx of French Creole refugees from Haiti, who were, however, expelled to New Orleans in 1809 when Spain defected from an alliance with the French and joined with the British.

By 1827 Cuba had over three hundred distilleries hissing and bubbling away, and by 1860, there were over a thousand. Spain had noticed an imperial rum gap and tried to get the planters to make it up. Like Voodoo in Haiti, Santeria in Cuba demands rum for its rituals. Allegedly even non-Santeria Cubans spill a drop of rum for a libation before drinking, although one has to doubt whether the waste will survive the current hard times.

The early Cuban rum-makers relied upon the primitive French *guildives* or alembics, possibly imported from Saint-Domingue by fleeing refugees, and the product was not too good. With the example of Jamaican rum close at hand, Cubans knew that it could be better, and they experimented. Fernando de Arritola produced a swan-neck still with coils that represented a big step forward. But they were still missing out on something. They knew that foreign rums were aged, but did not appreciate the effect of the wooden containers. One enterprising innovator, Pedro Diago, tried burying rum in pottery jars in the ground. It did not work.

In the nineteenth century, in the Spanish-speaking islands that were all that was left of the empire after the mainland revolted, the royal Spanish government decreed standards for rum that were designed to make it fit to serve at the court in Madrid. The Crown had offered a prize for the creation of a rum that would be "more delicate, lighter, and able to satisfy the taste of the Court and the elite of the Empire."[267] Hence the snobbishly titled *el Ron Superior*, which anticipated the French branding coup of *rhum agricole*.

That did not stop renowned distilling dynasties like the Bacardi family from supporting Cuban rebels against Spain. Rum has always tended to favor and flavor rebellion. Several rum-distilling families from Cuba also supported Fidel Castro in the years before the revolution. One such family was the company that made Rum San Pablo, and its story was told to me by Willem Jonckheer, whose family now makes it in Curaçao, the Dutch semi-desert island just off the coast of the Spanish Main.

Señor Justo Gonzales, had been happily making and exporting Rum San Pablo to Curaçao for many years, where his agent, August Damian Jonckheer, known as "A. D." distributed it to eager local customers. Then in 1960 an unusual request was brought to the table. Could A. D. Jonckheer place an order for the entire stock of rum in the factory, 150 barrels? However, could he also not pay as promptly as he usually did? In fact, would he hold it until Gonzales came to collect it himself?

When he arrived in Curaçao, Gonzales explained to A. D. that the cash from the rum and the recipe for making more of the same were now his only worldly assets. Castro had nationalized the rum distilleries—it could have been because he considered them essential public services, but then he nationalized pretty much everything else, down to the hotdog sellers at the baseball stadiums. Gonzalez had gone to see him and remonstrated—after all, they had sent money to Fidel and the rebels in the Sierra Maestra to fight the dictator Batista.

Over a glass of San Pablo in Curaçao, Billy, A. D.'s son recounted, "He said Fidel turned round to his secretary and told her, find out how much he sent—and write a check to him for that amount." The nationalization went ahead. San Pablo rum ended up being made with imported molasses in dry, sugar-cane-free Curaçao to the recipe that Gonzales had smuggled out.

Jonckheer went into partnership with Gonzales and, on the death of his exiled Cuban friend, Justo Gonzales, A. D., Jonckheer continued the business which is still in operation, run by his children and grandchildren. In 2005, sixty years after its birth, San Pablo was finally launched on the North American market, from Cuba via Curaçao.

Batty about Rum

Bacardi has a similar tale, but somehow less affecting. Certainly in any telling of the David and Goliath story, Bacardi and its bat logo come out more like Goliath. Bacardi was the very reason I was talking to Billy Jonckheer. I was in Curaçao for a conference on sustainable tourism, which is supposed to support local industries and businesses. In the bar of the resort hotel at which I was staying, like so many across the Caribbean, there was only one rum brand available, Bacardi, so I had gone to seek out the local producers— in this case, Jonckheer.

Not only do tourists bring in dollars to the countries they visit, they often develop tastes and create markets for local products. But for a few thousand dollars, Bacardi, registered in the Bahamas, made in Puerto Rico, and with its management mostly living in Florida, monopolizes the local markets across the Caribbean and the world with its bland, branded spirit. The major hotel chains will all stock Bacardi rums, but few carry any serious sample of the islands' scintillating variety of spirits. Fifty years of marketing have made Bacardi almost synonymous with rum in much of North America, and as Thierry Gardère of Barbancourt pointed out with a pained expression, "They always advertise it as mixed with something else."

In civilized countries, drinkers go to the corner bar for a tipple. In Prohibition-era America, lots of them went to Cuba, and what they drank there, in keeping with the ambience, was rum, usually in cocktails and often in bars favored by Fidel's onetime fishing partner, Ernest Hemingway. "My mojito in La Bodeguita, my daiquiri in El Floridita," he distinguished. Cuba made great rums and had some of the world's most renowned bars.

Like most nations that get into rum, the Cubans act as if they own it and invented it. On one visit I met Fernando G.

Campoamor the author of *The Happy Child of the Sugar Cane,* his history of Cuban rum, in which he happily echoed another writer from 1925: "Indeed, there never has been and never will be rum as good as ours. Those made outside Cuba do not have the best raw material that exists, molasses made from Cuban sugarcane." Sadly, the aged author lives in a shabby apartment that shows the decayed chic of more than forty years ago when he was one of Havana's jet set, hobnobbing with Hemingway and others. His boxes of clippings are mildewed, and the furniture is decaying. The bottle of Havana Club we brought along with us was the first decent rum he had tasted for a long time. Cuban pensions don't run to export-quality rum anymore.

In 1999, Castro, who had already given up the trademark cigars that regularly put him on the cover of *Cigar Aficionado* magazine, went one step further; he urged Cubans to give up rum as well and warned that anyone who wanted rum over the New Year "will pay dearly for it." He asked an assembly of medical students, "How much damage has rum caused in any society?" He even lamented that there were "supporters of the revolution who like to toss down a few once in a while."[268] Cynics assumed that the supplies for the growing export market for Cuban rum were threatened by domestic demand.

Still a Cuban nationalist, Fernando held to the line of his book: that Cuba has for almost two centuries made better rum than anyone else. It is, as the philosophers say, an eminently falsifiable premise. But they do make good rums now, Havana Club being the most lucrative. When I was there in the mid-nineties, they had run out of the top-of-the-range seven-year-old Anejo. When I returned at the

turn of the century, they were selling fifteen-year-old—at
an extortionate price. The math did not add up, but a rep
resentative of the company admitted that it was *una media,*
an average. One should always be wary of numbers in cen-
tralized economies.

The most renowned step forward for rum in Cuba was
when a wine merchant, Don Facundo Bacardi y Maso, an
immigrant from Spain, set up his Bacardi distillery in Santiago. The family takes it very seriously. I have a bronze
keepsake of the original distillery, showing the iconic palm
tree that they kept alive through many subsequent expan-
sions and remodelings of the distillery. Many rum connoisseurs now think that modern, deracinated, and
globalized Bacardi is best suited to Cuba Libre—a rum and
coke, the product of two mighty brand-building empires,
Coca Cola and Bacardi. The palm tree died. For political
reasons, Bacardi would bring Cuba Libre back to life.

The company is steeped in the phantasms of its own
mythology. The black bat trademark was allegedly inspired
by the bats nesting in the proto-distillery or in the palm
tree. And the family makes much of its patriotic endeavors
for Cuban independence yet, at the same time, claims that
the young King Alfonso of Spain was rescued from near
death by a tot of the family specialty in 1892. The rum
was already "by appointment" the official rum for the royal
family. There are unexplained gaps, biographical blind
spots. One of the founders and the person who taught the
Bacardis how to make rum was a distiller of French origin,
José Leon Bouteiller, who was dropped from the company
and its attendant mythos in 1874. He is not mentioned in
any of the company histories.

The distillery was even more antique than the family Hernando Ospina, author of a critical history of the family claimed. 1862 was the year they actually bought it from an Englishman, John Nunes, who had been making rum in Santiago since 1838. The still that Nunes had installed twenty-four years earlier went on working for another half-century after 1862. The date of 1838 is significant. Jamaican sugar production was plummeting following the emancipation of the slaves in the British Empire in 1833. Emancipation would take another forty years in Cuba, so there was cheap sugar and molasses to be had there. And as for those bats: it is said that Bacardi used to retail Nunes's rum in old olive oil containers that had a trademark bat on them.

The company really rose to prominence after the American occupation, or liberation, of Cuba, at the turn of the twentieth century, when Cuba became the playground for its northern neighbor. Bacardi consolidated that with its adroit positioning around Prohibition. When the Eighteenth Amendment took force, Bacardi USA sold sixty thousand shares, closed down the company, and distributed its assets, coincidentally sixty thousand cases of Bacardi rum, to the stockholders. During the dry years of Prohibition, shiploads of Bacardi went to rendezvous with the rumrunners on Rum Row, just outside American territorial waters. At the height of Prohibition, the company's order books would suggest that there were unquenchable thirsts in Shanghai, Bahamas, and tiny islands like the French enclave of Saint Pierre and Miquelon, off Newfoundland.

As soon as repeal was in sight, Bacardi litigated all the way up to the Supreme Court to open its business in Puerto Rico, where it was eager to get Caribbean costs combined with American nationality. Its rivals in Puerto Rico used the same style of targeted retrospective legislation that Bacardi later did against Castro's Cuba in an attempt to keep Bacardi out. In the first year after Prohibition, Bacardi sold almost a million bottles to the United States. But soon it was not selling it from Cuba. Despite the family's overt and noisy Cuban patriotism, the company supplied the United States from Puerto Rico, and Cuban rum's share of American imports dropped from 52 percent in 1935 to 7.3 percent in 1940.

In 1955 Bacardi moved its trademark to the Bahamas, perhaps in gratitude for the islands' help in keeping the product moving during Prohibition, and also because that made it eligible for British Commonwealth preferences. Its offshoring from Cuba proved very prescient when Castro nationalized the Cuban operations in 1960, which was as much a shock to Bacardi as it was to the San Pablo company. The Bacardi building had greeted the arrival of Fidel, Che, and the *compañeros* with a banner saying simply "Gracias, Fidel!"[269] In 1959, Castro's delegation to the United States had included Juan Pépin Bosch and Daniel Bacardi, two of the family's heads.

The company is still held by six hundred descendants of the founder, so it does not have to file financial statements or submit to valuations as if it were listed on stock exchanges, and in any case, with sales in two hundred countries adding up to 200 million bottles, no one could be sure which exchange it would list on. As its record shows, it is the original multinational. Its trademark is now held in Liechtenstein, one of the most secret and secure banking centers in the world which contrives to be "offshore" in the middle of the Alps.

However, while attending to business, the Bacardi family has never missed a chance to pay back Castro. Juan Pépin Bosch brought a touch of the old connection between buccaneering and rum back to life in 1961 by buying a surplus U.S. Air Force B-26 Marauder medium bomber in order to bomb a Cuban oil refinery. Later he was the money behind a plot to assassinate Castro.[270] Bosch remained the patriarch of the clan. For many years he was a major funder of the Cuban American Lobby and a major litigator who has brought the United States to the verge of trade wars with the rest of the world. The technique has been to lobby legislators to exercise their anti-Cuban prejudices, regardless of general principles of international or indeed domestic law, and then to pay lawyers to implement the resulting legislation.

One such piece of legislation, the Helms-Burton Act, which allowed people whose property in Cuba had been expropriated or nationalized to sue for compensation in the U.S. courts, produced an amusing closing of the rum circle and put a swizzle stick in lots of international affairs. Claiming parity with former Cuban property owners, Canadian descendants of Loyalists expelled and dispossessed because of the last big Rum War in 1776 threatened to sue for the return of the center of Philadelphia, from which they had been driven during the Revolution—and not compensated. Israeli lobbyists rushed in and, fearful of Palestinian refugees suing for the land from which they were driven in 1948, secured from Senator Jesse Helms, a notorious United Nations baiter, a clause stating that the law would not apply to countries set up by UN resolution—which effectively meant Israel, although Namibia could perhaps claim some dubious benefits from the clause.

Bacardi was spurred into action when Castro's government went into partnership with the French liquor giant, Pernod, to market the renowned Havana Club internationally. The multinational Pernod, even though excluded from the U.S. market by the embargo, was able to sell 38 million bottles in the first few years. In anticipation of an end to the Cuban embargo, it was gearing up for big sales in the United States. This was a challenge, both political and commercial to Bacardi, which set to firing retaliatory legal broadsides and to the rediscovery of its Cuban roots.

Bacardi, wherever it is made, had for some decades tried to bury its Cuban origins, but in the 1990s it went into reverse. Its labels began to mention prominently that the company was founded in Santiago de Cuba in 1862 while eliding mention of where the rum was actually made currently. In 1998, "rum and Coke" or "Bacardi and Coke" suddenly became known as a Cuba Libre again. To match the myths, various stories were circulated to celebrate Cuba Libre, claiming that it had been invented by an American in 1898 to celebrate the American victory over the Spanish in Cuba. Of course, like the Filipinos, the Cubans, who had been fighting the Spanish for some years, tended to believe that they had pretty much freed themselves before the gringos arrived to take the prize.

The original makers of Havana Club, the Arechabala family, had fled the country after the revolution, leaving the distillery and the brand behind. The family did not renew its trademark, which lapsed in 1973, and in 1976, the Cuban state export company registered the century-old brand with the U.S. Patent and Trademark Office. Twenty years later, Bacardi sought out the Arechabalas and bought their residual claim. Reportedly, Bacardi paid them $1.25 million after the family had spurned offers from Pernod Ricard, which was attempting to cover its back.

The Bacardi company, happy to tweak Fidel's beard, began selling a rum with the Havana Club label (made in the Bahamas) in the United States in 1995, and Pernod sued. The case was going in Pernod's favor, as the Manhattan judge initially made her rulings based on existing law. Then the Bacardi family cut the Gordian knot. Using political clout in Florida, it got the law changed by persuading the Floridian senators to smuggle a clause into a large spending bill specifically to exempt trademarks nationalized by the Cubans from the usual international protections unless the original owner had agreed to hand them over. And of course, the Arechebalas had not.

In the end, the judge broke new legal ground by accepting this retrospective and clearly privileged legislation as binding, since Pernod wanted an injunction against future use of its trademark. Judge Shira Scheindlin decided:

At this point, because plaintiffs can sell no product in this country and may not be so able for a significant length of time, they suffer no impairment of their ability to compete as a result of defendants' actions. Any competitive injury plaintiffs will suffer based upon their intent to enter the U.S. market once the embargo is lifted is simply too remote and uncertain to provide them with standing.

It was yet another case of the United States flouting treaties and international law, and the judgment is not recognized anywhere else in the world—a point emphasized by the World Trade Organization (WTO) shortly afterward.

Even so, the U.S. Patent Office threw out Bacardi's attempt to register six other names containing Havana, which were variously Little, Old, Silver, Clipper, Clasico, and Primo. It allowed Little Havana perhaps because that is a district in Miami, but disallowed the others because the company was claiming a spurious connection to Havana, which could have confused drinkers who thought they were buying rum from Cuba.

When Pernod pushed the European Union into filing a dispute with the WTO, Bacardi complained, in a manner that almost defines the term "disingenuous" from a family that had just secured private legislation: "Pernod Ricard has pressured the EU into filing a claim with the WTO in an attempt to politicize a purely civil dispute. Bacardi views this as a private civil matter and one that is not connected in any way to world trade laws or the WTO." Others begged to differ, not least when Castro announced that Cuba could abrogate U.S. trademarks, such as Coca Cola, in retaliation. The WTO itself found in 2001 that the American law violated free-trade agreements, and the U.S. trademark office has refused to revoke Pernod's registration despite even more litigation and lobbying by Bacardi, helped by alleged illegal campaign contributions to Senate leader Tom DeLay. In response to the Trademark Court's rebuttal to Bacardi in 2004, a string of Delay client congressman returned to Capitol Hill trying to squeeze in new privileged laws for the company.

Perhaps the ultimate weapon was when Castro, despite his strictures on rum drinking, threatened in 2001 to start producing a rum in Cuba called Bacardi. The U.S. State Department, not good at seeing itself as others see it, promptly declared this to be a provocation. In the meantime, the European Union has effectively been bullied into taking no action to enforce the case it has won at the WTO, although at one point the British Office of Fair Trading was threatening to fine Bacardi up to £40 million for its efforts to secure exclusive selling rights in bars— seen in Britain as a direct attack on burgeoning Havana Club sales.

While Fidelistas may berate Bacardi for its feud, rum aficionados almost universally deplore the company for the effect it has had on rum. Gresham's law observes that bad money drives out good; Bacardi has achieved this with rum. Its bland ubiquity has been driving the distinctive rums of the world from the mass consumer market. It is the equivalent of American cheddar driving out the three hundred cheeses of France. Its monopoly power has been used to keep much better, genuinely local Caribbean brands from reaching takeoff. Many of them consider Bacardi to be industrial spirit with flavorings.

All across the Caribbean, other rum distillers examine each others' product jealously, and the more modern distillers all have gas chromatographs, which analyze the complex organic compounds in their rivals' rums. Three of them told me during visits about "spikes" in the chromatography for Bacardi's Anejo aged rum, and suggest a naturally aged rum would have a smoother curve of compounds. Instead of Bacardi relying on Father Time for aroma and savor, its rivals suggest that a beaker of "essence" of Anejo has been added. Such claims are indignantly denied by Bacardi, but one thing that struck me on a trip to the huge Bacardi plant in Puerto Rico is how little the flocks of tourists see of the actual process. There are lots of historical mock-ups and barrels, but the only part of the process that I could see open to visitors was the bottling plant. It was a strange contrast to some other distilleries, where the visitors could wander through the vats, the stills, and the warehouses. But then, maybe I am just the suspicious type.

22. PROHIBITION AND THE END OF THE HEROIC AGE OF RUM?

There is some historical irony in the fact that in the 1960s, John F. Kennedy, the heir to a rum-runner's fortune, discussed with Juan Pépin Bosch of Bacardi, who provided so much of that fortune, how to overthrow Fidel Castro, who was, in those days, styling his revolution as the Cuban equivalent of 1776. As we have seen throughout this book, the wheels of history wobble in strange ways when rum is involved. It is doubtless impolite to mention it, but the financial foundations of the New Camelot were built on the proceeds of rum-running.

The great days of Prohibition allowed the New England states to return to their historical roots—as rum smugglers. And just as the movers and shakers of the new American republic came to prominence, wealth, and influence as a result of their smuggling and rum trading with the connivance of ineffective enforcement, so too did the new dynasty of the later republic, the Kennedys, owe their origins to the trade.

Rum and slavery, abolition and prohibition, all shared similar roots in the American mind-set. Oglethorpe, the founder of Georgia, banned slaves and rum—and ended up with both. But the same New England Protestant fervor that cried down slavery also cried down the demon rum. It was not always a well-advised demand. Abraham Lincoln declared in 1840, when he was an Illinois legislator:

> Prohibition will work great injury on the cause of temperance. It is a species of intemperance within itself, for it goes beyond the bounds of reason in that it attempts to control a man's appetite by legislation and makes a crime of out of things that are not crimes. A prohibition law strikes at the very principle upon which our government was founded.[271]

As so often in American history, Lincoln's good sense was ignored. The pressure for temperance, for personal redemption, was fine, but for the spiritual descendents of the Pilgrim Fathers, it was never enough to be good yourself. That was mere Quakerism and similarly dangerous effete and ineffective piety. No, Our Lord wanted you to force your neighbors to be good whether they liked it or not. Rarely has a democracy taken such a nannying attitude to its citizens as the United States, filling its prisons with perpetrators of victimless crimes, whether in the name of a war on drugs, homosexuality, prostitution, or, for so many years, the war against the demon rum. White,

Anglo-Saxon, Protestant Republican clergymen castigated the Democrats as "the party whose antecedents have been Rum, Romanism, and Rebellion," shorthand for Southerners and Irish.

Insanity can be infectious. Much of Canada was afflicted, but mercifully for only a short period before seeing the folly of the project. Discussions of prohibition in the United States often overlook the Canadian experience, which began by allowing localities to declare themselves dry and moved on to a prohibition referendum in 1898, which was won by 51 percent of the vote. Quebec exceptionalism saved the day however. Prime Minister Sir Wilfred Laurier had counted the votes as well, and he noted that French Catholic Quebec, one of his major support bases, had voted by 81 percent against this crazy Anglo-Protestant idea. He realized that a federally enforced prohibition would precipitate much unease among his French-speaking voters, and so he did not try to implement it.

In the end, the matter was left to the provinces, some of which tried prohibition, while others made liquor a government monopoly. In the Maritime Provinces, such as Nova Scotia, rum had its strongest hold, and they returned large majorities for prohibition. Nova Scotia mandated prohibition everywhere except Halifax, which is where most of its people lived, but then it extended it to cover the entire province. Newfoundland, independent at the time, voted for prohibition in 1915 but had the good sense to repeal it in 1924, just in time to benefit from the Americans' mistake—Newfoundland made the rum-running ships for the trade down the coast. It would compete with the French islanders from Saint Pierre and Miquelon in smuggling rum—and whiskey, gin, and anything else potable—down the New England coast.

But the cunning Frenchies, vestiges of the eighteenth-century rum wars, were quicker off the mark, because they had begun by supplying Newfoundland when it introduced prohibition in 1915. The rum that the Newfoundlanders imported was, according to Warner Allen, "portentous," and the sometime thriller writer and wine expert used his literary skills to describe it: "Neat, it was the most awe-inspiring liquor I ever tasted. Its smell was terrific, compounded of tar, and leather, and strange sea scents, and if ever there was a drink strong enough to float a handspike, it was the contraband rum of Saint Johns, Newfoundland."[272]

The paradox is that most Americans were drinking whiskey rather than rum as the American temperance movement lurched on toward Prohibition. But Rum had become exalted as the demon spirit, a sort of Platonic idea of mother's ruin, and to be paired with anything with which the preacher disapproved.

Just as the South's absence from the debate during the Civil War allowed prohibition to take over in the navy, it could be said that the nullification of the power of the beer-drinking German-American lobby during the First World War allowed the prohibitionists to get away with a surprise victory with the Eighteenth Amendment. As with any law with which a significant part of the population strongly disagrees, Prohibition turned the United States into an alcoholic vacuum sucking in booze from wherever it would come—towed on cables under border lakes and rivers, taken over the ice on trucks, flown in on dubious biplanes, and shipped in from the Rum Rows where the ships from Cuba and the Bahamas in the south and New-foundland in the north, lined up just outside territorial waters to sell to the fast motor launches from the shore.

The traditional expertise that had fought the excisemen since colonial times was now recalled into play. In North and South Carolina, people used molasses to make moon-shine rum. But generally they used anything that would ferment, and refined sugar was often added to the mash. This was not an age for connoisseurs. People wanted ethanol without worrying too much about taste or congeners, and aging was too much of a luxury with Prohibition agents on the prowl.

The risks of the trade were low and the profits high. Five thousand cases of liquor loaded for $125,000 at Nassau would double in value when sold at Rum Row. On the beach, the price doubled again to $500,000, and by the time the cargo had been cut with water and sold in New York, it was worth $2 million. Bill McCoy, "Bartender to the whole nation," boasted of his exploits with his fleet of eight ships plying to Rum Row off Long Island where, beyond the twelve-mile limit, they serviced the fast rum boats that came out on a cash-and-carry basis. Of course the rumrunners had to face the risk of revenue cutters, but it seems that the law officers often performed their duties with the same lack of assiduity as their New England predecessors had done during colonial times.

While much of the rumrunners' stock-in-trade was whiskey, gin, and Champagne, there was a lot of rum, not only to meet the historical northeastern tastes but also for companies like Bacardi to meet the new upmarket taste for rum that American tourists had acquired in Cuba. New England rum had never been a drink for gourmets, and its patrons were always more interested in the alcohol than the flavor.

Alcoholic Amnesia

It's easy to see why this important part of American heritage is now all but forgotten except by historians. Quite apart from the perennial American amnesia about history, Prohibition helped erase the importance of alcohol in general and rum in particular to the country's development. Anything alcoholic became so thoroughly disreputable that to say that a founding father took the occasional drink is on a par with suggesting that George W. Bush sniffed cocaine: it may be true, but it is not polite to talk about it.

As the prohibition and temperance movements grew in strength, patriotic prints of the first president and his officers were bowdlerized. The Currier and Ives print of Washington's farewell toast to his officers that was published in 1848 showed a glass in his hand and a decanter on the table. By 1867, the glass had disappeared, leaving him with his hand on his chest in Nelsonian mode, and the decanter had been converted to a hat! Successive biographers of Patrick Henry turned him from a former tavern keeper to an occasional tavern visitor, before dropping the tavern entirely from his life story.

We enter the hypocritical version of American idolatry, which overlooked its idols' feet of clay while primly

ignoring their rum-soaked livers entirely. This dry spirit
ran deep and long. Ezra Pound had to make his way to
Europe when he was fired from Wabash College. His land-
ladies had reported him for having a woman in his rooms
overnight, and his protestations that she slept on the floor
were not believed. The college elders showed scant sympathy, since not only did he smoke, but he took rum in his
tea as well. Even so, the very land their college was built
on was allegedly purchased from the Indians for fifty
pieces of silver and a hogshead of rum.[273]

At the end of Prohibition, several companies tried to
revive the centuries-old tradition of New England rum.
One valiant effort was Pilgrim rum, whose efforts to evoke
Yankee history did not work out in the marketplace. The
taste for rum, already declining under the assault of
whiskey, never really recovered from Prohibition, and just
like their forebears, Americans who did drink the stuff
preferred Caribbean imports, not least Bacardi, whose
generic spirit and commercial power drove out many of its
competitors. By the modern age, only Felton was left of
the New England rums. In 1983, the plant was sold and
mothballed, and so ended the tradition. New England rum
survives only in the rarified world of bottle collectors,
where their embossed pint bottles' depictions of sailing
ships and black-hatted pilgrims evoke a bygone era.

Boston had some unusual casualties from the old rum
connection, and none more so than the Great Boston
Molasses flood which ominously opened the new era of
drought. On January 15, 1918, a fifty-eight-feet-high tank
built by the Purity Distilling Company split open and dis-
gorged its 2.3 million gallons—14,000 tons—of molasses.

Like some glutinous volcanic lava flow, it gurgled across the North End of the city in a flood five feet deep that ran at thirty-five miles an hour, taking over twenty people in its path to the stickiest of sticky ends.

The final vote for the last state necessary to ratify the Eighteenth Amendment was due to take place the following day and in anticipation, Purity had sold the operation to the United States Industrial Alcohol Company, which claimed that a dynamite charge had crashed open the tank, but the courts ruled otherwise and ordered $1 million in compensation. The suspicious may have wondered at the coincidence of impending prohibition and its significance for all the molasses, which could either be distilled or used with baked beans. It would take an awful lot of beans to use up that much molasses.

More to the point, despite attempts to revive New England rum afterward, Prohibition effectively put an end to the centuries-old tradition. That ominous flood of molasses was almost a murky-brown epitaph to the old days that had given birth to the nation, even if its spirit did live on in the Kennedy dynasty and its Cuban connections. And the ghost of the tradition survives on New England taste buds—for example, Mount Gay rum from Barbados still has one of its best American markets in the Boston area. Bostonians claim that you can still smell the molasses in the vicinity of the disaster, but it is at best as ephemeral as the aroma of rum in the city's bars, a ghost of its former self.

Modern Rum: Matured but No Longer Piratical

Indeed, after Prohibition, rum became so passé that even preachers stopped inveighing against it. The post-Prohibition era was a brave new age in which white spirits like gin, white rum from Bacardi, and later vodka were the basis for the cocktails. "Brown spirits" went into something of a depression, except for high-end whiskies and Cognac. Rum was not in a position to compete on quality or branding, since, apart from some Cuban and French Antillean rums, it suffered from its previous plebeian popularity.

It was only toward the end of the century, as the niche market for single malt scotches, VSOP Cognac, and even aged tequilas took off, that rum-makers really began to appreciate the importance of branding. As vodka—40 percent ethanol and 60 percent water—showed, the difference between $10 a bottle and $80 a bottle was the bottle and the label. Bacardi epitomized that marketing, with its rootless spirit made from any sugarcane, anywhere.

But this posed a problem for the more traditional rum-makers in the Caribbean. To age rum means tying up capital for five or more years. You pay for expensive spirit and the expensively hand-coopered barrels, and you have to pay to warehouse them and give them tender loving care, knowing that each year 10 percent of your stock evaporates through the wood. The business entails money for marketing and brand-building, for distribution and advertising.

While the Caribbean had once been the cockpit of empires, it was now an embarrassing backwater for many of the former imperial powers. First coal and then oil had replaced sugar as the most lucrative carbon-based commodity and foundation of empire. A combination of Napoleon's sugar beet, European protectionism, and high American tariff walls designed to protect Archer Daniel Midland's high-fructose corn syrup, made sugar a drug on the world market. Even Cuba, faced with Gorbachev's fight against alcoholism, lost first its Soviet rum exports, then its sugar markets. Many islands, once the sugary equivalent of oil-gushing Gulf states, gave up sugar plantations entirely. Golf courses were more lucrative and tourism more dependable than sugar mills. The imperial powers had some vestigial sense of responsibility for the islands they had populated with kidnapped Africans and reduced to backbreaking monoculture—but not too much.

The British government, influenced as ever by the Trea-sury, could see that these islands were now loss-making assets and happily encouraged independence. The French, still dreaming of glory, incorporated their islands as integral parts of France. When the Europeans got together at the Lomé Convention to try to help their former colonies in the developing world with trade preferences, uneasy com-promises were made. Martinique and Guadeloupe were officially part of France, so their rums were guaranteed preferential access, and to protect them while extending a helping hand to the former colonies, the European Union agreed to a quota system for rum entering the Continent from former colonies. It tied the Caribbean rum producers to what looked like a secure arrangement that would, however, do little to encourage them to take the necessary steps toward the product development, branding, and marketing that they needed. And whatever they did was in the face of a near-monopoly from Bacardi—not just on the rum market, but with the very concept of rum in the biggest markets.

In the ultimate show of ingratitude, almost in a fit of absentmindedness, the European Union agreed with the United States during trade talks at the World Trade Organization in Singapore 1997 to end the quotas and protective tariffs for spirits, throwing the market open. It was a sweetener for a deal that gave the European Union better access to the U.S. technology market. The beleaguered rum producers of the Caribbean suddenly found themselves facing open competition from countries where sugar production was subsidized and where unions were unknown. For example, the fuel that was going into Brazilian cars could theoretically now be exported as cheap rum. Caribbean rum was providing thousands of jobs in the region—and $260 million a year in foreign exchange.

Some of the producers, such as Appleton in Jamaica and Mount Gay in Barbados, went into alliance with the handful of major global spirits companies and began to emphasize quality and age in order to develop a premium market. And Bacardi also developed its "aged" or Anejo products. But many small distilleries on the various islands were not in a position to fight trade rules and Bacardi.

It took four years of conscience-tugging at the European Union to produce a $70 million aid package to help the Caribbean rum distillers develop production techniques and market their product. With tourism surging in the islands, exposure to the local product should help marketing, but as we have seen, chain hotels are often tied to major international companies such as Bacardi for what they offer to their visitors. With all the barriers against

them, the genuine Caribbean rum producers are surviving. Whether they will thrive remains to be seen. Certainly, it makes more sense for the island nations to turn
their sugar into high-value-added premium rum than to
sell it undervalued on a grossly protected world market.

Even allowing for future World Trade Organization battles, short of the oil wells gurgling dry and leaving the
world dependent on sugarcane alcohol—rum—for fuel
supplies, neither rum nor molasses is likely to play the
major motive role in history that it once did. So it seems
that the heroic, buccaneering, and blasphemous age of
rum, of kill-devil, of the libation that, for better or worse,
has shaped the American character and the modern world
has passed.

Whether it was the blood of slaves or of Nelson, rum
soaks into the pages of battlefields from Haiti to Yorktown,
from the Somme to Gallipoli, from Trafalgar to Jutland,
liquid history as well as liquid sunshine. Still, even if rum
may not shape our history so directly now, in these stressful
times a therapeutic response to history is to hang loose and
savor yet another tot of the global spirit that still has its
warm heart in the Caribbean. "Life Needs the
Caribbean," claimed the post–September 11 travel ads
trying to coax timorous Americans on to flights south. And
what is the Caribbean without rum—the only common
essential factor apart from sunshine in that richly multi-
cultural region whose current polylingualism reflects its
historical role as a great power battleground. A good life
still needs a good rum.

BIBLIOGRAPHY

Adams, John. *Diary & Autobiography.* Cambridge: Harvard University Press, 1961.

Adams, John and Abigail. *The Letters of John And Abigail Adams,* London & New York: Penguin Books, 2004.

al-Hassan, Ahmad Y. *Alcohol and the Distillation of Wine in Arabic Sources from the Eighth Century Onwards.*
http://www.gabarin.com/ayh/alcohol.htm

Alderman, Clifford Lindsey. *Rum, Slaves, and Molasses: The Story of New England's Triangular Trade.* New York: Crowell-Collier, 1972.

Allen, Everett S. *The Black Ships: Rumrunners of Prohibition.* Boston: Little, Brown, 1979.

Allen, H. Warner. *Rum: The Englishman's Spirit.* London: Faber & Faber, 1931.

Allison, Robert J. ed. *The Interesting Narrative of the Life of Olaudah Equiano.* New York: Bedford, 1995.

Andrews, William L, and Henry Louis Jr., Gates. *Slave Narratives.* New York: Library of America, 2000.

Andrieux, J. P. *Over the Side: Stories from a Rum Runner's files from Prohibition days in Atlantic Canada and Newfoundland.* Lincoln, Ontario: W. F. Rannie, 1984.

The Angostura Story. Port of Spain: Angostura Holdings, 2001.

Angeloni, Umberto. *Single Malt Whisky: An Italian Passion.* New York: Brioni, 2001.

An Outline of American History. US Information Services. www.usemb.se/usis/history/outline.pdf 1994.

Anon. *A Lover of Mankind: The Trial of the Spirits: or some considerations upon the pernicious consequences of the Gin Trade to Great Britain, as it is so Destructive of the Wealth and Lives of his Majesty's subjects.* London: 1736.

Anon. *An Eulogium on Rum.* Boston 1837.

Arkell, Jule. *Classic Rum.* London: Prion, 1992.

Avery-Stuttle, L. D., and J. E. White. *The Man That Rum Made.* Nashville, TN: Southern Publishing Association, 1912.

Aykroyd, W. R. *The Story of Sugar: A Remarkable Account of the World's Search for the Precious Sweetener.* Chicago: Quadrangle, 1967.

Barbados Rum Book. London: Macmillan Education, 1985.

Baines, Thomas. *History of the Commerce and Town of Liverpool.* London: Longman Brown, Green, and Longmans, 1858.

Barrows, Susanna & Robin Room. *Drinking: Behavior and Belief in Modern History.* Berkeley: University of California Press, 1991.

Barry, William David, and Nan Cumming. *Rum, Riot, and Reform: Maine and the History of American Drinking.* Portland: Maine Historical Society, 1998.

Barty-King, Hugh, and Anton Massel. *Rum Yesterday and Today.* London: Heinemann, 1983.

Baynham, Henry. *From the Lower Deck: The Royal Navy, 1780-1840.* Massachussetts: Barre Publishers 1970.

Beckles, Hilary McD. *Natural Rebels: A Social History of Enslaved Black Women in Barbados.* New Brunswick, N.J.: Rutgers University Press, 1989.

————. *A History of Barbados: From Amerindian Settlement to Nation-State.* Cambridge: Cambridge University Press, 1990.

Behr, Edward. *Prohibition: Thirteen Years That Changed America.* New York: Arcade, 1996.

Bellesiles, Michael A. *Arming America: The Origins of a National Gun Culture.* New York: Knopf, 2000.

Benezet, Anthony. *The Potent Enemies of America* Philadelphia: printed by Joseph Cruikshank, 1774.

Bentham, Jeremy. *Works* Vol 2 *The Principles of International Law,* Essay 4, Volume 2. London: Bowring, Edition 1843. pp. 535—560).

Bolingbroke, Henry. *Voyage to Demerary.* London: Richard Phillips, 1807.

Bolster, W. Jeffrey. *Black Jacks: African American Seamen in the Age of Sail.* Cambridge, MA: Harvard University Press, 1997.

Bragg, Fanny Greye, Israel Putnam, *Connecticut Magazine.* May, 1899.

Brewer, John. *The Sinews of Power: War, Money, and the English State.* Cambridge, MA: Harvard University Press, 1988.

Brewer, John, Susan Staves. eds. *Early Modern Conceptions of Property.* London: Routledge, 1995.

Broom, Dave. *Rum.* New York: Abbeville, 2003.

Brown, Thurlow Weed. *The Rumseller's Daughters, or, Woman in the Temperance Reform.* New York: Henry S. Goodspeed, 1874.

Bryant, Arthur. *Samuel Pepys: The Saviour of the Navy.* London: Reprint Society, 1953.

Buckley, Norman Roger. *The British Army in the West Indies: Society and the Military in the Revolutionary Age.* Gainesville: University Press of Florida, 1998.

Burck, William. *An account of the European settlements in America. In six parts.* London: R. and J. Dodsley, 1758.

Burke, Edmund. Speech On American Taxation, April 19, 1774. Second Edition. London: Dodsley, 1775.

Bushman, Richard L. *The Refinement of America: Persons, Houses, Cities.* New York: Vintage, 1993.

Byrd, William. Westover Manuscripts Containing the History of the Dividing Line betwixt Virginia and North Carolina: A *Journey to the Land of Eden,* A. D. 1733; 45.

Byrn, John D., Jr. *Crime and Punishment in the Royal Navy: Discipline on the Leeward Islands Station 1784-1812.* Brookfield, VT: Gower, 1989.

Cadwallader, Thomas. *An Essay on the West Indies Dry Gripes.* Philadelphia, 1745.

Calloway, Colin G. *The American Revolution in Indian Country.* Cambridge: Cambridge University Press, 1995.

Cappon, Lester J., ed. *The Adams-Jefferson Letters: The Complete Correspondence Between Thomas Jefferson and Abigail and John Adams.* Chapel Hill: University of North Carolina Press, 1987.

Camard-Hayot, Florette, and Jean-Luc de Laguarigue. *Martinique: Terre de Rhum.* For de France Traces, 1997.

Campoamor, Fernando G. *El Hijo Alegre de la Cana de Azucar: Biografia del Ron.* Havana: Editorial Cientifico-Tecnica, 1988.

———, ed. *Cuba: The Legend of Rum.* Toulouse, France: Éditions Bahia Presse.undated, 1990s

Canot, Theodore. *Adventures of an African Slaver.* New York: World Publishing, 1928.

Cappon, Lester J. ed., *The Adams-Jefferson Letters.* Gainesville: University of North Carolina Press, 1959.

Carmichael, Gertrude. *The History of the West Indian Islands of Trinidad and Tobago 1498–1900.* London: Alvin Redman, 1961.

Carson, Gerald. *Rum and Reform in Old New England.* Portland: Maine 1966.

Chesterton, G. K. *The Flying Inn.* New York: Sheed and Ward, 1955.

Cheyne, George. *Practical Rules for the Restoration and Preservation of Health and the Best Means for Invigorating and Prolonging Life.* London: James Smith, 1823.

Clark, Norman H. *Deliver Us from Evil: An Interpretation of American Prohibition.* New York: Norton, 1976.

Clark, Roger S. "Steven Spielberg's 'Amistad,' and Other Things I Have Thought about in the Past Forty Years: International Criminal Law, Conflict of Laws, Insurance, and Slavery." Lecture delivered as Board of Governors Professor, Rutgers School of Law, November 19, 1998.

Clarkson, Thomas. *History of the Rise, Progress, and Accomplishment of the Abolition of the African Slave Trade by the British Parliament.* London: John W. Parker, 1839.

Cobbett, William. *Cobbet's America.* London: Folio Society, 1985.

Cockburn, Henry Thomas, Lord, *Memorials of His Time,* New York: D. Appleton, 1856.

Conneau, Theophilus. *A Slaver's Log Book, or 20 Years' Residence in Africa.* Englewood Cliffs, N.J.: Prentice-Hall, 1978.

Conroy, David W. *In Public Houses. Drink and the Revolution of Authority in Colonial Massachusetts,* Chapel Hill: The University of North Carolina Press, 1995.

Cotton, Leo, Ed. *Old Mr. Boston Deluxe Official Bartender's Guide.* Boston: Ben Burk, 1935.

Crawford, A. *Reminiscences of a Naval Officer: A Quarter-Deck View of the War against Napoleon.* London: Chatham, 1999.

Cuba: Culture in its Hands. Havana: Ministerio de Cultura, undated.

Dorchester, Daniel. *Liquor Problem in All Ages.* New York: Hunt, 1886.

Deerr, Noel. *Cane Sugar: A Textbook on the Agriculture of the Sugar Cane, the Manufacture of Cane Sugar, and the Analysis of Sugar House Products.* London: Norman Rodger, 1921.

Demachy, Jacques-Francois. *L'Art du Distillateur D'eaux-fortes &c.* Paris: L. F. Delatour, 1773.

Dening, Greg, ed. *The Marquesan Journal of Edward Roberts.* Canberra: Australia National University Press, 1974.

Dictionary of National Biography, Oxford: OUP, 2004.

Dobree, Bonamy, and G. E. Manwaring. *The Floating Republic: An Account of the Mutinies at Spithead and the Nore in 1797.* New York: Harcourt, Brace, 1935.

Doggett, Scott, and Leah Gordon. *Lonely Planet's Dominican Republic and Haiti Guidebook.* London: Lonely Planet, 1999.

Dorsainvil, J.C. *Histoire d'Haiti. Éditions Henri Deschamps. 1968.* Port-au-Prince.

Dunn, Richard S. *Sugar and Slaves: The Rise of the Planter Class in the English West Indies, 1624–1713.* New York: Norton, 1972.

Earle, Alice Morse. *Customs and Fashions in Old New England.* Boston: Tuttle Pub, 1974.

Earle, Alice Morse. *Sabbath in Puritan New England.* New York: Charles Scribner's Sons, 1968

Edwards, Bryan. *History of the British Colonies in the West Indies* London: 1793

Elkins, Stanley, and Eric McKitrick. *The Age of Federalism: The Early American Republicans, 1788-1800.* New York: Oxford University Press, 1993.

Evatt, H.V. *Rum Rebellion: A Study of the Overthrow of Governor Bligh by John Macarthur and the New South Wales Corps.* Sydney: Sirius Books, 1965.

Fennelly, Catherine, ed. *Rum and Reform in Old New England*. Sturbridge, Mass.: Old Sturbridge, 1966.

Foster, Peter. *Family Spirits: The Bacardi Saga of Rum, Riches, and Revolution*. Toronto: Macfarlane, Walter and Ross, 1990.

Franck, Henry A. *Roaming through the West Indies*. New York: Century, 1920.

Franklin, Benjamin. *Autobiography*. London: The Folio Society 1989

Franklin, James. *The Present State of Hayti (Saint Domingo), with Remarks on its Agriculture, Commerce, Laws, Religion, Finances, and Population*. London: John Murray, 1828.

Furnas, J. C. *The Life and Times of the Late Demon Rum*. New York: Putnam, 1965.

Getz, Oscar. *Whiskey: An American Pictorial History*. New York: David McKay, 1978.

Gipson, Lawrence Henry. *The Coming of the Revolution, 1763-1775*. New York: Harper Torchbooks, 1954.

Griffith, Paddy. *The Art of War in Revolutionary France*. London: Greenhill, 1998.

Hamilton, Edward. *Rums of the Eastern Caribbean*. Puerto Rico: Tafia, Culebra, 1995.

———. *The Complete Guide to Rum*. Chicago: Triumph, 1997.

Hannay, David, ed. *Letters of Sir Samuel Hood*. London: Navy Record Society, 1893.

Harmsen, Jolien. *Sugar, Slavery, and Settlement: A Social History of Vieux Fort St. Lucia from the Amerindians to the Present*. Saint Lucia: Saint Lucia National Trust, 1999.

Havana and Rum. Havana Club Collection Paris: Jazz Editions, undated

Hawkes, Alex D. *Rum Cookbook*. New York: Drake, 1973.

Hay, Douglas, Peter Linebaugh, John G. Rule, E. P. Thompson, and Cal Winslow. *Albion's Fatal Tree: Crime and Society in Eighteenth Century England*. New York: Penguin, 1977.

Haycock, David Boyd. "Exterminated by the Bloody Flux: Dysentery in Eighteenth-Century Naval and Military Medical Accounts." *Journal of Maritime Research*. January 2002.

Hayward, Tom, and Keith Ashton. *The Royal Navy: Rum, Rumour and a Pinch of Salt*. Glasgow: Brown, Son & Ferguson, 1985.

Huetz de Lemp, Alain. *Histoire du Rhum*. Paris: Édition Desjonqueres, 1997.

Hugill, Stan. *Shanties and Sailors' Songs*. New York: Praeger, 1969.

James, C. L. R. *The Black Jacobins*. New York: Random House, 1963.

Johnson, Samuel. "Taxation No Tyranny." In *The Works of Samuel Johnson*. vol. 14 93-144. Troy, N.Y.: Pafraets, 1913.

Johnson Samuel, *An Introduction to the Political State of Great Britain 1756. vol. 12, The Works of Samuel Johnson, LL.D.* London: F. C. and J. Rivington, et al, 1823. 47-70.

Johnson, Walter. *Soul by Soul: Life inside the Antebellum Slave Market.* Cambridge, Mass.: Harvard University Press, 1999.

Jones, Howard. *Mutiny on the Amistad.* Oxford: Oxford University Press, 1988.

Josselyn, John. *New-Englands Rarities Discovered.* Bedford, MA: Applewood, 1672.

————. *An Account of Two Voyages to New England.* London, 1663.

Kennedy, Roger G. *Mr. Jefferson's Lost Cause.* Oxford: Oxford University Press, 2003.

Ketchum, Richard M. *Divided Loyalties: How the American Revolution Came to New York.* New York: Henry Holt, 2002.

Knapton, Ernest John. *Empress Josephine.* Cambridge, Mass.: Harvard University Press, 1963.

Knight, Franklin W., ed. *General History of the Caribbean, Volume III: Slave Societies of the Caribbean.* Paris UNESCO Publishing: 1997.

Kolchin, Peter. *American Slavery, 1619–1877.* New York: Hill and Wang, 1993.

Kukla, Jon. *A Wilderness So Immense: The Louisiana Purchase and the Destiny of America.* New York: Knopf, 2003.

Kurlansky, Mark. *A Continent of Islands: Searching for the Caribbean Destiny.* Reading, Mass.: Addison-Wesley, 1992.

————. *Cod: A Biography of the Fish That Changed the World.* London: Jonathan Cape, 1998.

————. *Salt: A World History.* New York: Walker, 2002.

Labat, Jean-Baptiste. *The Memoirs of Pere Labat, 1693–1705.* trans. by John Eaden. London: Constable & Co, 1931.

Labistour, Patricia. *A Rum Do! Smuggling in and around Robin Hood's Bay.* Whitby, U.K.: Marine Arts, 1996.

Langguth, A. J. *Patriots: The Men Who Started the American Revolution.* New York: Simon and Schuster, 1988.

Lender, Mark. "Drunkenness as an Offense in Early New England." *Quarterly Journal of Studies on Alcohol* vol. 34 (1973), 353-366.

Lender, Mark Edward, and James Kirby Martin. *Drinking in America: A History.* New York: Free Press, 1982.

Leslie, Charles. *A New History of Jamaica.* London, 1740.

Leyburn, James G. *The Scotch-Irish: A Social History.* Chapel Hill: University of North Carolina Press, 1962.

Linvald, Steffen. *Sukker og Rom.* Copenhagen, Denmark: Foreningen Dansk Vestindien, 1967.

Lloyd, Christopher. *The British Seaman, 1200–1860: A Social History.* Cranbury, N.J.: Associated University Presses, 1970.

Lodge, Henry Cabot. *The History of Nations: Mexico, Central America, and the West Indies.* New York: P. F. Collier, 1913.

Mancall, Peter C. *Deadly Medicine: Indians and Alcohol in Early America.* Ithaca, N.Y.: Cornell University Press, 1995.

Martin, Michel, and Alain Yacou. *Mourir pour les Antilles: Independence Negre ou Esclavage.* Paris: Éditions Caribeennes, 1991.

Martínez-Fernández, Luis. *Fighting Slavery in the Caribbean: The Life and Times of a British Family in Nineteenth-Century Havana.* Armonk, N.Y.: M. E. Sharpe, 1998.

Mbaeyi, Paul Mmegha. *British Military and Naval Forces in West African History, 1807–1874.* New York: NOK, 1978.

McClellan, William S. *Smuggling at the Outbrak of the Revolution with Special Reference to the West Indies Trade,* New York: 1912.

McCusker, John T. "*The Rum Trade and the Balance of Payments of the Thirteen Continental Colonies, 1650–1775*". Ph.D. dissertation, University of Pittsburgh, 1970.

———, and Russell R. Menard. *The Economy of British America.* Chapel Hill: University of North Carolina Press, 1985.

Melloy, R. S. *Time Will Tell: Memoirs of a Kangaroo Point Kid, as told to Diane Melloy.* Australia Boolarang Publications, (1993).

Miller, Jon Stephen. "'Heavens Good Cheer': Puritan Drinking in the Meditations of Edward Taylor, 1682–1725." *Dionysos: Journal of Literature and Addiction* 8.2 (Summer 1998), 30–44.

Milton, Giles. *Nathaniel's Nutmeg: How One Man's Courage Changed the Course of History.* London: Hodder and Stoughton, 1999.

Mintz, Sidney W. *Sweetness and Power: The Place of Sugar in Modern History.* New York: Penguin, 1985.

Monzert, Leonard. *Practical Distiller* (reprint). Bradley, IL: Lindsay Publications, 1987.

Moreira, James, and James Morrison, eds. *Tempered by Rum.* Nova Scotia, Canada: Pottersfield, 1988.

Morgan, Edmund S. *Benjamin Franklin.* New Haven, Conn.: Yale University Press, 2002.

Morison, Samuel Eliot. *John Paul Jones: A Sailor's Biography.* Boston: Little, Brown, 1959.

Morris, Sam. *The Ravages of Rum.* Sam Morris, 1945.

Murray, Dea. *Cooking with Rum, Caribbean Style.* St. Thomas: Rolfe Associates, 1982.

Nelson, Derek. *Moonshiners, Bootleggers, and Rumrunners.* Osceola, Wis.: Motorbooks International, 1995.

Nevinson, Henry W. *A Modern Slavery.* Essex, U.K.: Daimon, 1963.

Newlands, Benjamin E. R., John A. R. Newlands, and Charles G. Warnford. *Sugar: A Handbook for Planters and Refiners.* London: E. & F. N. Spon, 1888.

Niles, Samuel. *A pressing memorial, circularly transmitted and humbly offered to the several very worthy bodies of justices, of His Majesty's quarter sessions of the peace, in their respective counties, and to the select-men in every town through the province [Regarding the] unnecessary multiplication of taverns, and licenses houses for retailing rum and strong drink.* Braintree, June 23, 1761.

Oberholzer, Emil. *Delinquent Saints: Disciplinary Action in the Early Congregational Churches of Massachusetts,* New York: Columbia University Press, 1956.

Oldmixon, John. *The British Empire in America.* 2 vols. London: J. Nicholson, B. Tooke, 1708.

O'Shaughnessy, Andrew Jackson. *An Empire Divided: The American Revolution and the British Caribbean.* Philadelphia: University of Pennsylvania Press, 2000.

Ospina, Hernando Calvo. *Bacardi: The Hidden War.* London: Pluto, 2002.

Owen, O. M. *Rum, Rags, and Religion, or In Darkest America and the Way Out.* Syracuse, N.Y.: A. W. Hall, 1894.

Pack, James. *Nelson's Blood: The Story of Naval Rum.* Phoenix Mill Alan Sutton, 1995.

Parry, J. H., and Philip Sherlock. *A Short History of the West Indies.* New York: St. Martin's, 1971.

Parsons, Elsie Clews. *Folk-Lore of the Antilles, French and English.* New York: American Folk-Lore Society, 1936.

Parsons, G. S. *Nelsonian Reminiscences: A Dramatic Eye-Witness Account of the War at Sea, 1795–1810.* London: Chatham, 1998.

Peeke, Hewson L. *Americana Ebrietatis; The Favorite Tipple of our Forefathers and the Laws and Customs Relating Thereto.* New York: Hacker Art Books, 1970.

Pegram, Thomas R. *Battling Demon Rum: The Struggle for a Dry America, 1800–1933.* Chicago: Ivan R. Dee, 1998.

Petitioners for the Abolition of the Slave Trade. *An Abstract of the Evidence Presented Before a Select Committee of the House of Commons.* Glasgow and Edinburgh Societies, 1791.

Philpott, Don. *Landmark Visitor's Guide to St. Lucia.* Derbyshire, U.K.: Landmark.

Pilgrim Rum: The True New England Flavor for Better Drinks and Food. Peekskill, N.Y.: Fleischmann Distilling Corporation, 1939.

Pokhlebkin, William. *A History of Vodka.* New York: Verso, 1992.

Pope, Dudley. *Life in Nelson's Navy*. Annapolis, Md.: Bluejacket, 1996.

Pope-Hennessy, James. *Sins of the Fathers: A Study of the Atlantic Slave Traders, 1441–1807*. New York: Barnes & Noble, 1967.

Price, Richard, and Sally Price. *Stedman's Surinam: Life in an Eighteenth-Century Century Slave Society*. Baltimore, Md.: Johns Hopkins University Press, 1992.

Prince, Nancy. *A Black Woman's Odyssey through Russia and Jamaica*. New York: Markus Weiner, 1990.

Quimme, Peter. *The Signet Book of Coffee and Tea*. New York: Signet, 1976.

Renault, Jean-Michel. *Bonjour le rhum*. Lyons, France: Pelican, undated.

Reynolds, Reg. *Gibraltar Connections*. Gibraltar: Guideline Promotions, 1999.

Rice, Kym S. *Early American Taverns: For the Entertainment of Friends and Strangers*. Chicago: Regnery Gateway, 1983.

Richards, John F. *The Unending Frontier: An Environmental History of the Early Modern World*. Berkeley: University of California Press, 2003.

Robinson, Charles N. *The British Fleet: The Growth, Achievement, and Duties of the Navy of the Empire*. London: George Bell, 1894.

Rodger, N. A. M. *The Wooden World: An Anatomy of the Georgian Navy*. New York: Norton, 1996.

Rodriguez, Jose Angel. *Los Paisajes Geohistoricos Caneros en Venezeula*. Academia Caracas, Venezuela: Nacional de la Historia, 1986.

Rorabaugh, W. J. *The Alcoholic Republic: An American Tradition*. New York and Oxford: Oxford University Press, 1979.

Ros, Martin. *Night of Fire: The Black Napoleon and the Battle for Haiti*. New York: Sarpedon, 1994.

Rum, Sonne der gluckenlichen Inseln: Geschichte, Bilder und Geschichten aus der Welt des Rums. Flensburg, Germany: H. H. Pott, undated.

Russell, Phillips. *Benjamin Franklin: The First Civilized American*. New York: Bretano's, 1926.

Schecter, Barnet. *The Battle for New York: The City at the Heart of the American Revolution*. New York: Walker, 2002.

Schwartz, Stuart B., ed. *Tropical Babylons: Sugar and the Making of the Atlantic World, 1450–1680*. Chapel Hill: University of North Carolina Press, 2004.

Schivelbusch, Wolfgang. *Tastes of Paradise: A Social History of Spices, Stimulants, and Intoxicants*. New York: Vintage, 1993.

Scott, Joseph, and Donald Bain. *The World's Best Bartender's Guide*. New York: HP Books, 1998.

Shenkman, Richard. *I Love Paul Revere, Whether He Rode or Not*. New York: HarperCollins, 1991.

Shields, David S. "The Demonization of the Tavern." In *The Serpent in the Cup*, ed. David S. Reynolds and Debra J. Rosenthal (Amherst: University of Massachusetts Press, 1997) 10-21.

Shuffelton, Frank, ed. *The Letters of John and Abigail Adams*. London: Penguin, 2004.

Silva, Ruth C. *Rum, Religion, and Votes: 1928 Re-examined*. University Park: Pennsylvania State University Press, 1962.

Simon, André L. *Wines of the World Pocket Library: South Africa*. London: Newman Neame, 1950.

————. *Wines of the World Pocket Library: Burgundy*. London: Newman Neame, 1950.

————. *Wines of the World Pocket Library: Champagne*. London: Newman Neame, 1949.

————. *Wines of the World Pocket Library: Claret*. London: Newman Neame, 1950.

————. *Wines of the World Pocket Library: Hock*. London: Newman Neame, 1950.

————. *Wines of the World Pocket Library: Rum*. London: Newman Neame, 1950.

————. *A Dictionary of Wines, Spirits and Liqueurs*. New York: Citadel, 1963.

Sloane, Hans. *Voyage to the Islands of Madeira, Barbados etc.* vol. 1. London: printed by B.M. for the author, 1707; Vol. 2. London: printed for the author, 1725.

Smith, Adam. *The Wealth of Nations*. New York: Modern Library, 1937.

Sovereign, T. *The American Temperance Spelling Book*. Philadelphia, Pa.: Perkinpine & Higgins, 1839.

Spavens, William. *The Narrative of William Spavens: A Chatham Pensioner by Himself*. London: Chatham, 1998.

Spears, John R. *The American Slave Trade* (abridged). New York: Ballantine, 1960.

Stedman, Captain John G. *Narrative of a Five Years Exhibition against the Revolted Negroes of Surinam etc.*

Stout, Nancy. *Habanos: The Story of the Havana Cigar*. New York: Rizzoli, 1997.

Stout, Neil R. *The Royal Navy in America, 1760–1775: A Study in the Enforcement of British Colonial Policy in the Era of the American Revolution*. Annapolis, Md.: Naval Institute Press, 1973.

Strong, L.A.G. *The Story of Sugar*. London: Weidenfeld and Nicolson, 1954.

Summers, Mark Wahlgren. *1884: Rum, Romanism and Rebellion, the Making of a President*. Chapel Hill: University of North Carolina Press, 2000.

Taussig, Charles William. *Rum, Romance and Rebellion*. New York: Minton, Balch, 1928.

————. *Some Notes on Sugar and Molasses*. New York: C. W. Taussig, 1940.

Taylor, Alan. *American Colonies*. New York: Penguin, 2001.

Taylor, Edward. *Minor Poetry*. Boston: Twayne Publishers, 1981.

Thomas, Hugh. *The Slave Trade*. New York: Simon and Schuster, 1997.

Thompson, Peter. *Rum Punch and Revolution: Taverngoing & Public Life in Eighteenth Century Philadelphia*. Philadelphia: University of Pennsylvania Press, 1999.

Touzeau, James. *The Rise and Progress of Liverpool from 1551 to 1835*. Liverpool: The Liverpool Booksellers Company, 1910.

Tree, Ronald. *A History of Barbados*. St. Albans, U.K.: Granada, 1977.

Dr. Trotter, Thomas. *Notes and Queries* 9 (1850), 168.

Unsworth, Barry. *Sugar + Rum*. New York: Norton, 1988.

Vandercook, John W. *King Cane: The Story of Sugar in Hawaii*. New York: Harper, 1939.

Ward, Ned. *Trip to New England 1698*. London, 1699.

Ward, W. E. F. *The Royal Navy and the Slavers*. London: Allen and Unwin, 1969.

Waugh, Alec. *In Praise of Wine and Certain Noble Spirits*. New York: William Sloane, 1959.

Weeden William B. *Economic & Social History of New England*. Boston: 1891

Wild, Antony. *The East India Company: Trade and Conquest from 1600*. New York: Lyons, 2000.

Wilder, Rachel, ed. *Insight Guides: Barbados*. Hong Kong: APA Publications, 1993.

Williams, Gomer, *History of the Liverpool Privateers and Letters of Marque, with an account of the Liverpool Slave Trade*. London: William Heineman, and Liverpool: Edward Howell, 1897

Willoughby, Malcolm F. *Rum War at Sea*. Washington, DC: U.S. Government Printing Office, 1964.

Wilson, C. Anne. *Food and Drink in Britain: From the Stone Age to the Nineteenth Century*. Chicago: Academy, 1991.

Wood, Gordon S. *The Radicalism of the American Revolution*. New York: Knopf, 1992.

Zumbado, H. Z. *A Barman's Sixth Sense*. Havana: 1980

Zunder, William, ed. *Paradise Lost, John Milton, (New Casebooks.)* London: Palgrave Macmillan, 1999.

ENDNOTES

i Taussig, xii.

ii Taussig, 250.

iii Huetz de Lemp, 8.

iv Taussig, 4.

1 Taussig.

2 Bermuda Assizes, November 27, 1660, cited in Allen, H. Warner, 12.

3 Aykroyd, 87.

4 Huetz de Lemp.

5 Huetz de Lemp.

6 see Barty-King and Massel, 6.

7 Aykroyd, 10.

8 Barty-King and Massel, 3.

9 Aykroyd, 19.

10 Huetz de Lemp, 12.

11 Taussig, 4.

12 Nevinson, cited in Aykroyd, 143.

13 Al-Hassan Islamic Science –

14 Oxford English Dictionary, entry on "rum," citing Anon, A Brief
   Description of the Island of Barbadoes. A French historian of rum,
   D. Kergevant, claimed that this oft-quoted Anon was referring to
   Jamaica, but since the British under Cromwell did not take Jamaica
   from the Spanish until 1655, perhaps we can discount this particular
   French *bon mot.*

15 Huetz de Lemp, 71.

16 Allen, H. Warner, 5.

17 Colt's Diary, cited in Dunn, 5.

18 Ligon.

19 Ligon, 86.

20 Ligon, 110.

21 Ligon, 43.

22 Ligon, 43.

23 Beckles, p. 581 in Brewer, J. & Staves, S. eds. Early Modern Conceptions of Property (1995).

24 *Oxford English Dictionary.* entry for "rum"

25 Dunn, 57.

26 Zunder.

27 Ligon, 46.

28 Beckles, Brewer & Staves, 579.

29 Ligon, 44.

30 Ligon, 29.

31 Ligon, 86.
32 McCusker, 200.
33 Dunn, 62.
34 Ligon, 56.
35 Ligon, index.
36 Ligon, 57.
37 Barty-King and Massel, 9.
38 Ligon, 33.
39 Ligon.
40 Ligon, 27.
41 Ligon, 40.
42 Ligon, 93.
43 Ligon, 102.
44 *Oxford English Dictionary,* 1654 (see entry on "kill-devil"). Tenison, T. *Twenty Seven Philosophical Letters upon Several Occasions.* London, 1684, cited in Taussig, 5.
46 Ligon, 93.
47 Ligon, 20.
48 Richards, 420.
49 Richards.
50 Dunn, 59.
51 Ligon, 37.
52 Ligon.
53 Ligon, 25.
54 *Mercurius Politicus,* no. 90, 1654.
55 Ligon, 101.
56 Tree, 35.
57 Allen, H. Warner, 14.
58 Allen, H. Warner, 14.
59 Oldmixon.
60 Oldmixon, cited in Allen, H. Warner, 14.
61 McCusker 219.
62 Tenison, cited in Taussig, 7.
63 Tree, 19.
64 Tree, 11, 12.
65 Beckles, History of Barbados, 33.
66 Washington Diaries, quoted in Taussig, 37.
67 Smith, 157.
68 Dunn, 337.
69 Taussig, 12.
70 Getz, 11.
71 Taussig, 13.
72 Taussig, 14.
73 Huetz de Lemp, 71.
74 McCusker 443.
75 Taussig, 15.

[76] Rorabaugh.
[77] Rorabaugh, 29.
[78] Taussig, 15.
[79] Mancall, 14.
[80] Burck, cited in Barty-King and Massel, 161.
[81] Ward, Ned.
[82] Cited in Taussig, 145.
[83] Taussig, 178.
[84] Rorabaugh, 31.
[85] Taylor, Edward, 235
[86] McCusker, 508.
[87] Rorabaugh, 26.
[88] Taussig, 212.
[89] Carson, 11. He actually says a pint of doctrine, but one cannot help feeling that this is a misprint, or even worse, he did not get the point of the joke.
[90] Taussig, 217.
[91] Taussig, 218.
[92] Earle, Customs.
[93] Earle, Customs. chap. 19.
[94] Taussig, 211.
[95] Taussig, 214.
[96] Franklin, Ben. quoted in Taussig, 216.
[97] Franklin Papers 2: 168, Yale: YUP, continuing.
[98] Taussig, 75.
[99] Taussig; Barty-King and Massel, 24.
[100] Rorabaugh, 20.
[101] Taussig, xi.
[102] McCusker and Menard, 508.
[103] Moreira and Morrison, 17.
[104] Huetz de Lemp, 77.
[105] McLellan quoted in Taussig, 37.
[106] Taussig, 38.
[107] Taussig.
[108] Huetz de Lemp, 76.
[109] McCusker and Menard, 468, 476.
[110] Thomas, 328.
[111] Huetz de Lemp, 88.
[112] Barty-King and Massel, 158.
[113] Weeden, cited in Taussig, 18.
[114] Taussig, 155.
[115] Taussig, xi.
[116] Taussig, appendix.
[117] Taussig, 102.
[118] Taussig, 97.
[119] Thomas, 328.

[120] Aykroyd, 92.
[121] Taussig, 27.
[122] Johnson "Taxation No Tyranny."
[123] Clough, "A Modern Decalogue."
[124] Mancall, 107.
[125] Franklin, cited in Taussig and Barty-King, 27.
[126] Mancall, 48.
[127] Huetz de Lemp, 79.
[128] Mancall, 53, 54.
[129] Taussig, 25.
[130] Mancall, 45.
[131] Mancall, 105.
[132] Adams, John Diary, November 10, 1771.
[133] Mancall 43.
[134] Peeke, 93.
[135] Peeke, 94.
[136] Lind.
[137] Haycock.
[138] Stout, Neil, 10.
[139] Stout, Neil, 9.
[140] Aykroyd, 44.
[141] Stout, Neil, 11.
[142] Taussig, 89.
[143] Stout, Neil, 17.
[144] Taussig, 39.
[145] Taussig, 40.
[146] Taussig 70
[147] Stout, Neil, 23.
[148] McCusker, 352.
[149] Linvald, 67.
[150] Williams, Gomer, 269
[151] 45 George II Cap 121.
[152] McCusker 985.
[153] Pack, 13.
[154] Stout, Neil, 19.
[155] Stout, Neil, 17.
[156] Stout, Neil, 22.
[157] Bentham, *The Principles of International Law*, Essay 4.
[158] Brewer, 91.
[159] Taussig, 68.
[160] Stout, Neil, 87.
[161] Taussig, 61.
[162] Burke,
[163] Franklin, Letters to the Press, cited in Stout, Neil, 88.
[164] Stout, Neil, 40.
[165] McCusker, 360.

[166] McCusker, 400.
[167] Peeke,
[168] Johnson, Samuel. *Taxation No Tyranny.*
[169] Taussig, 65.
[170] Smith, Adam, 20.
[171] Pack, 121.
[172] Ketchum, 206.
[173] Taussig, 68.
[174] *An Outline of American History*, U.S. Information Services.
www.usemb.se/usis/history/outline.pdf 1994
[175] Taussig, 67.
[176] Baines, 449.
[177] Baines, 450.
[178] Adams, Letters 10.
[179] Adams, John. *Works.* Boston, 1856, cited in Taussig, 10.
[180] Rorabaugh, 35.
[181] Taussig, 80.
[182] Bragg.
[183] Adams, Letters, 78.
[184] Rorabaugh, 65.
[185] Getz, 40.
[186] Adams, Letters 129.
[187] Taussig, 57.
[188] Taussig, 69.
[189] Rorabaugh, 91.
[190] Byrd, William.
[191] Sloane, cited in Barty-King and Massel, 19.
[192] Carson, 7.
[193] Simon, *Rum and Spirits,* cited in Allen, H. Warner, 15.
[194] Anon, *Short Animadversions on etc.,* cited in Allen, H. Warner, 16.
Kemays, J.G, *Free and Candid Relections occasioned by the Duties on
Sugar and Rum.* cited in Allen, H. Warner, 17.
[196] Josselyn, *Journey to New England.*
[197] Allen, H. Warner, 3.
[198] See http://www.diggerhistory.info/pages-equip/grog.htm.
[199] Cockburn, *Memorials,* 140.
[200] Cadwallader, cited in Rorabaugh, 39.
[201] Hunert, *Observations,* cited in Allen, H. Warner, 17.
[202] Niles.
[203] Rorabaugh, 43.
[204] Moreira and Morrison.
[205] Sovereign.
[206] AU.
[207] Benezet, cited in Rorabaugh, 37.
[208] Taussig, 44.
[209] Cowper, William, *Bristol Gazette,* June 12, 1788.

210 Taussig, II 35.

211 Avery-Stuttle and White.

212 Allen, H. Warner, 8.

213 Price & Price.

214 Huetz de Lemp, 43.

215 McCusker, 156.

216 Huetz de Lemp, 45.

217 Johnson. *An Introduction To The Political State of Great Britain.*

218 Demachy.

219 McCusker, 174.

220 Allen, H. Warner, 30.

221 Allen, H. Warner, 30.

222 Pack, 25.

223 Allen, H. Warner.

224 Allen, H. Warner, 29.

225 Allen, H. Warner, 27.

226 Allen, H. Warner, 3.

227 Huetz de Lemp, 37.

228 Allen, H. Warner, 18.

229 Cf Allen, H. Warner, 8.

230 Huetz de Lemp, 35.

231 Order signed by Pepys, March 3, 1688.

232 Andre Simon, cited in Allen, H. Warner, 29.

233 Pack, 10.

234 Pack, 37.

235 Dr. Thomas Trotter, Notes and Queries 9 (1850), 168

236 Aykroyd, 90.

237 Robinson, 138.

238 Pack, 95.

239 Pack, 127.

240 Quoted in Pack, 35.

241 Behr, 32.

242 Allen, H. Warner, 3.

243 Saintsbury cited in Allen, H. Warner, 3.

244 Melloy.

245 Evatt, 217.

246 *Dictionary of National Biography.*

247 Evatt, 96.

248 Huetz de Lemp, 39.

249 Huetz de Lemp, 60.

250 Huetz de Lemp, 25.

251 J. F. Charpentier de Cossigny, cited in Barty-King and Massel, 13.

252 Huetz de Lemp, 18.

253 Huetz de Lemp, 36.

254 Huetz de Lemp, 32.

255 Huetz de Lemp, 49.

256 Barty-King and Massel cited 13
257 Huetz de Lemp, 40.
258 Aykroyd, 98.
259 Huetz de Lemp, 52.
260 Franklin, James, 348.
261 Huetz de Lemp, 54.
262 Huetz de Lemp, 63.
263 Huetz de Lemp, 67.
264 Huetz de Lemp, 67
265 Huetz de Lemp, 68.
266 Huetz de Lemp, 56.
267 Campoamor, *The Son of the Sugar Cane,* 15.
268 EFE Spanish News Agency, Havana, December 4, 1999.
269 Ospina, 15.
270 Ospina, 23.
271 Foster, 34.
272 Allen, H. Warner, 23.
273 Reynolds, 198.

INDEX